P9-DXM-471

French Symbolism
and the Modernist Movement

John Porter Houston

 French
Symbolism
and the Modernist Movement

A Study of Poetic Structures

Louisiana State University Press
Baton Rouge and London

Designer: Patricia Douglas Crowder
Typeface: VIP Aldus
Typesetter: The Composing Room of Michigan, Inc.
Printer: Thomson-Shore, Inc.
Binder: John Dekker & Sons, Inc.

LIBRARY OF CONGRESS CATALOGING IN PUBLICATION DATA
Houston, John Porter. 1933–
    French symbolism and the modernist movement.
    Includes bibliographical references and index.
    1. Poetry, Modern—20th century—History and
criticism.   2. French poetry—19th century—History
and criticism.   I. Title.
PN1271.H6   809.1'04   79-23479
ISBN 0-8071-0593-7

For M. N. *and* J.

Contents

Preface

This book is intended to elucidate the structural and stylistic differences that distinguish what is usually called modern poetry from that which preceded it. The works of poets as varied as Stéphane Mallarmé, Federico García Lorca, Rainer Maria Rilke, and Ezra Pound are all felt to differ fundamentally from the bulk of nineteenth-century poetry. Although the new poetry first became prominent in France, I am not particularly concerned with the idea of influence; essays and even books have carried that subject as far as its limited interest warrants. Rather, my effort has been to study analogies between poets and poems without any attention to chronology and with only cursory suggestions, few of them especially original, about the filiation of poetic styles and forms.

As with the idea of influence, I am not concerned with finding one easily stated principle from which all of modern poetry could be said to derive. Often, of course, symbolism is invoked as just such a principle, but there are one or two things about the term which should make one wary. Its application to a literary movement is an accident of journalism and polemics, as with the near contemporary term impressionism. However much it may seem apt and the accident a happy one, we must remember that there is no sacred authority behind the broad use of the word, not even Mallarmé's: it was the inspiration of a quite minor poet, Jean Moréas, who had no particular distinction as a critic or discursive writer. His *Manifeste du Symbolisme*, published in the *Figaro* in 1886, had principally the merit of finding an alternative to the term decadent, in many ways appropriate as a designation of the new literature but involving too many distracting associations.

Much authority seems conferred in retrospect on Moréas' choice of term, owing to the proliferation of uses and senses of symbolism in logic, philosophy, psychology, and so forth, but we must try to imagine that we are approaching the subject of modern poetry without the word symbolism ingrained in our minds, in order perhaps to see that there are some other dominant aesthetic principles in it besides the symbol. As a matter of fact, we shall find that there are at least two kinds of symbolism in modern poetry; the use of the word in one special sense is sanctioned by Mallarmé and William Butler Yeats; in another it designates a more or less definable meaning beyond the literal and is related thereby to the higher tradition of allegory. In addition, symbol may mean an explicit analogy or a one-word metaphor, perhaps puzzling but of no great structural importance. We shall encounter all these senses while attempting to make clear the specific way the word is being used. In these pages Symbolism with a capital *S* or the French adjective *symboliste* will refer to late nineteenth-century French poetry, without any particular implication about whether symbolism with a small *s* is necessarily involved.

There has been one notable theoretical attempt to characterize modern poetry in the Western European languages, which is Hugo Friedrich's *Die Struktur der modernen Lyrik* (Hamburg: Rowohlt, 1956). Friedrich's approach consists in the drawing up of a series of "negative categories" which he finds present in Symbolist and more recent poetry. These include disorientation, incoherence, fragmentariness, sacrifice of order, abrupt perturbation, violent suddenness, dislocation, alienation, breaking up sequences, unpoetic poetry, sharp images, enumeratory style, astigmatic vision, reversability, contentless ideality, empty transcendency. The first eleven of these are closely related ways of perturbing unity of surface and introducing surprise into the texture of poems. Enumeration deals with syntax; reversibility with the logic of passages, while "contentless ideality" and "empty transcendence" are a judgement—perhaps valid, perhaps not—on the poet's philosophy. The problem with Friedrich's categories is that, while they are adequate for describing local effect in a surrealist poem, or even in *The Wasteland,* they say very little about the general conception of poems of any scope. They seem to me to reflect that inability, in European criticism deriving from Benedetto

Croce, to account for more than the passing impression. As an intellectucal exercise it might be curious to see whether one could put Friedrich's negative categories into some kind of dialectic progression and discover if they lead anywhere. My basic approach, in any case, is far more concerned with the mimetic principle and the relation of content and structure.

As a consequence of the attempt to correlate kinds of content with stylistic and structural features, I have been led to consider at times the relations between modern fiction, which we may date from Gustave Flaubert, and poetry. Old-fashioned schemes of literary history drew an absolute antithesis between the French novel of the second half of the nineteenth century and Symbolist poetry, an antithesis that was by no means so clear to all writers of the period. Actually, we see today that the real antithesis was between the new novel and poetry, on the one hand, and, on the other hand, the products of academic taste, a jejune heritage of earlier decades symbolized by François Sully-Prudhomme, the poet who won the first Nobel Prize for literature (1901). The evolution of the language of poetry cannot be separated from that of the novel in an age when the latter had assumed enormous aesthetic importance: poets do not work *en vase clos,* unaware of the spread of contemporary literature of merit, even if Paul Valéry said he could not read novels. Ezra Pound came much closer to the poets' real concern when he remarked that poetry should be at least as well written as prose. As it happens though, poets sometimes anticipate or discover on their own certain novelistic techniques.

I have drawn my examples from the works of the minor French poets of the late nineteenth century as well as the great figures; some of the former were far more original, in this age of stylistic experimentation, than secondary figures usually are, and they participated in the general high renown of French poetry among modernists in various countries. The reader in search of a greater sampling of their poetry, some of which is not to be found in any but the largest libraries today, is referred to the generally excellent *La Poésie symboliste,* edited by Bernard Delvaille (Paris: Seghers, 1971); bibliographical information is included which I have seen fit to omit. The old *Poètes d'aujourd'hui* by Paul Léautaud and Adrien Van Bever (Paris: Mercure de France, 1946), which contains fairly complete accounts of the poets' careers, went through various editions earlier in the century and for a long time was the only available anthology; its criteria for selection, however, were not especially *symboliste* or modernist. I have not dealt much with minor writers' turbid speculations on poetry; in these the eternal antinomies of art tend, as Giuseppe Ungaretti put it, to come down to *questioni di lana caprina*, and one senses a general inferiority of the discursive faculty to the poets' imaginative capacities.

The three opening sections of the first chapter are designed to put forth some basic considerations about French poetry in the nineteenth century. They are theoretical, necessarily somewhat abstract, and might be read as well after the bulk of the book. They contain reference points, however, to which I return again and again.

Translations are included for anything of length or difficulty: these, it should be noted, are more interpretive than literal when I feel the reader needs help. For Saint-John Perse's *Anabase,* the English text is that of T. S. Eliot's translation.

Acknowledgments

Grateful acknowledgment is made to the following publishers: Wallace Stevens' "Earthy Anecdote" and "On the Manner of Addressing Clouds," copyright 1923 and renewed 1951 by Wallace Stevens, reprinted from *The Collected Poems of Wallace Stevens* by permission of Alfred A. Knopf, Inc.; 5 poems from Jorge Guillén's *Cántico* reprinted and translated by permission of Editorial Sudamérica S. A.; excerpts from *Anabasis* by Saint-John Perse, translated by T. S. Eliot, are reprinted by permission of Harcourt Brace Jovanovich, Inc., copyright 1938, 1939 by Harcourt Brace Jovanovich, renewed 1966 by Esme Valerie Eliot; from *Anabasis: a poem* by St-John Perse, translated by T. S. Eliot, 10 lines from I, 2 short quotations from III, 13 lines from VIII, reprinted by permission of Faber and Faber Ltd; 13 lines from "Motetti, I," 48 lines from "Notizie dall'Amiata," 26 lines from "L'Ombra della magnolia," 27 lines from "Nuove Stanze" in Eugenio Montale, *Selected Poems*, copyright © 1948, 1949, 1957 by Arnoldo Mondadori Editore, all rights reserved, copyright © 1965 by New Directions Publishing Corporation; excerpts from *Four Quartets* by T. S. Eliot are reprinted by permission of Harcourt Brace Jovanovich, Inc., copyright 1943 by T. S. Eliot, renewed 1971 by Esme Valerie Eliot; 10 lines from "Burnt Norton" and other short extracts reprinted by permission of Faber and Faber Ltd from *Four Quartets* by T. S. Eliot; 11 lines from "Canto 3," 12 lines from "Canto 4," 14 lines from "Canto 8," 16 lines from "Canto 17," 17 lines from "Canto 64" reprinted by permission of Faber and Faber Ltd from *The Cantos of Ezra Pound* by Ezra Pound; 70 lines from cantos 3, 4, 8, 17, 64 in Ezra Pound, *The Cantos*, copyright 1934,

1940 by Ezra Pound, reprinted by permission of New Directions Publishing Corporation; 182 lines from *Collected Poems* by W. B. Yeats reprinted by permission of M. B. Yeats, Miss Anne Yeats and the Macmillan Co. of London and Basingstoke; 7 lines from "To His Heart, Bidding It Have No Fear," 10 lines from "He Remembers Forgotten Beauty," 13 lines from "The Secret Rose," 16 lines from "To Some I Have Talked with by the Fire" reprinted with permission of Macmillan Publishing Co., Inc., from *Collected Poems* by William Butler Yeats, copyright 1906 by Macmillan Publishing Co., Inc., renewed 1934 by William Butler Yeats; 17 lines from "The Double Vision of Michael Robartes" reprinted with permission of Macmillan Publishing Co., Inc. from *Collected Poems* by William Butler Yeats, copyright 1919 by Macmillan Publishing Co., Inc., renewed 1947 by Bertha Georgie Yeats; 8 lines from "Sailing to Byzantium," 16 lines from "Meditations in Time of Civil War," 18 lines from "Nineteen Hundred and Nineteen" reprinted with permission of Macmillan Publishing Co., Inc. from *Collected Poems* by William Butler Yeats, copyright 1928 by Macmillan Publishing Co., Inc., renewed 1956 by Georgie Yeats; 31 lines from "A Dialogue of Self and Soul," 32 lines from "Byzantium," 18 lines from "Blood and the Moon" reprinted with permission of Macmillan Publishing Co., Inc. from *Collected Poems* by William Butler Yeats, copyright 1933 by Macmillan Publishing Co., Inc., renewed 1961 by Bertha Georgie Yeats; 16 lines from "The Gyres" reprinted with permission of Macmillan Publishing Co., Inc. from *Collected Poems* by William Butler Yeats, copyright 1940 by Georgie Yeats, renewed 1968 by Bertha Georgie Yeats, Michael Butler Yeats and Anne Yeats; 28 lines from Saint-John Perse's "Anabase," in *Oeuvres complètes* (Bibliothèque de la Pléiade), copyright © Editions Gallimard, reprinted by permission of the publisher. Paul Valéry's "Les Vaines Danseuses," from *Album de vers anciens*, reprinted in *Oeuvres* (Vol. 1, Bibliothèque de la Pléiade), copyright © Editions Gallimard, and lines from his *La Jeune Parque*, reprinted in *Oeuvres* (Vol. 1, Bibliothèque de la Pléiade), copyright © Editions Gallimard, reprinted and translated by permission of the publisher. Lines from Guillaume Apollinaire's "La Chanson du mal-aimé," "Un Soir," "Le Voyageur," "Les Fiançailles," "Le Brasier," and "Zone," all from *Alcools*, reprinted in *Oeuvres poetiques* (Bibliothèque de la Pléiade), copyright © Editions Gallimard, reprinted and translated by permission of the publisher. Stéphane Mallarmé's *Un Coup de dés jamais n'abolira le hasard,* copyright © Editions Gallimard, reprinted and translated by permission of the publisher. Lines from Federico García Lorca's "Romancero Gitano" used and translated by permission of Isabel García Lorca. "Das späte Ich" by Gottfried Benn, from *Lyrik* by Gottfried Benn, published by Arche-Verlag, Peter Schifferli, copyright 1956, reprinted and translated by permission of the publishers.

French Symbolism
and the Modernist Movement

I
The Poetry of Consciousness

1. Some Ideas on Art, Life, and Nature

From the early nineteenth century on, there are aspects of French aesthetic thought which stand out from contemporary English and German theory and anticipate the characteristic ideas on art of a later period. In fact, the first deeply influential and significant volume of French romantic poetry, Victor Hugo's *Les Orientales* (1829), has, both in its preface and contents, features whose consequences extend beyond what we normally think of as the chronological limits of French romanticism. The poems, which are set in parts of the Mediterranean world remote from Paris, are presented as the reveries of a city-dweller. Their style is, in comparison to previous French poetry, rich in evocations of light, color, line, and detail. In the preface Hugo compares the individual poems to paintings and to the varied architectural monuments of an old Spanish city; the book as a whole he characterizes as a useless one of pure poetry. A work of art which is constructed with skill out of the dead materials of pigment, canvas, or stone is pure artifice, not a natural object; the additional presentation of it as resembling a reverie could, in a sense, imply a certain remoteness from the immediate emotions of life. Hugo's conception of his art in *Les Orientales* acquires significance when we compare it to the ideas of imagination and organic form typical of English and German aesthetics in the early nineteenth century. Certainly the English romantics' idea of imagination as the faculty encompassing the totality of human and natural experience conjoined resulted in poetry which embodied a greater span of vital perceptions and feelings than Hugo's notion of art implied. The theory of the imagination as it gave both shape and theme to poems was the most powerful aesthetic of the early nineteenth century.

The word imagination was current in eighteenth-century France as it was in England, and was similarly associated with poetry descriptive of nature—which, in France, was largely imitated from English work. The final philosophical elaboration of this term, however, did not occur; imagination did not take on the suggestion of an essential higher life force relating the ideas of God, nature, and love.[1] As a result, French nature poetry, as exemplified in the work of Alphonse de Lamartine and in Hugo's work of the 1830s, seems far closer to the aesthetic of James Thomson's *The Seasons*, the epitome of the eighteenth-century love of nature, than it does to William Wordsworth or Percy Bysshe Shelley. Personifications and pathetic fallacy, more than mythic life, generally inform it. Nature is simply the pleasant experience of the countryside uplifted with thoughts about life or God.[2] Even without knowing it to be the case, as with Hugo, one might have the impression nature poetry was written by someone who vacationed in the countryside but whose most decisive experiences were those of a city-dweller. On the other hand, the poetry of the English romantics or, especially among the Germans, of Joseph von Eichendorff, conveys the point of view of someone whose life is completely involved in nature, the inhabitant at most of a village. This is, of course, an artistic matter, not one of circumstances: one would never guess that Eichendorff spent his days toiling as a bureaucrat in large cities.

The idea that a poem is an object made from materials and not a living thing parallel to nature may seem to reflect on Hugo's part a continuing adherence to that side of neoclassical theory which saw art as craft. This is not at all surprising: neoclassicism was not, from the early nineteenth-century French point of view, merely an episode in the history of literature, it was the French tradition and French art itself, renaissance and baroque works constituting more a group of irregular forms than a coherent tradition of their own. For much of the nineteenth century in France, formal aesthetic questions continued frequently to be conceived according to basic assumptions of neoclassicism (imitation, unity of detail, symmetry).

Hugo's other major statement, besides the comparison of poems to the fine arts, takes on its significance only in regard to a favorite neo-classical dictum: his declaration that *Les Orientales* is a useless book is intended as an allusion to the theory, after Horace, of joining the *utile* to the *dulce*, which appealed to the unitarian thinking of neoclassicists. By the useful Horace meant, of course, the moral exemplum of art, and by useless Hugo meant, of course, that his poems were not didactic like eighteenth-century odes. The sense of these terms, however, was shortly modified by Théophile Gautier, principally in the preface to *Mademoiselle de Maupin*. The useful Gautier equated not with moral suasion but with the practically and commercially useful, and his example was the *lieux d'aisance*. This leap of ideas was not completely far-fetched: the bourgeois public's often conservative, neoclassical views of art were reinforced by the Saint-Simonian doctrine which maintained both that practical usefulness and flourishing commerce were a high goal and that art should make itself useful by lofty moral teachings. Gautier chose to reduce the two senses of the *utile* to one for polemical purposes. However, there is also a far-reaching implication in his talk of *latrines* and Ghiberti's doors; he has strengthened Hugo's perhaps largely implicit notion of the poem as a rich object and made it clear that this object has no place in the world of moral purposefulness. The character of the poem as artifact suggests, as Hugo's comparison already had, that the sensory value of art should predominate, that poetry should contain luxuriant imagery, as neoclassical poetry did not. Furthermore, the poem might not simply be morally useless, it might be antimoral or immoral. Beyond this lies a further dialectic step: it can be maintained that there is a higher code of values than that of the middle-class reading public, that there is a morality of art subsuming the ordinary notions of moral and immoral.

Gautier suggests the nature of such an ethic to some extent in the text of *Mademoiselle de Maupin*, but the poet most concerned with reconciling the notions of art and morality was Charles Baudelaire, who returned to the question time after time in his critical writings. What is perhaps most arresting about Baudelaire's thinking on the subject is the impression he gives that art contains morality: that art does not merely imitate the moral conflicts implicit in life but that nearly everything important in life, such as morality, is lesser than and embraced by art. This is, however, merely an impression, a tendency in Baudelaire's thinking; he was sufficiently under the sway of traditional religious conceptions that he could not replace God by art; something remained outside art and was at least of equal importance.

There is one other among Baudelaire's many and sometimes contradictory thoughts on art that is relevant here: the distinction between art and nature, implicit in both Hugo and Gautier's comparisons of poetry with carved stone or bronze, becomes explicit in Baudelaire's view of a hierarchy of values in which art is above nature, the latter being flawed by original sin. (Baudelaire sometimes takes the next step and identifies art with redemption.) This has consequences for poetic imagery; "la froide majesté de la femme stérile" and similar expressions convey the idea that beauty is opposed to life because it is opposed to nature. (This is by no means Baudelaire's only conception of beauty, but it was an influential one.) Another opposition between beauty and life, which is based on quite different assumptions, is found in Charles Leconte de Lisle's poetry and theorizing. There, present-day life, supposedly based on a commerce of the *utile* alone, is consciously ignored in favor of evocations of the remote in space or time. Nature appears, but is exotic and alien; life assumes a distant, heroic, and mythic character. Although Leconte de Lisle intended his poetry to exalt truth, beauty, and pristine vital forces, the embodiments of these are at such a remove from our ordinary sense of reality that they paradoxically have appeared lifeless to many readers despite intense sensory imagery.

Leconte de Lisle was content with the conception of poetry as a craft; Baudelaire timidly and metaphorically called it evocative sorcery, but Hugo, in the last phase of his career, and later poets found it necessary to have recourse to transcendental notions in order to account for their creative activity. The concept of the logos (*le Verbe*) occures in Hugo and Arthur Rimbaud, the supernatural "mystery of a name" in Mallarmé's picture of an Adam-poet ordering the world. Vision and sight, meaning the perception of normally invisible realms, are other terms common to the three poets; Mallarmé used the word "idea" as well, in the sense of a higher reality.[3] None of these notions is really explored: they serve their purpose of characterizing poetry as coming from beyond life or being above it, and the essential is that they do not put poetry in conflict with life, practical or otherwise, but obviate the possibility of comparing the two, just as one would not compare the infinite with the finite. The various oppositions typical of earlier poetic theory yield, especially in Mallarmé's thought, to a harmonious view of an ascending scale with art at its transcendental summit: art is no longer a beautiful object which can be placed opposite a practical one.

In *Hérodiade*, the mystery (the sense is religious and theatrical at once) which Mallarmé worked on at various times in the course of his life and never finished, Salome, who is here given her mother's name, and John the Baptist represent beauty and the artist: John's glance violates the princess, his death comes as a result, and the "cold jewels" of Hérodiade, her sterile nature, "open." It is from having absorbed John's life that she, no longer a princess, "triumphs as queen."[4] After the imagery of metal, moon, and ice, which has earlier characterized her, there is a synthesis symbolized by sexual union between life and the inorganic.

Hérodiade reflects the persistence in the nineteenth century of the belief that there is a category of things subsumed under the idea of the beautiful: of course, instead of the neoclassicists' version of the *beau idéal*, nineteenth-century poets chose their own imagery—in which we find the gold and jewels and decor of Mallarmé's poem—but the habit of thinking of the beautiful as a prestigious class of things remains a characteristic neoclassical one. At some point, however, Mallarmé began to realize that the beauty of a poem comes from structural relations, not just from specific images, and with this he moved into a new perspective on art. Up to this time, the English and German organic theory of poetic form was undoubtedly superior to any thinking done about it in France; now, however, Mallarmé's new definition of poetry as "music in the Greek sense, basically meaning a rhythm among relationships" avoided the distracting vegetal associations of the organic theory and permitted Mallarmé to use quotidian imagery like furniture and to focus on questions of design, the more essentially poetic element in poetry.[5] Mallarmé had arrived at this aesthetic conception by meditating on music, of which he knew little and had no technical knowledge. His ignorance, however, seems to have preserved him from the supposedly Wagnerian ideas current in late nineteenth-century France, according to which music is primarily a matter of repetition.

Mallarmé's theory of art as relationships is of considerable value in confronting many poems of the late nineteenth and twentieth centuries. It suits, for example, symbolic poems, like some of Wallace Stevens', in which the whole meaning depends on sensing the bonds between two or more somewhat cryptic objects or creatures. In a sense, it does for much modern poetry what the idea of imagination did for English romantic nature poetry: it is relevant to both the formal conception of the poem and its subject; it provides a general idea of much subtlety and flexible application.

The movements in French aesthetics we have been surveying are generally referred to as *l'art pour l'art*, a term I have avoided because it seems to say something rather simple but actually encompasses quite diverse positions and currents of thought. The evolution of ideas on art from the beginnings of romanticism to the final stage of Mallarmé's aesthetic has, as I have sketched it, certain correspondences to poetic imagery. It is by no means the only sequence of aesthetic conceptions that could be traced: indeed, the more closely one studies them, the more it appears that from each idea one could move to any one of several others in a proliferation of dialectic. The aesthetic thought of Baudelaire or Mallarmé, for example, can be reduced to a system only by ignoring various implications and by limiting the conflicting tendencies one allows to become apparent. The nineteenth century was not, as I choose to see it, so much a period of critics and doctrinaires as a time when the practical aesthetics of poets and novelists were both abundantly recorded and highly significant. Their wealth of ideas, set forth in a largely unsystematic fashion, makes every account of them an experiment in dialectic, and I have chosen the conceptions that seemed best to lead into the intense formal concerns of nineteenth-century poets.

2. The Morphology of Romantic Lyric

The shifts in the conception of poetry in nineteenth-century France are related to, if not completely identifiable with, changes in the actual shaping of poems. These changes cannot be fully appreciated, however, without reference to the forms that preceded and persisted alongside the new ones. I shall attempt briefly to outline a morphology of the lyric in its principal romantic manifestations, with some indication of how poets were to deviate from them.

While romantic types of poems could be exemplified by the work of all the many minor poets published in *Le Parnasse contemporain* (1866), which is interesting as a kind of encyclopedia of French poetic common practice on the eve of Symbolism, I shall refer rather to poems by more substantial figures. Perhaps an insignificant piece would, through its lack of general salience, illustrate more clearly this or that tendency in poetic structure; on the other hand, major poems, or at least the work of major poets, provide valuable examples of the range of effect possible within the limits of a specific rhetorical configuration. Reference can usefully be made not only to English and German romantic poetry but also to the work of the great French innovators of the late nineteenth century; in Rimbaud, and especially in Mallarmé, many basic patterns of earlier poetry persist, as they do even in Valéry. In the very middle of the century, Baudelaire is a particularly rich source of illustration of well-articulated rhetorical structures. What follows is based on extensive attempts to classify large bodies of poetry, such as all of John Keats and Shelley's lyrics, the complete works of the major French poets, William Blake's *Songs of Innocence* and *Songs of Experience*, Friedrich Hölderlin's body of work, a generous representation of Goethe's lyric poetry, and so forth. While I do not doubt that it has imperfections, there seems to be an undeniable and even surprising limit on the poetic structures one is likely to find.

The structures we are going to examine have, as their general characteristic, great clarity in rhetorical situations, by which I mean the relationships among author, speaker, person or thing addressed, subject matter, and reader, or whatever combination of them is relevant. This clarity is demonstrable on the levels of syntax, vocabulary, and figurative language. While the rhetorical relationships may be at least hypothetically formulated for any discourse, the body of poetry we are dealing with does not, as a rule, accidentally or intentionally create confusions between the speaking voice or subject, to use a grammatical analogy, and the various objects, as happens in modern poems rendering consciousness, where the speaker's mental activity and what he perceives may fuse. A noteworthy stylistic aspect of romantic lyric is the reader's ability to distinguish between concrete and figurative language or to recognize the simultaneous presence of both, distinctions which are often not at all clear in an inner monologue like "L'Après-midi d'un faune." Another characteristic of well-defined rhetorical forms is that we can perceive the poem's reference as general, exemplary, or particular; in Rimbaud's "Mémoire," on the other hand, we cannot readily be certain whether the experience is that of one person or not. Figurative language is often found in exemplary poems, where its symbols, if not transparent, suggest the tradition of the parable rather than the modern kind of symbolism, in which important words may be cryptic or a strange figure or object appear, like the grey jar set down in Tennessee in one of Wallace Stevens' poems. Visionary lyrics of great resonance in the larger context of the poetry of Shelley, Blake, or Novalis commonly lend themselves to an at least momentarily satisfactory limited interpretation. While longer works, notably those of Blake, may offer considerable difficulty, the short poem tends to illustrate readily the desire to move an audience in some way, the original sense of rhetoric, in virtue of which we can answer the questions of from whom, to whom, and about what. On the other hand, some modern poems, such as Valéry's "Les Vaines Danseuses," convey little about speaker, subject, or hearer.

Certain speech situations directed at second persons, present or absent, provide very clear-cut forms: invitation, prayer, invocation, question, command, prohibition, interlocution (of which only one side may be represented), and the hortatory kind of imperative found in Paul Verlaine's "Art poétique." Rhetoric has terms for these, whereas some modern uses of the second person, like that at the beginning of Verlaine's "Clair de lune," completely elude classification. In rhetorical poetry there are various ways in which content can be structured within the traditional second person categories, as we shall see later. What must be remembered, however, is that great ranges of tone and situation are encompassed within them, however elementary they seem when reduced to a list. Poems 25 to 55 of Les Fleurs du mal contain most of the second person patterns, and in them we can observe another strong rhetorical element, which determines not form in a narrow sense, but the purpose of communication: praise and blame. Ode and satire (which, of course, may be third person as well as second) are obvious forms of praise and blame, and the ode in particular, taken in this general sense of a poem exalting its subject, accounts for an impressive amount of high lyric poetry. It persists in some modern poems like Mallarmé's "Toast funèbre." Even in poems not normally thought of as odes, the matter of praise is abundantly found. In contrast, we might imagine a kind of modern poem in which praise or blame or their causes is entirely implicit. In Guillaume Apollinaire's "Un Soir," furthermore, we cannot easily tell whether it is praise or blame that is implicit, although one or the other clearly is. In romantic and earlier poetry, the definition of second persons and the attitude taken toward them are often clarified by their falling into certain traditional categories: mistress, fellow-poet, the Christian God, patron, king, and so forth. On the whole, the poem addressed to someone or something seems to show most distinctly the changes that have come over poetry in the last century or two: from Greek and Latin lyric through European neoclassicism and much romantic poetry, the conceiving of the poem as a well-delineated act of address, and the explicit use of the second person helps circumscribe genres within the lyric and generally to suggest the specific occasion, real or fictional, of which the poem is a record. Mallarmé's "Hommage" to Richard Wagner, on the interpretation of which there is little agreement, shows how the kind of occasion and the degree of praise can be quite enigmatic in more modern work.

The apostrophe or invocation directed toward something personified is a special case of poetry of the second person in that it often is joined with much self-revelation on the part of the speaking first person: the "Ode to the West Wind" is only one of many of Shelley's poems that have this dual character. Before the rise of the dramatic monologue, even poems dominated by the first person (like Keats' nightingale ode) often have some second person point of reference. Both romantic odes show, furthermore, the poem tending toward general statements about life, beauty, and art and making sense in a simple, limited way, if that is as far as the reader cares to go. Even first person poems we may think of as unrhetorical, such as the songs in Elizabethan plays, often are connected to the tradition of public utterance by the use of maxims or commonplaces, generalized wishes or deliberations. In the work of a number of modern poets, the place the ode had in English romanticism is occupied by the dramatic monologue, which is concerned with specifics rather than the general. The elusive, unrhetorical song, of which one authority said there were no examples in France before the last three decades of the nineteenth century,[6] is associated with Verlaine during the 1870s and 1880s before becoming abundant in volumes of poetry by 1900. These two genres, Verlainesque song and dramatic monologue, represent, in the Symbolist period proper, the farthest evolution away from traditional rhetoric. There are also other genres worth considering, which occupy a kind of borderline between specific and general reference.

As much as romantic poets were concerned with the individual and even the idiosyncratic, it is still quite perceptible in their work that experiences tend to be treated as something of general value to all. Poems of memory, which are characteristic of the nineteenth century and especially of Baudelaire, can be almost narrative in movement as recollections unfold ("La Chevelure"); their subject finds its justification in its exemplary quality. It is characteristic of first person poems to take what is local and individual and make of it something typical; anecdote and self-portraits (not necessarily presented as being of the poet) work this way. Blake's "Little Black Boy" and a number of other lyrics or Baudelaire's "Spleen" poems, "Je suis comme le roi" and "J'ai plus de souvenirs," illustrate the great possible range of self-portraits. Longer first person poems may have important narrative elements (Valéry's "Ebauche d'un serpent"), or various combinations of self-portrait, episode, and meditation. A special case of the latter occurs in Hugo, where reflective poems often lead to visions in which cosmic patterns are revealed ("Les Malheureux" and "Halte en marchant" in *Les Contemplations*). Such poems also show the difficulty of classifying sometimes ambiguous forms solely by grammatical persons: the import of Hugo's visions is never relevant only or primarily to the seer but carries the objectivity of third person accounts. Of course, the objectivity of generally valid statements and the truth to be found in human types underlies most romantic first person poems, and modern criticism's identification of fictitious speakers or personae in them, like the prophet of Hugo's visions, emphasizes this element of *ethos,* as traditional rhetoric called the creation of character based on moral-psychological types. It may be that with ingenuity we could classify the speakers of all modern first person poems, but the aim of the poet often seems to be the devising of some startling, elusive, and even mysterious figure. Many of Jules Laforgue's speakers in *Les Complaintes* are of this sort, like the virgin King of Thule or the Munis (sages) of Montmartre.

Third person poetic genres include anecdotes, short narratives, portraits, and scenes. Hugo's *Légende des siècles* abounds in the first two; in Rimbaud, "Les Assis" and "Le Forgeron" typify the others. Speeches and narrative may be joined, notably in some of Alfred de Vigny's poems like "La Colère de Samson" or "Le Mont des oliviers." Characteristic of all these are the great overtness of praise and blame, that is of the rhetorical motivation, and the frequency of historical or legendary material, with an attendant implication of exemplarity. These poetic narratives or fragments of narration make, if anything, only moderate use of novelistic plot devices like ellipsis. In Rimbaud's "Les Premières Communions" and some other poems, on the other hand, we shall find interesting parallels with modern fiction. Finally, from "Le Bateau ivre" to Dylan Thomas' "Ballad of the Long-Legged Bait," we find symbolic works with plot, or at least action, and some analogy to the allegorical tradition. In the case of the Thomas poem at least, it is clear that its technique goes beyond the romantic hermeticism of Blake and Gérard de Nerval.

In romantic poems which are not narratives, scenes, or portraits, we can distinguish structural principles shaping the body of the poem. Poetic arguments can be put together with an incremental movement, a unified tone, and perhaps rising intensity ("Au lecteur" in *Les Fleurs du mal*). Often this pattern seems enumeratory as in Baudelaire's "Les Phares." The opposite principle is conflictual movement, in which antithesis, with or without resolution, dominates (Mallarmé's "Las de l'amer repos" and Baudelaire's "Causerie") and may, in especially elaborate cases, be complicated by overt paradoxes ("Le Voyage" in *Les Fleurs du mal*). The conceit (Mallarmé's "La chevelure vol") is generally a paradoxical argument that makes ordinary logic untenable. In general, the arguments of antithetical or incremental poems have a reasonable show of logical coherence, and occasionally we find a poem with a fairly formal kind of reasoning (the first piece of *Les Contemplations*, for example). The great meditations like "Tintern Abby" have, of course, an important element of psychological development, as well as an adequate logical one, and this combination can be found in some modernist poems like Stevens' "Le Monocle de mon oncle" or "The Idea of Order at Key West" and Valéry's "Le Cimetière marin." These also show that stanzaic forms in meditation can lead to highly epigrammatic effects. What we do not find in all the poems we have mentioned is the seemingly irrelevant associative movement which imparts a deceptive stream-of-consciousness-like surface to many modern poems and of which an unusual, early example is to be encountered in Baudelaire's "Le Cygne."

Incremental and antithetical patterns of argument often are combined with other rhetorical units such as elaborate addresses in the second person, descriptions or the noting of perceptions, or analogies (which, by themselves, of course, constitute the whole of some short poems: Mallarmé's "Les Fenêtres," or, in a less formalized, bipartite manner, "M'introduire dans ton histoire"). Some poems, like Hölderlin's "Der Rhein," are great composite structures in which we see a number of elements: in the Hölderlin poem we find a narrative of the Rhine's birth and course, an expository meditation on the gods, an apostrophe to Rousseau, a generalization with the specific example of Socrates, and an address to the friend to whom the poem is dedicated. Finally, the ending of a poem is often a distinctive unit in itself, though following from what precedes: sententiae (Keats' "Grecian Urn"), images (Keats' gathering swallows in the "Ode to Autumn" and countless poems by Hugo), rhetorical questions (the "Ode to a Nightingale"), the dialectic resolution of an antithesis (Baudelaire's "Hymne à la beauté"), in French an imposing quadripartite line with special sound repetitions and deployment of long vowels ("Et l'avare silence et la massive nuit," Mallarmé: "Toast funèbre") or some other rhetorical pattern (Baudelaire's "Voyage à Cythère" with its prayer, or the apostrophe of "Au lecteur").

Modern poets have moved away from romantic poetic structures not only by using the dramatic monologue, which has a lesser degree of logical articulation than the meditation, but also in their tendency to use general statements without any easily traceable logical connection between them; rather, such disconnected statements often occur in dense patches of imagery, which is, itself, difficult to interpret. Apollinaire's "Le Brasier" and "Les Fiançailles" are excellent illustrations. Another feature of such statements is that they sometimes say exactly what one does not expect: "Beauty is momentary in the mind—/The fitful tracing of a portal;/But in the flesh it is immortal" (Wallace Stevens: "Peter Quince at the Clavier"). Countless poets have warned that beauty is most perishable in the flesh and survives only in verse. Modern poems that consist solely of juxtaposed images without commentary (like Mallarmé's "Ses purs ongles") are by no means necessarily harder to interpret than the mysterious sententiousness of Rimbaud, Stevens, Eugenio Montale, Hart Crane, and Dylan Thomas.

A last element of poetic texture, which we have only mentioned in passing, is natural description, bringing us to a significant characteristic of romantic poetry: while description is inseparable from the English concept of imagination and the French idea of the poem as a richly colored object, it is nearly always handled as a coordinate or subordinate in the poem rather than as an independent, autonomous rhetorical entity. (A special exception can be found, at least theoretically, in descriptions designed to dazzle through artfulness and *enargeia,* as vividness was called.) The reason for this is that description, unless accompanied by even a slight interpretive analogy, represents a kind of neutral discourse, which does not fulfill the rhetorical purpose of influencing or moving. In the rhetorical tradition, even what may seem the most obvious symbolic functions of description, such as the equivalence between a winter landscape and old age, cannot exist without an explicit correlative. A new autonomy of description will be seen in more recent poetry.

The possibility of formulating, however briefly, a morphology of lyric based on the rhetorical tradition suggests that deviations from these patterns may also present themselves in recurrent types, and, furthermore, that the very absence of certain rhetorical features will be of use in interpretation of these forms. Here is the place to consider the new ideas that came to modify poets' handling of traditional poetic structures.

3. Impersonality and Objectivity

The idea of impersonal poetry in France, free of an overt rhetoric of praise and blame, is usually thought of as evolving in reaction to an emotive theory of poetry current in the romantic period. Actually, as we have seen, the conception of the poem as a beautiful object, from which a notion of impersonal poetry is easily derived, is quite as characteristic of French romanticism, but for the general public, the seemingly personal work of Alfred de Musset and his imitators, detested by most later poets, occupied the foreground. There is definitely a question of the sociology of literature here: as the bourgeoisie of 1830 had seemed utilitarian and neoclassical in its taste and thereby hardly amenable to the idea of poetry as gratuitous beauty, the bourgeoisie now appeared in the mid-century, because of its sentimentality, hostile to the further evolution of aesthetic thought in the direction of the autonomy of art. Moreover, the emotive theory of poetry was an eighteenth-century development, already present in Lamartine's predecessors, and therefore quite as conservative as neoclassicism: hence the connection between the new antibourgeois society, bohemia, and the new poetics of art for art's sake.

The most insistent theorist and practitioner of impersonal poetry in the mid-century was Leconte de Lisle, and the interest of his poetry and polemics lies in the fact that he provided ideas about verse which were a point of departure for later theorists, as well as a model of style which persisted through to the early twentieth century. (Many poets were to write, in not necessarily any evolutionary sequence, "Symbolist" poems and Parnassian ones, by which is usually meant an imitation of Leconte de Lisle's manner.) Leconte de Lisle derived certain general principles of style from the practice of Hugo, Vigny, and Gautier: the cult of euphony and the *beau vers*, generous adjectivation, abundant descriptions of a highly *plastique* character, unity of tone (he differs considerably from Baudelaire on this score), and polished conclusions for his poems. He had little imagination for metaphor, which is surely a factor in the monotony of his admirably finished verse. There is a curious resemblance between Leconte de Lisle's idea of a style generally valid for all worthy subjects and neoclassical aesthetics; this did not escape him.[7] The idea uniting all these technical features is that of controlled emotion objectified and sustained through representations of things, figures, and events in all the elements of color, light, line, sound, and movement necessary to fix it. The narrow range of Leconte de Lisle's subjects, which, although vast as history and the greater continents, carefully excluded the local and modern, should not detract unduly from an interestingly thought-out ideal and achievement.

Impersonality is implicit perhaps in Leconte de Lisle's choice of subjects, but the technique of presenting the subject is also relevant. At the same time as Flaubert was working out the theory of the absent author in the novel, Leconte de Lisle was experimenting with poems devoid of the poetic equivalent of authorial intervention and therefore of the rhetorical persuasions of didacticism and sentimentality. By no means are all his poems free from commentary on their subject (any more than Flaubert's novels truly are). Some poems, like "La Mort de Valmiki," have an interventional narrative technique almost like that of passages in Honoré de Balzac; in other poems the presence of the author is a relative matter, best judged by the standards of contemporary or previous poetry. Occasionally Leconte de Lisle reaches a high degree of impersonality, as in "Paysage polaire," which in the quatrains exemplifies his command of imitative harmony and in the tercets his often elegant syntactic arrangements:

> Un monde mort, immense écume de la mer,
> Gouffre d'ombre stérile et de lueurs spectrales,
> Jets de pics convulsifs étirés en spirales
> Qui vont éperdument dans le brouillard amer.

> Un ciel rugueux roulant par blocs, un âpre enfer
> Où passent à plein vol les clameurs sépulcrales,
> Les rires, les sanglots, les cris aigus, les râles
> Qu'un vent sinistre arrache à son clairon de fer.

> Sur les hauts caps branlants, rongés des flots voraces,
> Se roidissent les Dieux brumeux des vieilles races,
> Congelés dans leur rêve et leur lividité;

> Et les grands ours, blanchis par les neiges antiques,
> Çà et là, balançant leurs cous épileptiques,
> Ivres et monstrueux, bavent de volupté.

A dead world, the sea's immense foam, an abyss of sterile shadow and spectral glimmers; bursts of convulsive peaks drawn out into coils, which move, dazed, through the bitter fog. A rough sky rolling in blocks, a harsh hell in which fly sepulchral cries, laughter, sobs, harsh shouts, and death-rattles, all torn from the sinister wind's iron horn. On the high, trembling promontories, gnawed by the ravenous waves, stiffen the misty gods of ancient races, frozen in their dream and leaden pallor. And the great bears, pale from the age-old snow, here and there, their epileptic necks quivering, drunk and monstrous, slaver with lust.

This kind of implicit commentary on the survival of the life force in horrible circumstances is much in the vein of Flaubert's conception of the artist as everywhere present in his work but nowhere visible.

"Paysage polaire" provides us with our first example of a description free from any coordinate statement. That it is not obscure comes from the contrast we immediately sense with landscapes of harmonious life, but ultimately we have to refer to the survival of the fittest, to nineteenth-century science and its hypothesis that the universe would perish in cold, and to the philosophical pessimism supported by that science, in order to see that this is not a poem primarily about hell or sexuality. In other words, the subject is covert, and the impersonality of technique permits an at least theoretical ambiguity. If the ambiguity here seems negligible, there are descriptions, and not only in more obscure modern poets, in which the sense of the poem is problematic. Shelley wrote an uncharacteristic piece of straight description called "Evening: Ponte al mare, Pisa" which is not easy to interpret, and the same is true of a rather impassive description from Verlaine's early period entitled "L'Heure du berger." Verlaine wrote in a letter some years later of his plans for long poems about things from which man would be completely banished.[8] He did not write the poems, but the technical and theoretical interest in the possibilities of this kind of poetry had occurred to him as it would, in various forms, to other poets.

The most elaborate theory of impersonal poetry is to be found in Mallarmé's letters of 1866 and 1867. Mallarmé went through an acute spiritual crisis in those years, which began with meditations on the buddhistic themes of Maya, the veil of appearances, the ultimate nothingness of the world, and the Glorious Lie which poetry therefore must be. (These notions were familiar from the work of Leconte de

Lisle, Mallarmé's friend Henri Cazalis, and the vulgarizers of the relatively newly translated oriental texts.) Through another friend or through a not very accurate article, Mallarmé next drew on Hegelian ideas, which he worked out in a highly personal way, the result being that, from despair over nothingness, he was saved by the triadic concept that Being and Nothingness are synthesized in an Absolute, which is art or beauty. Furthermore, beauty corresponds to the absolute idea of the universe, which presented itself to Mallarmé's mind. "Beauty . . . finds in the entire universe its correlative phases."[9] With this, beauty was removed from dream and chance, those being the characteristics of contingent, personal art. After the two-year crisis had passed, Mallarmé, who had undergone much physical suffering in the anguish of his discoveries, resigned himself to writing poems "merely tinged with the absolute."[10] The poetry of his maturity, as we shall see, reflects in its style a certain conception of impersonality.

With Rimbaud another term related to impersonality, but rather more problematic, enters our considerations. In the famous letters of May, 1871, Rimbaud contrasted objective poetry with its insipid subjective opposite. The prose is sometimes difficult to follow, but it is clear that Musset's personal poetry represents everything detestable in verse. Objective poetry, as it fitfully occurred in the romantics, comes from a force outside the poet of which he may even be unaware. This might be the sense of "Je est un autre," but the source of the other voice, at least as it has manifested itself already in other poets, remains obscure, although Rimbaud calls it universal intelligence. The imagery he uses suggests less intelligence than a collective unconscious, and the expression "plenitude of the great dream" confirms this. In any case, what the poet brings back from "down there" can be formless in its essential character and expression, by which Rimbaud meant that it does not have the symmetries and unity of tone proper to form in the neoclassical tradition; the idea of organic form, which was totally unfamiliar to Rimbaud, would better suit the case.

The significance of the formless becomes clear when we look at the poems included in his letters. One, "Le Coeur supplicié," is a kind of plaintive fool's song (fool's songs and mad songs occur in Hugo's *Cromwell* and Emile Verhaeren's *Les Campagnes hallucinées*; they are not so abundant as in English poetry). Other pieces are a repulsive portrait, "Accroupissements," a punning account of the crushing of the Commune, and a violent, obscure vituperation against "Mes Petites Amoureuses." Words and phrases in the latter sometimes border on the incomprehensible. The objectivity of these poems depends not only on their perhaps having been dictated by the universal soul (they are commonly taken as autobiographical); their dense, almost opaque style makes them indeed linguistic objects, which bear no resemblance to the transparent clichés of personal poetry. Here we have an important further development of the idea of the poem as object: obscurity of subject matter and complexity of expression give it the air of an artifact separated from its creator. Difficult poems have distance as much from the poet as from the reader, and the impossibility of readily seeing them as autobiographical or of penetrating the author's intentions, without special conjectures or information, precludes or should preclude local or anecdotal interpretations. Of course, the opposite argument can be maintained, that nothing is more subjective than hermetic language and, conversely, that commonplace idiom is objective; that, however, is a critic's point of view, not a poet's, and it is perfectly clear how, in the context of nineteenth-century French poetry and the prevalence in the reading public of a debased emotive theory of art as personal expression, Rimbaud evolved his theory of objectivity. Nor is this conception unique to him: it seems implicit in Tristan Corbière and later poets. Flaubert, speculating on possibilities in poetic style, suggested that for impersonality of subject matter, something related to the poet's life could be substituted, provided that it were "strange, disordered, so intense that it becomes creation." What Flaubert is tacitly admitting is that the genetic argument, which seems often to lie behind the theory of impersonality, is not the issue: the real question is one of stylistic expression, not whether the subject comes from outside the poet's experience. Personal poetry as practiced was the poetry of cliché: creative language, whether dealing with personal anecdote, the poet's unconscious, the lives of others, or the universal intelligence, is objectivity.

The paradox inherent in the idea that an almost impenetrable metaphor, say, is more objective than a commonplace which everyone understands and uses, can be dispelled if we refer to the modern conception of the persona in literature. The most ordinary, direct form of expression does not always give the impression of a real, distinct, concrete person speaking. The personality in such circumstances is not clearly constituted, as Flaubert put it, through lack of precise details. What comes forth is such general and therefore approximate language that it lacks individual objectivity. Those who respond better to generalities and abstractions may have more highly evolved minds, as Remy de Gourmont thought, but less capacity for aesthetic discrimination and creativity. There is a middle ground, however, between the extremes, and it is worth noting that the persona envisaged by Flaubert and evolved by Rimbaud is slightly to one side of it: much poetry of earlier centuries assumes a speaker who is the poet in one of his conventional roles, but a poet and not a generalized ordinary man. What Rimbaud's practice implies is actually personae individualized according to the modern novelist's habit of trying to form a distinct consciousness for a character (as opposed to the pure type-characters of much fiction). This relation between modern fiction and poetry is only the first of several such rapprochements we shall observe.

Precise details and the communication of a feeling of personality bring us to one further nuance in poetic theory and practice: the objective poem can be thought of as attaining its goal through the representation of objects. This means that descriptive poems can convey something slightly different from the kind of covert theme we found in Leconte de Lisle's "Paysage polaire." Their content may be a subjectivity whose rendering is objectified. Such an effect is clearly related to the idea of impersonality, but it is a further refinement and takes us beyond the domain of Leconte de Lisle's poetry and into the practice of poets associated with the term Symbolism.

4. Mood Poems

Of the various uses of the word symbolism in the late nineteenth century, only one is entirely new and cannot, through any equivocation, be assimilated to allegory and other traditional ideas of the symbol. This is its application to a group of poems that convey a state of mind, either permanent or mood-like and transitory, through a combination of primarily descriptive elements. Mallarmé, who rarely spoke of symbols or symbolism in his critical writings, uses it in this sense to describe the work of the younger poets of the 1880s and 1890s.[11] (We find few examples in his own work of poems whose only goal is to render a mood). Yeats also meant by symbolism an inextricable nexus of images which, as no individual word could, communicates an *état d' âme*. The significant novelty in this use of the word is that, unlike the earlier conceptions of symbolism, it does not point to one or more symbols, specific elements in a context, but rather to a complex whose components may be inexplicable in themselves; such antirationalism also distinguishes the new sense from older ideas of symbolism where logical analogies are strong.

In the elaboration of mood poems, it was often felt necessary to indicate in some way that the imagery referred to the mind of the poem's speaker, as in the last line of Emile Verhaeren's "Londres":

> Et ce Londres de fonte et de bronze, mon âme,
> Où des plaques de fer claquent sous des hangars,
> > Où des voiles s'en vont, sans Notre-Dame
> Pour étoile, s'en vont, là-bas, vers les hasards.
>
> Gares de suie et de fumée, où du gaz pleure
> Ses spleens d'argent lointain vers des chemins d'éclair,
> > Où des bêtes d'ennui bâillent à l'heure
> Dolente immensément, qui tinte à Westminster.
>
> Et ces quais infinis de lanternes fatales,
> Parques dont les fuseaux plongent aux profondeurs,
> > Et ces marins noyés, sous les pétales
> Des fleurs de boue où la flamme met des lueurs.
>
> Et ces châles et ces gestes de femmes soûles,
> Et ces alcools de lettres d'or jusques aux toits,
> > Et tout à coup la mort, parmi ces foules;
> O mon âme du soir, ce Londres noir qui traîne en toi! (*Les Soirs*, 1887)

And this cast iron, bronze London, my soul, where metal sheets clatter in warehouses, where sails vanish without Our Lady for a star, vanish toward chance. Sooty, smoky stations, where gas weeps its distant silver spleen toward lightning rails, where beasts of ennui yawn at the vastly aching hour ringing at Westminster. And the infinite embankments with fatal lanterns, fates whose spindles plunge into the depths, and the drowned sailors under the petals of mud flowers, where the reflection of the flame glints. And the shawls and drunken women's gestures, and the roof-high gold letters spelling names of liquors, and suddenly death amid the crowds. O my evening soul, the black London drifting in you! ("London")

The loose syntax of nouns does not give the pattern of an argument. There is no explanation or distribution of emphasis for the benefit of another person, as in a rhetorical situation; this is overheard poetry. The description is not, of course, autonomous, in that it is correlated to the speaker's soul, but the soul-cityscape is not presented as exemplary, but rather as individual, strange, and disordered, Flaubert's terms for objectifying the personal. Verhaeren went on in the 1890s to write volumes of poetry that were characterized by contemporary critics as outward-turning and socially conscious, yet his poems are still conceived of in obsessive images of things red, black, gold, and metallic, of staring eyes, hallucinations, and sinister animals. The characteristics of mood poetry often extend to poems with more elaborately articulated themes.

Mood poems were written before Mallarmé and Yeats defined the new sense of symbolism, and the writer who tended especially to be associated with such effects was Verlaine. Here and there in his early volumes, and especially in *Romances sans paroles* (1874), we find complexes of images which, taken separately, are not particularly suggestive but which work as a whole:

> La fuite est verdâtre et rose
> Des collines et des rampes,
> Dans un demi-jour de lampes
> Qui vient brouiller toute chose.
>
> L'or, sur les humbles abîmes,
> Tout doucement s'ensanglante,
> Des petits arbres sans cimes,
> Où quelque oiseau faible chante.
>
> Triste à peine tant s'effacent
> Ces apparences d'automne,
> Toutes mes langueurs rêvassent,
> Que berce l'air monotone. ("Bruxelles: Simples Fresques")

The flight is greenish and pink of hills and ramps, in a half-light of lamps mingling everything. Gold over the low chasms softly grows blood red. Topless little trees where some bird sings weakly. Barely sad, because the autumnal appearances grow so faint; all my languor daydreams, rocked by the monotonous air. ("Brussels: Simple Frescoes")

Here the correlation between speaker and landscape is made; elsewhere in Verlaine it may be absent. In any case, the mood expressed by the description, whether autonomous or not, has no general or exemplary value. The imagery of *effacement* is especially characteristic of Verlaine, and what might be called its vagueness deserves a particular word. Verlaine's verse is often termed musical (he suggested the comparison himself), and vagueness is one of the qualities often ascribed to music by late nineteenth-century French writers. Music is not, of course, obscure for anyone trained in it, as Verlaine was not, and the analogy, while meaningful for Verlaine personally, is ultimately false, distracting, and useless. We might substitute the unpejorative word indeterminacy for vagueness and observe that it describes important kinds of perceptions that are remarkably rendered by Verlaine's imagery, with its subtle and original use of the verbal noun *fuite* with color adjectives of durational value and in the stylized spatial configurations. As in Verhaeren's "Londres," the creation of a mood poem leads to some innovation in the syntactic and lexical domain, which makes the presence of a new genre especially easy to identify. Verlaine was concerned that his mood poems not be assimilated to traditional description; he gave them unusual titles like *ariettes* and *simples fresques* to suggest that they followed a new aesthetic. A minor genre of the late nineteenth century that originated in *Romances sans paroles* (the paradox of that title is significant) is the impersonal mood poem cast in prosodic forms associated with song and consisting of fragments of description. These songs have no words in the traditional sense of a well-defined rhetorical situation in which a clear episode is communicated.

The fragmentary and indeterminate aspect of the description in "Bruxelles" and similar poems led to the question being occasionally raised whether the mood or the landscape came first, in other words, whether the origin of the poem was subjective or objective. Obviously only the poet could know—if even he could—but the fact that the issue was brought up shows the concern with the *ignes fatui* of subjectivity and objectivity. On the one hand, the fact that a poem abounded in objects seemed, in comparison with the not very concrete yet very emotive poetry of Musset and his imitators, to justify crediting it with both impersonality and objectivity; on the other hand, the

relative obscurity of the new imagery suggested a high degree of sub-
jectiveness. Verhaeren's generation often resolved the question in a
way unknown to Verlaine's, which was the affirmation of solipsism.
The latter was fancifully attributed to Arthur Schopenhauer, then a
fashionable name, probably because the title of *Die Welt als Wille
und Vorstellung* becomes in French *Le Monde . . . comme idée.* Solipsism never amounted to much as a practical philosophy of life, but it
was useful as a way of accounting for poems like "Bruxelles," in that
the tension between the subjective and objective was eliminated, the
subjective ceasing to be somewhat limited and incidental in order to
become the only possible vision. All manner of strange diction could
be justified by it. Finally, solipsism was theoretical grounds for the
destruction of rhetorical situations and their distinctions. In a solipsistic world apostrophes to nature or any other second person are meaningless, eliminating the relations characteristic of previous nature
poetry; autonomous descriptions of landscape no longer need an expressed correlative with the speaker, although poets frequently continued to make one. Exemplarity and generality are impossible. The
most radical implications of solipsism were not, however, exploited
during the 1880s and 1890s; mood poems came to have certain recurrent traits belying total subjectivity.

Verlaine created the prototype of the mood poem in "Clair de
lune" in *Fêtes galantes* (1869). Its opening line, perhaps addressed to
the self, "Votre âme est un paysage choisi" is the model for the correlative phrases widespread in poets of the 1880s and 1890s like
Georges Rodenbach, Albert Samain, Stuart Merrill, and Ephraïm
Mikhaël. In these poets, as in Verhaeren and Verlaine, the symbols of
mood recur in poem after poem; there is a great consistency in their
imagination, so much so that the correlative expression hardly seems
necessary. Especially frequent are fire, water, air, and qualities of
light and darkness. Gaston Bachelard and his followers have made
much of the presence of these in poetry, and in the static mood poem
their potential for embodying states of mind is perhaps greater than in
more dynamic poetry of the elements like André Breton's or Paul
Eluard's. (The moods of surrealist poetry differ in that they are often
expressed with many verbs of change and movement.) Rodenbach, for
example, creates a universe that is to some extent airy and chthonic

but above all filled with water, whether in aquariums, fountains, or the canals of Bruges, which becomes a stylized mood city in his verse. Rodenbach's imagery of the elements, like that of other mood poets, has no univalent or isolated meaning; the symbolism functions in complexes.

While the symbolism of mood poems may be irrational, it is not obscure, and indeed may be reinforced by the coloring of certain words. Verhaeren's "Londres," like many of Rodenbach's poems about things, uses a certain amount of emotive vocabulary like "weeps," "spleen," and "ennui." Obviously a mood poem could be written that would dispense with such terms: it would represent the objective idea of style evolving contemporaneously in the novel and would evoke emotion from descriptions while not naming the emotion. If, at the same time, any obvious correlation was avoided between the speaker's state of mind and the landscape, the result would be of considerable technical interest, even though the likelihood of its having great poetic intensity seems slight. (The larger structures of fiction can support bare description more easily than a short poem.) Such poems exist, of course: extreme examples are the first of Eliot's "Preludes," which might be little known were it not for the rest of Eliot's work, and some of William Carlos Williams' poems. A truly zero degree of emotive vocabulary is rare in nineteenth-century French poetry although examples of something attempted in that direction are to be met with as early as *Romances sans paroles*. Henry Bataille's verse offers examples of it, an especially good one being "Le Mois mouillé" (from *La Chambre blanche*, 1895):

> Par les vitres grises de la lavanderie
> J'ai vu tomber la nuit d'automne que voilà . . .
> Quelqu'un marche le long des fossés pleins de pluie . . .
> Voyageur, voyageur de jadis qui t'en vas,
> A l'heure où les bergers descendent des montagnes,
> Hâte-toi! Les foyers sont éteints où tu vas,
> Closes les portes au pays que tu regagnes.
> La grande route est vide et le bruit des luzernes
> Vient de si loin qu'il ferait peur . . . Dépêche-toi:
> Les vieilles carrioles ont soufflé leurs lanternes . . .
> C'est l'automne: elle s'est assise et dort de froid
> Sur la chaise de paille au fond de la cuisine . . .

L'automne chante dans les sarments morts des vignes . . .
C'est le moment où les cadavres introuvés,
Les blancs noyés, flottant, songeurs, entre deux ondes,
Saisis eux-mêmes aux premiers froids soulevés,
Descendent s'abriter dans les vases profondes.

Through the grey panes of the washhouse I saw this autumn night fall. Someone is walking along the ditches filled with rain. Traveler, long ago traveler passing by at the hour when shepherds come down from the mountains, hurry! The hearthfires where you are heading have gone out; closed the doors in the village you are going back to. The highway is empty, and the rustle of alfalfa comes from so far away it is frightening. Hurry! The lights are out on the old wagons. It is autumn: she has sat down and sleeps from the cold on the cane chair in the back of the kitchen. Autumn sings in the dead vine branches. Now is the time when missing bodies, white drowned men, floating dreamily among the eddies, seized by the first cold weather, sink to shelter in the deep mud. ("The Wet Month")

These alexandrines are relaxed by traditional standards with their frequent tripartite movement; such prosaic rhythm is accompanied by a certain prosaicness and restraint in diction. The address to the imaginary wayfarer is not a real apostrophe but a kind of inner monologue and thus, aside from the mild personification of autumn, the only conspicuously heightened effect is the substantial image of the corpses. The rhetorical gesture of the speaker's identifying his soul with the landscape has vanished, along with most other kinds of distinctly poetic language, so that the whole emphasis rests on that image.

The corpses in Bataille's poem are at the extreme limit of realistic description because of their mysterious plurality. When we observe the general consonance of Bataille's style with fiction and prose grammar, we must remember that the best French realist narratives are much studied in respect to stylization and symbolic configurations and that no absolute cleavage existed for someone like Mallarmé between some kinds of poetry and Emile Zola's most distinguished work. The prosaicness of Bataille's style was contemporary with novels given to poetic uses of imagery. An element we do find in Bataille which can specifically be called prosaic is the tendency to avoid interpretation and commentary: Flaubert's example here antedates any prominent one in French poetry.

In general, the role played by ideas of prose in the elaboration of mood poems and others in French is different from that in poetry in English, notably William Carlos Williams'. French conceptions of prosaic verse tend to have to do with rhythm and syntax, while not in the least excluding figurative language, as in these lines of Blaise Cendrars written in 1913 ("Contrastes," *Dix-huit Poèmes élastiques*), which are an evocation of light in the late afternoon following a rain:

> Il pleut les globes électriques
> Montrouge Gare de l'Est Métro Nord-Sud bateaux-mouches monde
> Tout est halo
> Profondeur
> Rue de Buci on crie "L'Intransigeant" et "Paris-Sports"
> L'aérodrome du ciel est maintenant, embrasé, un tableau de Cimabue
> Quand par devant
> Les hommes sont
> Longs
> Noirs
> Tristes
> Et fument, cheminées d'usine

It's raining electric lightbulbs. Montrouge, Gare de l'Est, North-South subway line, boats, world. All is halo, depth. On the Rue de Buci they're hawking *L'Intransigeant* and *Paris-Sports*. The celestial airport is now, flaming, a painting by Cimabue, while in the foreground men are long, dark, sad, and are smoking, factory chimneys. ("Contrasts")

Cendrars' lines seem initially quite different from the preceding mood poems we have looked at, and, indeed, the images are set forth in oppositions of high and low, light and dark, rather than in an incremental sequence. While this is not enough to be called an argument—there is no dialectic movement—it seems to have a different kind of effect. But the imagery of the elements—here fire, water, air—so frequent in mood poems, recurs, and, as in the others, the mood might most succinctly be described as melancholy, for, with all the variations in style and technique we have seen, these poems move in a somewhat narrow emotional ambit. To be sure, melancholy, as the term is used just by nineteenth-century poets, covers shades of feeling from deep depression to pleasant sadness, but in the face of all possible emotions they seem to favor a narrow part of the spectrum.

While a contrast, as between a factory chimney and a Cimabue, is the structural limit of the mood poem, more often perhaps its imagery tends to be uniform and incremental, focusing either on the chimney or the art work. That these are very restricted poems in their import does not, however, lessen their great technical interest: the effects of tone and imagery evolved for them often served their creators in far more elaborate works. One of the arresting examples of this is Yeats, some of whose early poetry, as we shall see, constituted a phase of experiment in the impersonal and archetypal, which left important traces later in his work. Yeats' poems belong to the other large group of mood poems, those which create an effect of impersonality not so much through objectifying an *état d'âme* in description as by evoking contemplatively images of the beautiful, which, by its supposedly transcendental nature, is objective. Curiously enough the same poets rarely wrote both kinds of mood poems.

The early poems of Yeats I want to look at have a semblance of movement absent in the mood poems examined until now. However, on closer analysis, we perceive the static character of those lyrics which Yeats published in *The Rose* (1893) and *The Wind among the Reeds* (1899) and which deal with the Danaan folk, beauty, and the rose. Not only is this a curious kind of cycle in that, instead of narrating, it presents a series of closely related moods, but also its imagery has a particular cast in having been adapted from Celtic mythology. The latter provides a picture of the world that has all the more poetic advantages in that no one—poet or reader—is distracted by believing in it, while at the same time it has just enough analogies with Christianity—a heavenly host and an end to time—as not to be utterly strange in its shape. The Celtic mythology Yeats drew on is aristocratic in origin and envisages a supernal world reflecting earthly nobility:

Be you still, be you still, trembling heart;
Remember the wisdom out of the old days:
Him who trembles before the flame and the flood,
And the winds that blow through the starry ways,
Let the starry winds and the flame and the flood
Cover over and hide, for he has no part
With the lonely, majestical multitude. ("To his Heart, Bidding it have no Fear")

It is not relevant to attempt to decide whether this refers to initiation or to an afterlife: the poem describes the contemplation of something both in and beyond change, in language suitable for a poet who disliked abstractions: the multitude is permanent, in, and yet distinct from, movement. The elements, which recur again and again in this early poetry of Yeats', as in so much mood poetry, do not form the traditional symbolic patterns of opposition but are grouped together, suggesting a flux. Instead of the distinctions of a poetry of discrete symbols, we have here an all-embracing associationism without contrasts. We know from the tone that this multitude is beautiful and are hardly surprised when elsewhere the imagery associates the fiery host and beauty:

> When my arms wrap you round I press
> My heart upon the loveliness
> That has long faded from the world . . .
> . . . .
> And when you sigh from kiss to kiss
> I hear white Beauty sighing, too,
> For hours when all must fade like dew,
> But flame on flame, and deep on deep,
> Throne over throne where in half sleep,
> Their swords upon their iron knees,
> Brood her high lonely mysteries. ("He remembers Forgotten Beauty")

I do not see any contrast here between dew and flame, but rather Yeats' peculiar way of suggesting flux and stability all at once, which makes little sense in the traditional language of symbolism but conveys that feeling of beauty's being at once transitory and permanent which is Yeats' mood and very difficult to reduce to an idea.

The invocation to the rose, which is synonymous with beauty, the ideal, heaven, and repose, describes an intimation of the other world:

> Far-off, most secret, and inviolate Rose,
> Enfold me in my hour of hours; where those
> Who sought thee in the Holy Sepulchre,
> Or in the wine-vat, dwell beyond the stir
> And tumult of defeated dreams; and deep
> Among pale eyelids, heavy with the sleep
> Men have named beauty . . .

. . . .
. . . I, too, await
The hour of thy great wind of love and hate.
When shall the stars be blown about the sky,
Like the sparks blown out of a smithy, and die?
Surely thine hour has come, thy great wind blows,
Far-off, most secret, and inviolate Rose? ("The Secret Rose")

The poem renders a mood of expectancy, whether of the speaker's death or the end of change ("until God burn time") is carefully left ambiguous, which is suitable in the context of an unbelieved-in mythology, whose function is to provide an emotive complex. The end of change is not meant to designate some literal metaphysical event but to describe what the contemplation of beauty makes one long for. "He remembers forgotten beauty" and other pieces are love poems of an almost impersonal sort, and the imagery relating to time is part of the lover's array of emotions. Likewise the poems on the supernatural beings are an essential part of the total mood rather than having any folkloric purpose:

While I wrought out these fitful Danaan rhymes,
My heart would brim with dreams about the times
When we bent down above the fading coals
And talked of the dark folk who live in souls
Of passionate men, like bats in the dead trees;
And of the wayward twilight companies
Who sigh with mingled sorrow and content,
Because their blossoming dreams have never bent
Under the fruit of evil and of good:
And of the embattled flaming multitude
Who rise, wing above wing, flame above flame,
And, like a storm, cry the Ineffable Name,
And with the clashing of their sword-blades make
A rapturous music, till the morning break
And the white hush end all but the loud beat
Of their long wings, the flash of their white feet. ("To Some I have talked with by
   the Fire")

Mankind's infirm aspirations and divine "fire-born moods" are the theme. These poems do not contain esoteric symbolism, much less a doctrine, as is sometimes thought; the only thing approaching a symbol in the traditional sense is the rose, which is more an overt analogy as it is in Dante. Rather, Yeats has devised an interrelated group of images informing a series of mood poems. Love for Maud Gonne is expressed quite impersonally and as part of a vaster picture, one which seems at first to have metaphysical dimensions, although actually the mythology serves as a psychological symbolic complex. For example, the expression "God's war" in "The Rose of Peace" is meant to convey not so much the kind of battle fought by Michael and Satan as change and restless movement.

Yeats' early lyrics appear more complicated than purely descriptive mood poems; what seem to be elements of theology provoke the urge to find some intellectual construct behind them, to treat them as something other than mood poetry and to look for the contrasts, conflicts, and resolutions of symbolic poetry in the traditional sense. The images, however, appear as an associative group, without articulation among them, and the technique he uses might be described as a pseudoargument: in "To his Heart, Bidding it have no Fear," some immensely significant distinction seems to be made dealing with a trial, but a trial indeterminate enough that we are hard put to fit it into a scheme of thought, and we then realize that the trial is not the point of the poem but rather the association of a noble multitude and the elements. This is an extraordinary achievement in ambiguity; the poem suggests a metaphysical conception but is not really about it. Yeats described his early poetry as a "mood of pure contemplation of beauty."[12] Moods are both emotions and ideas, and this poetry employs fragments of ideas the way other mood poems may use fragments of description. With some poets—such as Mallarmé—there is a risk of reducing a symbolic figure of thought to a poem expressive of mood; with Yeats' early work, however, as we can see in his essay on symbolism in poetry (in *Ideas of Good and Evil*), the mood was the overriding consideration.

Poems of the pure contemplation of beauty, like other mood poems, cannot by nature have an argument, a considerable limitation often compensated for by density of images. Some attempt to give an impression of movement in the sequence of images can prevent a totally static feeling, and Valéry in his poems of the 1890s (collected as the *Album de vers anciens*) is a particular master of this:

Celles qui sont des fleurs légères sont venues,
Figurines d'or et beautés toutes menues
Où s'irise une faible lune... Les voici
Mélodieuses fuir dans le bois éclairci.
De mauves et d'iris et de nocturnes roses
Sont les grâces de nuit sous leurs danses écloses.
Que de parfums voilés dispensent leurs doigts d'or!
Mais l'azur doux s'effeuille en ce bocage mort
Et de l'eau mince luit à peine, reposée
Comme un pâle trésor d'une antique rosée
D'où le silence en fleur monte... Encore les voici
Mélodieuses fuir dans le bois éclairci.
Aux calices aimés leurs mains sont gracieuses;
Un peu de lune dort sur leurs lèvres pieuses
Et leurs bras merveilleux aux gestes endormis
Aiment à dénouer sous les myrtes amis
Leurs liens fauves et leurs caresses... Mais certaines,
Moins captives du rythme et des harpes lointaines,
S'en vont d'un pas subtil au lac enseveli
Boire des lys l'eau frêle où dort le pur oubli. ("Les Vaines Danseuses")

They who are light flowers have come, gold figurines and tiny beauties glowing with weak moonlight. Now they melodiously flee in the glimmering wood. Mallows, iris, and night roses are the nocturnal graces opened beneath their dances. So many dim scents emanate from their golden fingers! But leaves of gentle azure fall in the dead grove, and slim water barely gleams, at rest like a pale treasure of ancient dew from which the flower silence arises. Here again they flee in the glimmering wood. Touching the dear blossoms, their hands are full of grace. A bit of moonlight sleeps on their pious lips, and their wonderful arms, with sleepy gestures, like to undo, beneath the friendly myrtles, their tawny bonds of hair, and their caresses... But a few, less imprisoned by the rhythm and distant harps, go off with subtle steps to the buried lake and drink the lilies' frail water, in which pure oblivion sleeps. ("The Vain Dancers")

Another poet might have framed these lines as a dream or fantasy, thus creating something closer to a conventional rhetorical situation. But Valéry, here as elsewhere in the *Album de vers anciens,* is careful not to attenuate the effect of his imagery by qualifying it. The result may be ambiguity for the unprepared reader who could wonder if the dancers do not represent something specific and perform symbolic actions. This, however, is the imagery of contemplation of beauty: the transcendent, supernal beauty at the top of the hierarchy of existence;

the dancers' movements are merely poetic graces with no particular allegorical value implied.

Valéry's images are favorite ones of transcendent beauty in late nineteenth-century French poets: flowers, the moon, gold, music, dancers, perfumes, and water, all infused by a lifeless quality that is not so much that of death, which after all is the result of organic decay, as of a virginal, prenatal, or otherworldly state. The only images frequent in this category which Valéry changes or omits are the park, jewel-plants, and birds such as swans or white peacocks. Objective descriptive poems are a common form for the imagery of pure beauty, and their characteristic texture is one of highly sensory imagery that strives through figurative language like Valéry's "frail water" to suggest ineffable yet perceptible qualities. This way of being at once lifeless but not death-like, sensible but impalpable, is a paradox proper to the divine, and of course beauty occupies that transcendental place for many late nineteenth-century poets. In Schopenhauerian terms the contemplation of beauty hushes the will and dispels the tension between the subjective and the objective which we may find in our earlier category of mood poems. While Schopenhauer should not be considered an "influence" on French poets, despite the modish regard for his philosophy in the 1880s and 1890s, he often provides interesting ways of looking at the literature of the end of the century.

The imagery of pure beauty has its sources in late romanticism: Baudelaire, Gautier, and Leconte de Lisle had variously contributed to it in the noting of refined sensations, the description of artifacts, and sensuous renderings of landscapes. For all the instances in which we find elements of the imagery of pure beauty, however, no one poem before Mallarmé's "Scène" from *Hérodiade*, published in *Le Parnasse contemporain* in 1869, contains the whole of it, in detail and in apparent general intention. Since the "Scène" alone does not make entirely clear what the allegory of *Hérodiade* was to be, younger poets took it as a work of absolute art, divorced from normal rhetorical expectations of subject and development. *Hérodiade* in its truncated form seems to have been at the origin of a good many visions of beauty in late nineteenth-century poetry. In the search for a distinctive note within the general type of imagery suggested by Mallarmé's poem, Valéry sometimes used classical subjects such as Helen and substituted pure sunlight for the lunar world.

While poems of the pure contemplation of beauty seem inextricably bound with nineteenth-century concepts of the poem as artifact, some poets managed to salvage a good deal of this imagery, which they integrated into other kinds of poetic structures. In his later poetry, *La Jeune Parque* and *Charmes*, Valéry remained in many ways faithful to the aesthetics of his youth: *La Jeune Parque* in particular has often been compared to *Hérodiade* for the exquisiteness of the speaker's view of herself. Stevens' "one of fictive music," wearing, on her "pale head," "a band entwining set with fatal stones," suggests something of the same refined vision of the aesthetic. Another poet is Ezra Pound, who in his imagist poems like "Actaeon" or "Alba" created pictures of medieval and Greek beauty, only later to make of them a contrasting, dramatic element, part of the mental furniture of Hugh Selwyn Mauberley and the speaker of the *Cantos*. Despite Pound's lack of interest in French aesthetic poetry after Gautier and his very different conceptions of stylistic detail, he perpetuated a similar conception of poetry's highest vision. There are many shades of difference in style between Pound's imagist poems and the invocation to the Lynx and Aphrodite in the *Pisan Cantos* (LXXIX), and Pound's critics find neoplatonic and mystical elements in his mature poetry, but at the origins of Pound's "mysticism" is the late nineteenth-century representation of transcendental beauty. Finally, a most extraordinary adaptation of this imagery remains Yeats' "Sailing to Byzantium," which, although it surpasses all the earlier poetry of transcendental beauty except Mallarmé's, is unthinkable without it.

The later Valéry, Yeats, and Pound offer examples of the transformation and integration into more elaborate poetic schemes of the imagery of pure beauty. In the 1890s, however, there are earlier examples of the way it could be used in poems and poem cycles that are not exclusively descriptive, and these belong in our present considerations because their significance is determined solely by this imagery. Like the young Yeats, Stefan George was concerned with expressing beauty and melancholy, but he did not have the advantages of Celtic mythology or Maud Gonne to organize his creative activity. In part of *Algabal* (1892), in *Das Buch der Hirten- und Preisgedichte* (1895), and occasionally later, George showed great skill at poems in which the speaker portrays himself in a specific situation; they are as dramatic as all but a very few of Robert Browning's monologues. Beginning, however, with *Das Buch der hängenden Gärten* (1895) and in a more pronounced way in *Das Jahr der Seele* (1897) and the "Gezeiten" section of *Der siebente Ring* (1907), George somewhat surprisingly abandoned this genre which, one would have thought, should have continued to interest him because of its newness and range of still unexplored possibilities. Instead, he created cycles of *I-and-you* poems in which the dramatic element is minimized through the indeterminacy of the situations evoked. There is an anticipation of this kind of poem in Verlaine's *Romances sans paroles*, which George had doubtless carefully studied around the time of his stay in Paris in the early 1890s, when he was especially interested in the innovations of contemporary French poetry.

Reading *Romances sans paroles*, and some of Verlaine's other poetry, was, in the 1890s, quite different from what it can be today, with copiously annotated editions and the availability of detailed biographies of the poet. Poems which we know to have reference to events and moments in Verlaine's life were elusive; others which we suppose to be fictive or whose biographical allusion escapes us, mingle with them. The whole must have formed an extraordinarily *insaisissable* texture, full of delicate shifts of tone and mood but impossible to construe as telling coherently of events. Verlaine, of course, was hardly unaware of this; he was living during 1872 and 1873 with a poet who was perfecting techniques of subtle evasiveness in subject matter. Verlaine, in short, created a volume expressive above all of *états d'âme*, even if specific poems do not always follow the patterns of mood poetry we have already seen.

We happen to know a certain amount about whatever autobiographical elements are behind George's lyrics, thanks to the vast *Kommentar* of his friend Ernst Morwitz.[13] It appears, from reading Morwitz, that George tended to embroider rather banal situations into ones more fraught with emotion, as well as to invent hazy

details, events, and figures, which can in no textual way be distinguished from those which have some scrap of autobiography in them.
Occasionally a poem is openly and carefully based on the poet's life.
The result of all this playing with imagination and reality is not
creation of sharply dramatized situations but of events that are alluded
to without their forming any coherent pattern. The aesthetic unity of
the cycles is elsewhere:

> Noch zwingt mich treue über dir zu wachen
> Und deines duldens schönheit dass ich weile;
> Mein heilig streben ist mich traurig machen
> Damit ich wahrer deine trauer teile.
>
> Nie wird ein warmer anruf mich empfangen;
> Bis in die späten stunden unsres bundes
> Muss ich erkennen mit ergebnem bangen
> Das herbe schicksal winterlichen fundes.

My loyalty obliges me to watch over you, and the beauty of your suffering compels
me to remain with you; I devoutly strive to make myself sad in order more truly to
share your mourning. Never will a warm cry greet me; until the late hours of our
union I must recognize with resigned dread that it is the bitter fate of winter's find.

The whole poem's justification is the last line, an example of the
French type of *beau vers* which George assiduously worked at in
German. "Waller im Schnee," from which this poem comes, is the
second of the autumn, winter, and summer cycles from *Das Jahr der
Seele*. There are allusions to both pleasant moments and disunity between the *I* and *you* in "Waller im Schnee," but close reading reveals
generally something implied in the last line above: the *you* is a function of winter; she has no existence apart from the landscape. Whatever episode of George's life may have inspired the cycle, the *you* has
become a winter fantasy, from which he will part as a consequence
of the change of season: "Ins frühjahr darf ich dich nicht mit mir
nehmen." The presence of the *you* creates intimacy of tone without
there being much objectivity embodied in the second person. It is
wrong to object that rhetorical and dramatic situations are so poorly
realized in *Das Jahr der Seele* and elsewhere: the whole aesthetic
is counter to them. Often the *you* is an inconsequential pretext, and

George wrote many occasional poems in which two people contemplate the surroundings but what is important is the description: they are mood poems *à deux*, in which there happens to be someone besides the speaker sharing the space. In the preface to the second edition of *Das Jahr der Seele* George notes that *you* and *I* have rarely been so much the same soul as in this book. Furthermore, the natural scene tends to have a special character.

As titles like *Das Jahr der Seele*, "Gezeiten," and *Das Buch der hängenden Gärten* imply, nature plays a dominant role in George's poetry, but it is a quite different role from that of nature in German and English romantic poetry. George's *Wandern* has little promise or fulfillment about it, just as companionship is more incidental than purposeful. There are no revelations in these nature poems, merely the presentation of a sustained contemplation of beauty. In the following poem the speaker and his companion fall silent on an "evening of inner companionship," because the spectacle of light is more voluptuous than anything they can imagine. Their words fall:

Sie sanken hin wo sich am fruchtgeländer
Der purpurschein im gelben schmelz verlor;
Sie stiegen auf zum schmuck der hügelränder
Wo für die dunkle lust die traube gor.

Ich wagte dir nicht, du nicht mir zu nahen
Als schräger strahl in unsre häupter schoss,
Noch gar mit rede störend zu bejahen
Was jetzt uns band; was jedes stumm genoss

Und was in uns bei jenes tages rüste
Auf zu den veilchenfarbnen wolken klomm:
Was mehr als unsre träume und gelüste
An diesem gluten-abend zart erglomm. ("Reifefreuden," *Das Jahr der Seele*)

They fell where, in the orchards, the purple gleam grew lost in molten yellow; they rose for the adornment of the hillcrests, where clusters of grapes fermented for dark pleasure. I dared not approach you, nor you me, when the oblique beam shot on our heads, nor dared by speaking to disturb what now bound us, what each silently enjoyed, and what in us, as that day set, climbed to the violet-colored clouds; what more than our dreams and longings glimmered softly in the evening incandescence. ("Ripening Joy")

George did not care much for real landscapes, according to Morwitz. Rather, he cared for the arrangement of words designating light and color in elegant sound patterns such as in the verb rhymes or in the last line above. It is the poem as a beautiful object that claimed his entire attention, which explains the insignificance of the *I* and *you* relations, the absence of drama and conflict. At the same time George did not write poems about absolute beauty like "Les Vaines Dan-seuses"; he followed the Verlainean model of the initimate lyric but handled the natural descriptions in a peculiar way, which is related to the French imagery of beauty. Nature first appears in his work as inorganic, jewel-like, precious, or even in the form of the antinatural, decadent black flower. In famous lines George expressed how, failing in his ideal of grey, austere verse, he was resigned to sumptuous effects:

> Ich wollte sie aus kühlem eisen
> Und wie ein glatter fester streif;
> Doch war im schacht auf allen gleisen
> So kein metall zum gusse reif.

> Nun aber soll sie also sein:
> Wie eine grosse fremde dolde
> Geformt aus feuerrotem golde
> Und reichem blitzendem gestein. ("Die Spange," *Pilgerfahrten*)

I wanted it made of cool steel and like a smooth firm band, but from no tunnels of the mine was such a metal ready for casting. Therefore let it be so: like a great strange umbel formed of fire-red gold and rich flashing jewels. ("The Clasp")

It is not that nature is transformed in George's poetry. In the first place there is no idea of a living, organic, whole called nature that could undergo a change; nature is only a complex of forms, textures, and colors, which present themselves to the melancholic contemplator of beauty:

> Nun säume nicht die gaben zu erhaschen
> Des scheidenden gepränges vor der wende;
> Die grauen wolken sammeln sich behende;
> Die nebel können bald uns überraschen.

Ein schwaches flöten von zerpflücktem aste
Verkündet dir dass lezte güte weise
Das land (eh es im nahen sturm vereise)
Noch hülle mit beglänzendem damaste.

Die wespen mit den goldengrünen schuppen
Sind von verschlossnen kelchen fortgeflogen;
Wir fahren mit dem kahn in weitem bogen
Um bronzebraunen laubes inselgruppen. (*Das Jahr der Seele*)

Now do not hesitate to snatch at the gifts of the parting pageantry before the season's turn. The grey clouds are swiftly gathering; mists may soon overtake us. A faint fluting from the tattered branch announces that a last indulgence sagely covers the land in shining damask, before it ices over in the coming storm. The wasps, with their gold-green scales, have flown away from closed blossoms. We are rowing in a wide curve around groups of islets of bronze-brown foliage.

All this metallic and textured magnificence is oddly lacking in the traditional correspondences between autumn and human life; the elegiac sentiments are absent. The main emotion detectable in George's *Das Jahr der Seele* and other volumes of the same period is a kind of dissatisfaction, quite unlike what Valéry's vain dancers are meant to inspire. Beauty here is never fixed or absolute, no image ever dominates the rest. George came, later in his career, to write poetry on the divine and regeneration, and to speak against the *Purpurgluten* of melancholy. But in his middle work we find a sustained, causeless, somewhat monotonous procession of images of the beautiful, which fail to halt or redeem the slow, sad passage of time.

The use of the imagery of pure beauty in poems in which no truly pure contemplation of it is achieved, is characteristic of the work of various minor French poets of the day—Samain, Pierre Louÿs, Laurent Tailhade, Charles Van Lerberghe, and Merrill, among others. Their art is less important in the context of French poetry than George's is in that of German, which is why I have chosen examples from his work. But the general aesthetic question is a similar one. For them there existed, as for the young Mallarmé, a quite absolute idea of beauty implied in the imagery that recurs in their poetry, and this idea did not have to share the poet's allegiance with God, as was the case in Baudelaire's work. Nor were they especially encumbered by the desire to write exemplary or dramatic poems on the incidents of life: pure imagination was their realm, and their poetry was to justify itself solely on the grounds of beauty. The notion of beauty expressed, however, has a certain philosophical ambiguity: we are led, on the one hand, to see beauty as transcendent, as the substitute for a nonexistent traditional deity; at the same time, the imagery used to convey transcendentality suggests that the beautiful consists of a small number of quite terrestrial properties. Among those which figure prominently, for example, are the fire and gleam of precious stones and metals. By these poets' attempt to make clear the metaphysical character of beauty, its content is narrowed. Perhaps the same might be said of some depictions of God, but we have a long enough tradition of representing deity that we do not perceive them as limiting. Furthermore, beauty may appear in minor Symbolist work to have what has been called empty ideality: the absence of contrasts, of dialectic patterns impairs the power of beauty's imagery, which seems merely obsessive and not transcendent. Yeats' early poetry is given strength by its peculiar mythology, and in *Hérodiade* the imagery of the beautiful is employed in a dialectic dealing with art and life. However, many of the minor poems of the period like "Les Vaines Danseuses" rely on assumptions the reader is expected to bring to the text: beauty is an absolute value and requires no more preparation for its appearance than does an object of religious veneration.

At the origins of the mood poem lies the feeling that traditional poetic language does not fully render states of mind, whether they be evanescent perceptions of emotion involved with a landscape or aesthetic man's reverie of the absolute. The shape of the poem is partly determined by what it is not; there is a refusal of some of the generalizing, abstracting, and stylizing characteristics of rhetoric. A mood poem is not a self-portrait, defining the self for an audience; it avoids developmental argument, ostentatious endings (a simple image in tone with the rest of the imagery suffices), exemplarity, metaphysical conceptions of nature as a living organism in face of the poet (its apparent solipsism is more elemental and primitive), and revelations and time schemes (these are characteristic, as we shall see, of other new kinds of poems). It follows that a sustained texture and tone informs it, with no symbol standing out against others, since the symbols are meaningful only as an associative complex, not as conflictual, antithetical elements. New kinds of poetic syntax may be employed to break down the synthesizing quality of traditional style. The poem may have the impersonality of a mood purely objectified; it is possible that the first person be only implied. In the case of poems of the pure contemplation of beauty, the seemingly ritualized imagery may suggest an analogy with the poetry of religious contemplation, but it should be remembered that, while religious contemplation is an exercise with a structure, the contemplation of beauty implies no form imposed on it, the free consciousness moving as it will.

Taken together these principles delineate a postrhetorical kind of first person poem, but not the only one possible, for the monologue is also first person but is more developed in the direction of movement, conflict, and plot. For this reason I shall turn to it along with another group of forms.

5. *The New Portrait, Narrative, and Monologue*

New ways of rendering psychological content extend beyond the mood poem, which we might consider merely the simplest unit in the depiction of mental activity. The analogies I have occasionally made with the art of prose narrative become more pronounced in the poems we are going to examine now, which constitute early examples in French and English of fully developed representations of the dynamics of inner life.

In his early, derivative poetry of 1869–1870, Rimbaud was attracted to the established rhetorical patterns of narrative, scene, portrait, and anecdote in which the conveyance of an authorial attitude is simple, direct, and immediate. One peculiarity, however, is that certain anecdotes ("Le Châtiment de Tartufe," "Au Cabaret-Vert") do not have any apparent exemplary significance: Rimbaud was beginning to move toward the feeling of particularity which is characteristic of modern fiction. This tendency is realized in his work of the following year, where anecdotes ("Les Chercheuses de poux") and portraits ("Oraison du soir," "Les Assis") seem so specific that the only commentary they usually receive is an elaborate, conjectural biographic one. The most circumstantial portrait of this period, however, is sufficiently rich in larger associations (freedom, maternal and filial relations, the renewal of society) that it stands easily by itself: biographical commentary is superfluous for "Les Poètes de sept ans," which has the perfect balance between the individual and the general which realist fiction after Flaubert strove for.

It is not idle to mention Flaubert in connection with "Les Poètes de sept ans." Although nothing permits us to suppose Rimbaud read any fiction more advanced in technique than Hugo's novels, he employed the same device of fusion of narrative elements that fourteen years earlier had marked *Madame Bovary* as a new departure in the aesthetics of fiction. Flaubert merged external events, mental activity, and description in a stylistic continuum; Rimbaud was working toward the same unified texture. Here are examples of the varied elements of the narration, inner and outer, including (in second place) silent free indirect discourse, which is an essential characteristic of the French novel after Flaubert:

> Quand, lavé des odeurs du jour, le jardinet
> Derrière la maison, en hiver, s'illunait,
> Gisant au pied d'un mur, enterré dans la marne
> Et pour des visions écrasant son oeil darne,
> Il écoutait grouiller les galeux espaliers.
> . . . .
> Et si, l'ayant surpris à des pitiés immondes,
> Sa mère s'effrayait; les tendresses, profondes,
> De l'enfant se jetaient sur cet étonnement.
> C'était bon. Elle avait le bleu regard, —qui ment!
> . . . .
> Il n'aimait pas Dieu; mais les hommes, qu'au soir fauve,
> Noirs, en blouse, il voyait rentrer dans le faubourg
> Où les crieurs, en trois roulements de tambour,
> Font autour des édits rire et gronder les foules.
> —Il rêvait la prairie amoureuse, où des houles
> Lumineuses, parfums sains, pubescences d'or,
> Font leur remuement calme et prennent leur essor!

When, laved of the day's odors, the little garden behind the house lit up with moonlight in winter, lying at the foot of the wall, covered with clay, and rubbing his dizzy eyes to create visions, he listened to the swarming sound of the mangy espaliers. . . . And if, having caught him at filthy acts of pity, his mother was horrified, his deep tenderness forced back her shock. That was all right. She had that blue glance—which lies! . . . He didn't like God, but the swarthy men whom, in the tawny evening, wearing overalls, he saw going home to the workers' quarter, where the towncriers with three drumrolls make the crowd laugh and roar over edicts. He dreamed of a love-bound pasture, where gleaming swells of beings, wholesome scents, golden puberties calmly move and soar off. ("Poets of Seven")

The early part of the poem consists of sentences in which description, gesture, and sensation are mingled; they follow the boy's activities seen from without and within. Gradually, the point of view becomes predominantly interior, as his dreams are told. The sobriety and discipline of the style are increased by the general adherence to prose word order. The imagery of mental life slowly grows more complex and culminates at the end of the poem in a remarkable daydream of a room-boat. Here the syntax is finally permitted to expand in a way only verse can accommodate (the displacement of *seul* and *couché* far from the antecedent *il*):

> Et comme il savourait surtout les sombres choses,
> Quand, dans la chambre nue aux persiennes closes,
> Haute et bleue, âcrement prise d'humidité,
> Il lisait son roman sans cesse médité,
> Plein de lourds ciels ocreux et de forêts noyées,
> De fleurs de chair aux bois sidérals déployées,
> Vertige, écroulements, déroutes et pitié!
> —Tandis que se faisait la rumeur du quartier,
> En bas,—seul, et couché sur des pièces de toile
> Ecrue, et pressentant violemment la voile!

And how he especially enjoyed dark things, when, in the bare room with closed shutters, high and blue, sourly humid, he read his endlessly meditated novel full of heavy ochreous skies and drenched forests, of flesh-flowers, opened wide in the sidereal woods—dizziness, crumblings, flights and pity!—while the noise of the town went on beneath, as he lay alone on pieces of unbleached cloth and violently anticipated a sail!

The *comme*-clause is a characteristic device of free indirect discourse as practiced by Flaubert, and the whole passage presents that extraordinary imagistic mingling of external description and inner consciousness which makes the texture of mental life accessible in fiction as it had never been before *Madame Bovary*. At the same time, the expanded syntax of verse creates a more intricate nexus of images than would be possible in prose and one displaying great elegance in the asymmetrical rhythm of the last two lines, which constitute a quite rare cadence.

Rimbaud's other great realistic portrait-narrative dates from about the same time as "Les Poètes de sept ans"; "Les Premières Communions" is longer and differs in technique by the use of authorial intervention in the narrative, but of a highly calculated sort (just as Flaubert occasionally used an intervening narrator for special effect despite his general disapproval of the device). The narrative voice at the beginning of "Les Premières Communions" does not resemble the traditional personae of the poet but rather the condescending, ironic speaker of the opening of, say, *Le Rouge et le Noir*, or the one describing provincial mores in Balzac's *Illusions perdues:*

> Vraiment, c'est bête, ces églises des villages
> Où quinze laids marmots encrassant les piliers
> Ecoutent, grasseyant les divins babillages,
> Un noir grotesque dont fermentent les souliers:
> Mais le soleil éveille, à travers des feuillages
> Les vieilles couleurs des vitraux irréguliers.

Really it's awful, these village churches, where fifteen ugly brats making dirty marks on the pillars listen to a grotesque black priest, whose shoes reek, rasp out the divine babble. But shining through the trees, the sun awakens the old colors of irregular stained glass. ("First Communions")

The notation of beauty after ugliness is very much in the ironic-lyric tone Flaubert devised for *Madame Bovary;* this tone persists through the ample presentation of village life centering on the catechumens and employing familiar expressions and prose word order. As the narrative focuses on the little girl about to make her first communion, the rhythm grows more sustained, the syntax expands:

> La veille du grand Jour, l'enfant se fait malade.
> Mieux qu'à l'Eglise haute aux funèbres rumeurs,
> D'abord le frisson vient, —le lit n'étant pas fade—
> Un frisson surhumain qui retourne: "Je meurs..."
> ....
> Adonaï!... —Dans les terminaisons latines,
> Des cieux moirés de vert baignent les Fronts vermeils
> Et tachés du sang pur des célestes poitrines,
> De grands linges neigeux tombent sur les soleils!

The eve of the great day, the child grows sick. At first, stronger than in the high nave with it funereal echoes, the shudder comes—the bed being fresh—a superhuman shudder that rolls her over: "I'm dying . . ." Adonai!—In the Latin endings, green-shimmering heavens bathe the golden brows, and, spotted with pure blood from celestial breasts, great snowy sheets fall onto the suns!

Sensation and remembered sound help induce the vision, which has the great sweep of baroque pictures of the Assumption, while at the same time suggesting its origin in illness. The rising in her emotions is rendered by a combination of rhythm and imagery, as is the drop that follows:

> Puis la Vierge n'est plus que la vierge du livre.
> Les mystiques élans se cassent quelquefois . . .
> Et vient la pauvreté des images, que cuivre
> L'ennui, l'enluminure atroce et les vieux bois;

Then the Virgin is only the one in the book. Mystic exaltations sometimes break off. And then come the wretched pictures darkened by boredom, dreadful colors, and crude printing.

The first two sentence verses are flat, and the next sentence lacks élan. A new vision follows, a highly erotic one of Jesus, which occupies her mind in what is either sleep or an intense reverie. As she awakens, there is another drop in tone registered by the prosody, but the rising and falling pattern continues; her feelings ascend in a new climax:

> A son réveil,—minuit,—la fenêtre était blanche.
> Devant le sommeil bleu des rideaux illunés,
> La vision la prit des candeurs du dimanche;
> Elle avait rêvé rouge. Elle saigna du nez,
>
> Et se sentant bien chaste et pleine de faiblesse
> Pour savourer en Dieu son amour revenant,
> Elle eut soif de la nuit où s'exalte et s'abaisse
> Le coeur, sous l'oeil des cieux doux, en les devinant;
>
> De la nuit, Vierge-Mère impalpable, qui baigne
> Tous les jeunes émois de ses silences gris;
> Elle eut soif de la nuit forte où le coeur qui saigne
> Ecoule sans témoin sa révolte sans cris.

When she awoke—midnight—the window was white. In front of the blue sleep of the moonlit curtains a vision came over her of Sunday's purity. She had dreamed red. Her nose bled, and feeling very chaste and full of weakness, to enjoy her reviving love amidst God, she thirsted for the night, in which the heart rises and falls under the eye of the soft heavens, whose presence the heart divines—for the night, ineffable Virgin Mother, which bathes all young girls' anguish in its grey silence; she thirsted for the powerful night in which a bleeding heart can pour out unwitnessed its silent resistance.

This impassioned rhetoric, moving from abrupt sentences to the great flowing central one, with its eloquent repetitions and the striking *beau vers* concluding it, is almost without parallel in Rimbaud as far as its techniques go; it is called forth by the need to render the emotion of this particular character in this particular situation. The interplay of surroundings and inner life is conveyed in what, compared to previous poetic narratives, is a highly novelistic technique; the poetic realism, the sense of detail, has strong resemblances to that of Flaubert:

> Et faisant la victime et la petite épouse,
> Son étoile la vit, une chandelle aux doigts,
> Descendre dans la cour où séchait une blouse,
> Spectre blanc, et lever les spectres noirs des toits.
>
> Elle passa sa nuit sainte dans des latrines.
> Vers la chandelle, aux trous du toit coulait l'air blanc,
> Et quelque vigne folle aux noirceurs purpurines,
> En deçà d'une cour voisine s'écroulant.
>
> La lucarne faisait un coeur de lueur vive
> Dans la cour où les cieux bas plaquaient d'ors vermeils
> Les vitres; les pavés puant l'eau de lessive
> Soufraient l'ombre des murs bondés de noirs sommeils.

And imitating the victim and the little bride, her star saw her go down, with a candle in her hand, to the courtyard, where a shirt was drying—like a white specter, and put to flight the black shadows of the buildings. She spent her holy night in the outhouse. Near the candle, through the holes in the roof drifted the white air, and a purple-black overgrown vine on this side of a crumbling nearby courtyard. The skylight made a spot of warm glowing in the courtyard, where the low skies plated the windowpanes with gold; the paving stones, stinking of wash water, made sulphurous patches in the shadow of the walls dense with black sleep.

The sudden shift in the penultimate section of the poem to a scene years later, on the morning after the girl's wedding night, shows the boldest kind of narrative invention, and the apostrophe to Christ at the conclusion is all the more powerful in that such a characteristically poetic device is largely avoided up to this point.

In its subject, "Les Premières Communions" strongly resembles the naturalist novels, which, a few years later, would deal with the deleterious effects of religion on naïve young souls, on the unwholesomely erotic character of certain strains of Catholic devotion, and on sexual maladjustment in marriage. Later the tone of irony and constrained indignation is very much one of Zola's weapons. But Rimbaud's command of imagery, expressive rhythm, and syntax far surpasses the novelist's; the depiction of the successive waves of emotion experienced by the communicant draws on complex resources of language, and the sympathetic rendering of a consciousness so remote from that of the intervening authorial voice supposes a fictional technique which was not to exist in the novel for some time to come.

The major portrait-narrative poems of Eliot and Pound also have a significant relationship with modern developments in the novel. The name of Henry James has often been brought up in regard to Eliot's "Portrait of a Lady," and Pound specifically called "Hugh Selwyn Mauberley" an "attempt to condense the James novel."[14] Whatever we think of so specific a comparison, it is certainly clear that the narrative elements of the poems do not derive exclusively from the verse tradition, even if the presence of Laforgue in Eliot and Gautier in Pound is occasionally perceptible. "Portrait of a Lady" employs an especially subtle form of first person narration in that the speaker's presence is necessary to bring out the qualities of the character portrayed in the third person. But since that character can only be reflected in the speaker's mind, and he himself is a character, the whole poem-narrative gives the impression of being caught in another's subjectivity, with no possibility of objectively understanding the situation. The technique of the monologue is ingenious in that the beginning and end, always particularly difficult points in the establishment and maintenance of the fictional illusion, are hypothetical fantasies:

We have been, let us say, to hear the latest Pole

. . . .

Well! and what if she should die some afternoon

For a moment distance is created between the narrator's subjectivity and the actual course of events: the felicitous effect of the poem as fiction is to a large extent dependent on the fading in and out of actual scenes, with their most concrete element, the lady's conversation, alternating with the flow of the narrator's mind.

In "Hugh Selwyn Mauberley" and "Mauberley 1920" the fiction consists of a series of fragments depicting Mauberley's inner life, contacts in society, and ultimate fate. The first group of poems, numbered 1 to 12, employs both first and third person, the former principally in anecdotes. The third person poems at the beginning (1, 2, 4, 5, 6, and perhaps the ambiguous 3) involve the more complicated problem in narration. The urbane voice, at once ironic and sympathetic to Mauberley, speaks in a style akin to his in its use of vocabulary and imagery: there is no mistaking this anonymous narrator for a remote or neutral one. By having this voice be not merely favorably disposed, through its irony, toward Mauberley but actually merging in tone with his, as if he were telling his own story in the third person—a Jamesian technique—it becomes possible to employ third person summary narration with an air both of objectivity and participation, the great advantage of this device. Summary narration is always completely dependent on stylistic detail for the difference between dead or mechanical-seeming recounting and a vivid perception of time's inexorability; Flaubert had provided an especially great model in the penultimate chapter of *L'Education sentimentale*, in which the main character's state of mind is perfectly rendered by rhythm and sentence structure. Pound obtains the maximum of narrative power in the third person sections of "Hugh Selwyn Mauberley" by a similar combination of grandeur and irony—reflecting the character's self-irony. In the shorter "Mauberley 1920" there are further experiments in technique. In poems 1 and 2 we find attempts at a drifting, fragmented inner monologue but in a third person context, a very original kind of compromise between Flaubert's free indirect discourse and broken, first person musings:

> For three years, diabolus in the scale,
> He drank ambrosia,
> All passes, ANANGKE prevails,
> Came end, at last, to that Arcadia.
>
> He had moved amid her phantasmagoria,
> Amid her galaxies,
> NUKTIS 'AGALMA
> . . . .
> Drifted . . . drifted precipitate,
> Asking time to be rid of . . .
> Of his bewilderment; to designate
> His new found orchid. . . .

The possibility of such a curious and ambiguous device rests on the stylistic unity of first and third person. The range of effect within this unity permits, however, the contrast in vocabulary and syntax between the summary narration of Mauberley's leaving the literary world (poem 3), and his inner monologue in his South Pacific retreat (poem 4). The Mauberley peoms reflect a rare technical inventiveness in narration.

Third person summary narration and first person monologue are two extremes in technique between which most fiction moves. The scene of solitary inner life in the third person was Flaubert's attempt to bridge the two. The curious quality of such scenes is their possibility of temporal expansion and contraction: the tense frequently does not betray whether the mental action is punctual or iterative. This ambiguity can be an important source of effect. One of Rodenbach's best poems departs from his usual mood poem type and consists of a scene exploring the feelings of an anonymous sick person:

> Le malade souvent examine ses mains,
> Si pâles, n'ayant plus que des gestes bénins
> De sacerdoce et d'offices, à peine humaines;
> Il consulte ses mains, ses doigts trop délicats
> Qui, plus que le visage, élucident son cas
> Avec leur maigre ivoire et leurs débiles veines.
> Surtout le soir, il les considère en songeant
> Parmi le crépuscule, automne des journées,
> Et dans elles, qui sont longues d'être affinées,
> Voit son mal comme hors de lui se prolongeant,

Mains pâles d'autant plus que l'obscurité tombe!
Elles semblent s'aimer et semblent s'appeler; ("Les Lignes de la main" II, *Les Vies encloses,* 1896)

The sick man often examines his hands, which, so pale, barely human, no longer have any but benign, priestly, ritual gestures. He consults his hands, his too delicate fingers, which, more than his face, make clear his case, with their thin ivory and faint veins. Above all in the evening he gazes at them at twilight, the day's autumn, and in them, lengthened by its refining process, he sees his illness extending from him; hands all the more pale in that darkness is falling, they seem to love and call each other. ("Lines of the Hand" II)

The adverbs present the scene as happening recurrently, but the increasing particularity of the images will suggest, as no more adverbs of repetition come forth, that the scene is focusing on a specific evening:

> Elles ont des blancheurs frileuses de colombe
> Et, sveltes, on dirait qu'elles vont s'envoler.
> Elles font sur l'air des taches surnaturelles
> Comme si du nouveau clair de lune en chemin
> Entrait par la fenêtre et se posait sur elles.
> Or la pâleur est la même sur chaque main,
> Et le malade songe à ses mains anciennes;
> Il ne reconnaît plus ces mains pâles pour siennes;
> Tel un petit enfant qui voit ses mains dans l'eau.

They have the chilly whiteness of doves and, slender, seem about to fly off. They make supernatural spots in the air, as if new moonlight in passing had come in the window and touched them. Now the pallor is the same on each hand, and the sick man thinks of his former hands. He no longer recognizes these pale hands as his own, like a small child seeing his hands in water.

The complex of extraordinary perceptions is the finest characteristic of Rodenbach's poetry, and here the imagery undergoes a remarkable shift from the airy and illuminated to the dark and submerged:

> Puis le malade mire au miroir sans mémoire
> —Le miroir qui concentre un moment son eau noire—
> Ses mains qu'il voit sombrer comme un couple jumeau;
> O vorace fontaine, obstinée et maigrie,

Où le malade suit ses mains, dans quel recul!
Couple blanc qui s'enfonce et de plus en plus nul
Jusqu'à ce que l'eau du miroir se soit tarie.
Il songe alors qu'il va bientôt ne plus pouvoir
Les suivre, quand sera total l'afflux du soir
Dans cette eau du profond miroir toute réduite;
Et n'est-ce pas les voir mourir, que cette fuite?

Then the sick man watches, in the memoryless mirror—the mirror concentrating for a moment its black water—his hands, which he sees sink like a twin pair. Oh voracious fountain, stubborn and narrowing, in which the sick man follows his hands—at what a distance!—the white pair sinking ever deeper and ever more inexistent until the mirror's water is dried up. He thinks then that soon he will no longer be able to follow them, when evening's flood will be complete, in the deep mirror's diminished water. And is this flight not watching them die?

This is more than simply metaphoric writing: the imagery represents hallucination, as is clear from the well-like spatial dimensions gradually acquired by the mirror. The elemental air and water recall mood poems, although the scene is recounted as part of a third person consciousness; the resemblances are indeed quite close, with the exception that the shift in imagery depicts a psychological process, whereas mood, as we have defined it, is more static. In any case, and here the Rimbaud poems as well as the Rodenbach are pertinent, the images function as a symbolic whole. In poems related by their technique to the presentation of consciousness in modern fiction, mood poems, narratives, scenes, or monologues, individual images are usually not independent symbols but acquire meaning only as part of a complex.

As we see in the Rodenbach, there is psychological movement that one would hesitate to call plot; so there are monologues that are progressive, unlike mood poems, but which stop short of anything one might consider narrative. Here again, in Maurice Maeterlinck's "Hôpital" (Serres Chaudes, 1889), the imagery is that of hallucination:

Hôpital! hôpital au bord du canal!
Hôpital au mois de juillet!
On y fait du feu dans la salle!
Tandis que les transatlantiques sifflent sur le canal!
(Oh! n'approchez pas des fenêtres!)

Des émigrants traversent un palais!
Je vois un yacht sous la tempête!
Je vois des troupeaux sur tous les navires!
(Il vaut mieux que les fenêtres restent closes,
On est presque à l'abri du dehors.)
On a l'idée d'une serre sur la neige,
On croit célébrer des relevailles un jour d'orage,
On entrevoit des plantes éparses sur une couverture de laine,
Il y a un incendie un jour de soleil,
Et je traverse une forêt pleine de blessés.

Oh! voici enfin le clair de lune!

Hospital! Hospital beside the canal! Hospital in the month of July! They've lit a fire in the ward! While the transatlantic ships whistle on the canal! (Oh! don't go near the windows.) Emigrants are going through a palace! I see a yacht in the storm! I see flocks of sheep on all the ships! (The windows had best stay closed; we're almost sheltered from the outside.) You think of a hothouse in the snow; it's like celebrating a churching on a stormy day. You see plants scattered on a woolen blanket. There is a fire on a sunny day, and I'm crossing a forest full of wounded men. Oh here at last is the moonlight!

The origins of this kind of monologue, which is far more abrupt and chaotic in imagery than the mood poems we have examined, are to be found in Maeterlinck's way of reading Rimbaud, and specifically certain of the *Illuminations* such as "Enfance." (Whether or not Rimbaud intended to imply hallucination in the *Illuminations* is another question.) As in many mood poems, elemental and cosmological imagery (fire, water, sun, moonlight) is intense:

Oh! mais la soeur de charité attisant le feu!

Tous les beaux roseaux verts des berges sont en flamme!
Un bateau de blessés ballotte au clair de lune!
Toutes les filles du roi sont dans une barque sous l'orage!
Et les princesses vont mourir en un champ de ciguës!
Oh! n'entrouvrez pas les fenêtres!
Ecoutez: les transatlantiques sifflent encore à l'horizon!

Oh, the Sister of Charity stirring the fire! All the beautiful green reeds on the banks are on fire! A boat of wounded men is pitching in the moonlight! All the king's daughters are on a boat in the storm! And the princesses are going to die in a field of hemlock! Oh! don't even open the windows a little! Listen: the transatlantic boats are still whistling on the horizon!

In "Hôpital" we finally have the approximation of a shifting stream-of-consciousness, as opposed to the more static imagery of mood; the difference between the two is not absolute in practice, and, of course, the present tense is potentially ambiguous in that it can be durative or perfective and successive. Nevertheless, the free verse of Maeterlinck's poem would seem to indicate a forward, successive movement, as does the parataxis. (This stream-of-consciousness owes nothing to the first novel in that form, Edouard Dujardin's *Les Lauriers sont coupés* [1888]: like other striking similarities between modern verse and fiction, the technique emerges from experiments in poetic language.) "Hôpital" has historical significance aside from its aesthetic value in that this kind of freely constructed, progressive sequence of images in parataxis is a formal arrangement developed and refined by Apollinaire, Cendrars, and Breton. It gives the greatest prominence to imagery. While Maeterlinck uses it to render hallucination, it will be capable of portraying more subtle shades of consciousness.

Avoidance of syntactic subordination is not the only significant grammatical device in creating inner monologue. Maeterlinck's poem uses *on*, *vous*, and *il y a*, as well as *je* to produce a special nuance: the mind perceiving the world does not necessarily make a sharp subject-object distinction. The subjective *I* may be only partially or intermittently felt as experiencing a clear I-am-seeing-you relation; consciousness may have a more blurred focus. Verlaine wrote a sonnet on the borderline between inner monologue and the mood poem, in which the experiencing *I* does not designate itself by the subject pronoun, just as indeed we do not always think in *I* subjects:

> Ah! vraiment c'est triste, ah! vraiment ça finit trop mal.
> Il n'est pas permis d'être à ce point infortuné.
> Ah! vraiment c'est trop la mort du naïf animal
> Qui voit tout son sang couler sous son regard fané.
>
> Londres fume et crie. O quelle ville de la Bible!
> Le gaz flambe et nage et les enseignes sont vermeilles.
> Et les maisons dans leur ratatinement terrible
> Epouvantent comme un sénat de petites vieilles. ("Sonnet boiteux")

Ah! it's truly dreary; it's turning out too badly. You can't be wretched to this point. It's really the death of an innocent animal, seeing its blood flow beneath its faded glance. London is smoking and crying out. What a city out of the Bible! The gas lamps flare and swim and the signs are gold. And the horribly shrunken houses are terrifying like a congress of little old women. ("Lame Sonnet")

Verlaine had an extraordinary gift for communicating uneasy states of mind of all kinds. Here the juxtaposition of the colloquial in the vocabulary of the first quatrain and the grand and grotesque in the second convey the intimate anguish of a situation that is not revealed; Verlaine was especially given to poems with concealed subjects, in which the emotion but not the cause is given.

The rare thirteen-syllable line, which gives the "lame" to the title "Sonnet boiteux" renders, along with parataxis, the gait of the dying animal; solidity is further undermined in the tercets by the disintegration of rhyme:

> Tout l'affreux passé saute, piaule, miaule et glapit
> Dans le brouillard rose et jaune et sale des *sohos*
> Avec des *indeeds* et des *all rights* et des *haôs*.
>
> Non vraiment c'est trop un martyre sans espérance,
> Non vraiment cela finit trop mal, vraiment c'est triste:
> O le feu du ciel sur cette ville de la Bible!

The whole dreadful past leaps, cheeps, mews, and yelps in the pink and yellow and dirty fog of the Sohos, with indeed's, and all right's and Oh's. No, really, it's too much a hopeless martyrdom; no, really, it's turning out too badly; it's truly wretched. Oh, the fire from heaven on the city out of the Bible!

The intermingling of inner and outer, mind and circumstances is accomplished in the development of the animal imagery, applicable both to memories and the half-invisible London crowd, and the abrupt contrast between polysyndeton and asyndeton in the tercets is remarkably expressive. While its form will not be the prototype Maeterlinck's inner monologue is, Verlaine's sonnet remains a very early (1873) and subtle example of using imagery to convey the movement of consciousness.

The concealed memories of "Sonnet boiteux" (and some other Verlaine poems) are related to another poetic device that assumes great importance in certain modern poems, especially monologues: this is the covert plot, or allusion to a complex of actions and circumstances of which the reader is given only a part. The effect is found in "Ulalume" and other pieces by Edgar Allan Poe, while a sonnet of Verlaine's, contemporaneous with "Sonnet boiteux" and famous for its obscurity, is, to my knowledge, the first example of this in French, after Baudelaire's "La servante au grand coeur":

> L'espoir luit comme un brin de paille dans l'étable.
> Que crains-tu de la guêpe ivre de son vol fou?
> Vois, le soleil toujours poudroie à quelque trou.
> Que ne t'endormais-tu, le coude sur la table?
>
> Pauvre âme pâle, au moins cette eau du puits glacé,
> Bois-la. Puis dors après. Allons, tu vois, je reste,
> Et je dorloterai les rêves de ta sieste,
> Et tu chantonneras comme un enfant bercé.

Hope gleams like a straw in the barn. What do you fear from the wasp drunk with its own crazy flight? See, the sunlight is still filled with dust motes in some hole. Why weren't you trying to fall asleep, leaning on the table? Poor pale soul, at least drink this water from the icy well. Then sleep afterwards. Come, you see, I am staying, and I will cosset the dreams in your nap, and you will hum like a child.

The end-stopped lines (contrary to Verlaine's usual practice) and inner pauses create an effect of quiet, slow speech. Aside from the first line, a simile deliberately reversed (straws shine like hope) for the sake of a mildly cryptic quality, the sentences clearly establish the scene as being in a barn in the heat; the person addressed does not feel well. The first tercet adds another character:

> Midi sonne. De grâce, éloignez-vous, madame.
> Il dort. C'est étonnant comme les pas de femme
> Résonnent au cerveau des pauvres malheureux.

Noon is ringing. Please, go away, Madame. He is sleeping. It is amazing how women's footsteps echo in poor wretches' heads.

Most of the commentary this sonnet has received consists in the invention of anecdotes about Verlaine, Rimbaud, Mathilde Verlaine, and Madame Rimbaud mère. (The two men, incidentally, are not known ever to have been in a barn with one or the other of the women.) The bankruptcy of the biographical method still prevalent in French studies could not be more complete. The very value of the poem, its mysterious effectiveness, lies partly in our knowing no more than what is stated and feeling that there is much more implied that we can never know. This is not a puzzle, because puzzles are intended to be solved; here we have a perfect example of the beautiful suggestiveness of concealed plot.

"L'espoir luit" has a mood and structure that are independent from the knowledge of what we can never know about the cause of the second person's illness, and so forth. The future reference of the initial word "hope" is reinforced by a repetition of the image of shining with a slight variation near the end of the sonnet:

> Midi sonne. J'ai fait arroser dans la chambre.
> Va, dors! L'espoir luit come un caillou dans un creux.
> Ah! quand refleuriront les roses de septembre!

Noon is ringing. I have had the room sprinkled down. Come, sleep. Hope shines like a pebble in a hole. Ah, when will September roses flower again!

The time structure of the poem is clear if we work back from the anticipation of September. Noon rings; it is the *partage de midi* between the rising and falling of the heat. The sick man falls asleep, a step toward recovery, and so the division of the day is correlated with the division of the year into periods of rising and diminishing heat: September is the afternoon of the year, and its roses the realization of the hope for health again. The great beauty of the poem lies in the interplay between the understated yet transparent time scheme and the unknown reaches of emotion and complication in the figures' lives. The use of the sense of time is one of the most interesting ways to give urgency and tension with a concealed plot; it is part of the foreboding effect Eliot creates, for example, in "Sweeney among the Nightingales" or parts of *The Wasteland.*

As a monologue "L'espoir luit" has a strangely broken style which gives a remarkable, laconic effect but would be obviously unsuitable to a regular verse poem much longer than a sonnet. Much greater elaboration of language is to be found in "L'Après-midi d'un faune," Mallarmé's only monologue (aside from those in *Hérodiade*), and the first example in French of the fully developed dramatic monologue, in which a scene is implied or described, inner thoughts and spoken words occur, and some element of plot stretching into the past or future informs the poem. Mallarmé devised the genre independently from Browning, just as Laforgue was to do a few years later. I do not think we can speak of the dramatic monologue, English or French, as growing out of romantic first person poems, even such as "Tintern Abbey" or the "Ode to a Nightingale," however much those do stand out in the early nineteenth century for their remarkable feeling of scene. Keats' poem is unique in his work for its pronounced associative movement, particularly between the last two stanzas; at the same time the apostrophe to the bird at the most intense point of the ode clearly places it in a traditional rhetorical structure. On the other hand, while "L'Après-midi d'un faune" contains an address to the landscape, the second person expresses the primitive character of the faun's mind, which sees the landscape as filled with life. Figures of rhetoric in Mallarmé's poem, although they derive from neoclassical sources, convey something quite different; they acquire a new psychological value.

The monologue Mallarmé originally wrote, in the hope of seeing it staged, is not at all a dramatic monologue in the customary modern sense; it resembles the deliberative rhetoric of neoclassical theater ("J'avais des Nymphes! Est-ce un songe? Non").[15] Apostrophes are used stiffly (Mallarmé's stage directions indicate that at times the faun turns to and harangues the *décor*). In the more than ten years that elapsed between the first and final versions of "L'Après-midi" Mallarmé rethought both the character of his faun and the means of expressing it. The opening of the poem was considerably modified to express more subtly the uncertainty in the faun's mind as to whether he had encountered real nymphs or ones in a dream. Short, jerky clauses were changed to ones embodying the involution of his processes of thought and perception:

> Ces nymphes, je les veux perpétuer.
> Si clair,
> Leur incarnat léger, qu'il voltige dans l'air
> Assoupi de sommeils touffus.
> Aimai-je un rêve?

Mon doute, amas de nuit ancienne, s'achève
En maint rameau subtil, qui, demeuré les vrais
Bois mêmes, prouve, hélas! que bien seul je m'offrais
Pour triomphe la faute idéale de roses.

I would perpetuate these nymphs. So bright their light flesh-pink that it leaps in the air drowsy with bushy sleep. Did I love a dream? My doubt, a mass of primeval night, ends up in many a subtle branch, which, remaining the real woods themselves, proves, alas, that quite alone I offered myself for my victory the ideal absence of roses. ("Afternoon of a Faun")

The demonstrative *ces*, the reprise pronoun construction in the first line, and the use of a sentence fragment ("Si clair") immediately establish this as syntax colored by psychological movement in a situation that is already underway. A combination of transferred epithets ("sommeils touffus," "rameau subtil"), indirectly stated comparisons (woods in the dream and real woods, flesh-pink and roses), and unusual connotations (*faute*—absence, *idéal*—existing only in the mind) conveys the faun's confused wondering. The effacement of distinctions between the abstract and the concrete (the *rameaux* are *ramifications*) also contributes to the rendering of the faun's elaborately primitive command of language. The faun's apperceptions, which are at once very subtle, as he observes the color of roses to be the same as that of the nymphs' skin, and crude, when he fails to differentiate clearly between the dream and what happened before it, suggest a mind that is capable of a complicated but not entirely rational discourse.

The plot and themes of "L'Après-midi" were also transformed over the years Mallarmé worked on it. In the earliest version we have, the faun had indeed raped the nymphs; the heavy self-assertion of this first faun, who seems very un-Mallarmé-like, yielded to the confused and frustrated faun who confides his emotion to song. But Mallarmé clearly wanted to avoid the poem's seeming primarily an allegory about the consolation of art: a dramatic monologue should preserve its integrity as a psychological representation and not lose its individual character in some general symbolic significance. The faun is only incidentally an artist. The dramatic release Mallarmé devised for the final version was to have the faun masturbate, which is marked by the words, "Je tiens la reine," and a special descending typography. This leads nicely to his desire to nap in the afternoon (the afternoon of the title, which takes place *after* the poem) during which he will "perpetuate" the nymphs in dream. The corporeal proves more satisfying than art.

Dramatic monologues are a striking poetic form and tend to stand out in a poet's production, as does "L'Après-midi" in Mallarmé's. Browning's most fully dramatic pieces like "The Bishop Orders His Tomb," "Andrea del Sarto," and "My Last Duchess," or Alfred Tennyson's "Tithonus" and "Ulysses" suggest a powerful new aesthetic in a way their other shorter poems do not. The comparison with speeches in Shakespeare is commonly made with regard to Browning, but, of course, the peculiar beauty of dramatic monologues is that they depend on suggestion and are not part of a large-scale rhetorical development such as the unfolding of the argument in sixteenth- and seventeenth-century theater. This is even more true of the monologues of Mallarmé and Valéry, for, while they share with neoclassical tirades some ornaments and figures, French dramatic poetry relies to a great extent on context for its force, and it uses but sparingly the *beau désordre* or alogical expression of feeling, although rhetoricians accepted it in theory. In the development of a neoclassical speech there are conflictual or incremental patterns; when the show of logical movement is interrupted by violent emotion, the break in texture is sharply underscored, so that the irrational itself can enter into a pattern. On the other hand, in "L'Après-midi d'un faune" the faun seems to reach one conclusion to his story, then starts the narrative again, without the reader's being able initially to perceive the covert plan involved; the sequence is apprehended as depending on some hidden psychological order, which is neither logical nor antilogical. The rhetorical tradition tended to stylize psychological movement, giving full force to the extremes of rational and antirational thought processes. The dramatic monologue may embody other kinds of shifts of consciousness, such as association of words or ideas, partial analogies, forgetfulness, ellipsis, tangential memories, and so forth.

We have been concerned in this section with the depiction of characters in situations where there is shifting mental activity or some element of plot. Such shifts or the psychological movement implied by plot may be very slight: some of these poems, like Rodenbach's on hands, may seem to differ but very little from the mood poems we have earlier examined. In the particular case of the Rodenbach, we could say the growing premonition of death is the principle difference from the static mood poem. At times, the most elaborate imagery has been brought forth in the service of some simple unified effect: Eliot's statement that "Sweeney among the Nightingales" was meant merely to convey foreboding is an excellent example. Eliot and Pound were not altogether the first to so puzzle the reader by confounding his sense of what to look for in a poem. The prototype seems to be certain "Complaintes" of Laforgue which appear to contain little more than the projection of a mood and which are mingled in with thematically elaborate and even philosophical "Complaintes." Such difficulties in interpretation must be solved poem by poem.

Like mood poems with their symbolism of *états d'âme*, the portrait as practiced by Rimbaud, the novelistic narrative, and the dramatic monologue are not presented as typical or exemplary, at least to begin with; if anything, unusual patterns of imagery tend to imply individuality and uniqueness. The connection with human experience in general is made only after we have focused on the special and private quality of the character's thought and feelings. Thus the narrating voice at the beginning of "Les Premières Communions" treats humorously and condescendingly the "mysticités grotesques" to be found in village religious life; he is as far removed as possible from such experience, only to come, at the end of the poem, to a sympathetic and indignant perception of how such religious devotion can impair normal feelings. This great emphasis on the particular, sometimes at the expense of the general altogether, becomes a characteristic of the poetry of Corbière. The dramatization of the first person in Corbière and Laforgue goes far beyond any other portrayal of characters in nineteenth-century poetry in the special stylistic techniques they created for monologue.

6. Characters in Situations: Corbière and Laforgue

The novelistic side of *Les Amours jaunes* (1874), like that of "Hugh Selwyn Mauberley," is clearest in plot at its beginning and end: the poet comes to Paris, lives his yellow loves, grows old, dies, writes his own epitaph, and survives himself. In later chapters of the book we have his vision of Brittany and seafaring life, poems not without thematic relation to the Paris chapters. The whole is characterized not only by extraordinary stylistic invention but by specific linguistic traits that make its rendering of personality something quite new.

The quality of particularity which characterizes the experiences of the book's voice makes generalizations about them far more difficult than in the case of, say, *Les Fleurs du mal,* where abstractions like "Spleen et Idéal" are reflected in the detail of the work. Corbière's section titles, "Les Amours jaunes," "Sérénade des sérénades," and "Raccrocs" mean simply individual examples of situations deriving from promiscuity, attempted seductions, and idle happenings; the quality of the situations is not characterized. Furthermore, in individual poems which are presented as summations of experience, there is a tendency toward enumeration rather than synthesis. The "Epitaphe" is all in antitheses:

> Il ne naquit par aucun bout,
> Fut toujours poussé vent-de-bout,
> Et fut un arlequin-ragoût,
> Mélange adultère de tout.
> . . . .
> Coureur d'idéal,—sans idée;
> Rime riche,—et jamais rimée.
> . . . .
> Poète, en dépit de ses vers;
> Artiste sans art,—à l'envers,
> Philosophe,—à tort à travers.
> . . . .
> L'esprit à sec et la tête ivre,
> Fini, mais ne sachant finir,
> Il mourut en s'attendant vivre
> Et vécut, s'attendant mourir.

He wasn't born in any special way, was always pushed along by the wind. He was a stew of second-hand scraps, an adulterous mixture of everything. Pursuer of the ideal, without an idea, a rich rhyme never rhymed . . . A poet, despite his verse, an artist without art, inside-out, a philosopher—muddled . . . His mind sober and his head drunk, finished, but not knowing how to end, he died expecting to live, and lived expecting to die.

There are themes here which the reader is left to formulate: first, chance, then the confusion of abstractions, and finally the feeling that there are no beginnings and ends, no center to experience. Corbière's language, however, avoids stating things in terms of ideas. When he moves toward a conclusion, it is often a negative one or the absence of one. The greater part of "Laisser-courre" consists of lists after the verb *j'ai laissé*, whose import is that of stripping down, doing away with. As a summary:

> Sous le temps, sans égides
> M'a mal mené fort bien
> La vie à grandes guides . . .
> Au bout des guides—rien—
> . . . Laissé, blasé, passé,
> Rien ne m'a rien laissé . . .

In all weather, without a shield, life, with free reins, ill-treated me very well. At the end of the reins: nothing . . . Left, blunted, passed, nothing has left me nothing. ("Laying-on the Pack")

Life is one of the few abstractions Corbière is fond of using, but, like his other favorite one, love, it has a very concrete meaning: the rubbing and erosion the individual perceives as the condition of living. It conveys the opposite of vitality. Love is an itch, an irritation, and the hostile, rejected lover of "Sérénade des sérénades," contemptuous of women and himself, is motivated to his buffoonish performances by an instinct as annoying to him as it is to its object. Perhaps the woman who is given a monologue about her erotic twitches ("Femme") wearily sums it up best: "une nuit blanche . . . un drap sali."[16]

The emptiness of abstractions, their reducibility to sharp or deadened sensation is nicely illustrated by "Libertà," which takes up a favorite poetic theme of the nineteenth century. Freedom in Corbière's poem is a stay in jail, defined first by what it avoids: "No more the sky . . . Existence that sticks to you is stuck away . . . No more bailiffs with dirty hands, no more friends' hands!" The suggestion of unpleasant sensations on the skin is a particularly good example of an abstraction like the tedium of life being replaced by sensations. Concrete objects, on the other hand, take on ironic abstract values: a pitcher is called "puits de la vérité," but remains empty when it is drunk; the idea of emptiness, the vacuity of an inflated abstraction, is bound to a specific case of genuine and acceptable emptiness. The wretched day when *truly* condemned he leaves prison, for a freedom whose lack of direction is expressed by "galley-rowing," he will go "there, anywhere, outside." The alternatives are empty idleness and idle motion not fulfilling anything, a strange and striking example of the plain physical feeling to which thought and experience are frequently reduced in Corbière.

> Ma pensée est un souffle aride:
> C'est l'air. L'air est à moi partout.
> Et ma parole est l'écho vide
> Qui ne dit rien—et c'est tout. ("Paria")

My thought is a dry breath, air. Air is mine everywhere. And my speech is the empty echo, saying nothing, and that's all. ("Pariah")

These monologues contain a totally new way of expressing the relation of the *I* to generalities: experience is grounded in the senses, and the mind does not synthesize or elaborate greatly on it. Modern novelists have at times made considerable efforts to recapture this quality of Corbière's.

The enumeration, antitheses, and highly specific images like those of life's stickiness are not only a way of avoiding abstractions in general, but especially a way of avoiding the abstractions of wholeness and consistency applied commonly to life in literature. Although the fate or destiny of the individual is constantly being suggested, these two words are absent, because of the plan and coherence they imply. Corbière does use the word *hasard*, as well as the more picturesque *raccroc*, but not to designate any metaphysical entity. Chance is the word for the absence of pattern and meaning, of any transcendency. The absence of concepts and the phenomenological concern for consciousness of the texture of experience give one emotion in particular a strikingly modern quality: the ennui rendered in Corbière is much closer to Samuel Beckett than to Baudelaire's *acedia* with its strong Christian resonances. Above all, damnation and salvation are empty notions just like fate. In one sonnet ("Heures") the poet, who thinks himself untouched by grace, hears the "male heure" ring in the night, but, counting, discovers that fourteen hours have rung and the tolling still continues: there is no decisive hour. The most extreme example of the absence of the complex of abstractions involved with time is found in "Paria":

> Mon passé: c'est ce que j'oublie.
> La seule chose qui me lie
> C'est ma main dans mon autre main.
> Mon souvenir—Rien—C'est ma trace.
> Mon présent, c'est tout ce qui passe
> Mon avenir—Demain . . . demain.

My past is what I forget. The only thing binding me is my hand in my other hand. My memories—nothing—my footsteps. My present, everything passing; my future—tomorrow, tomorrow.

The speaker can connect nothing with nothing except his hands; causality in the widest sense has disappeared with the temporal sense.

Ugliness, deafness, blindness, unpleasant sensations, the deprivations of poverty, insomnia, the pain of wounds, the irritant of libido, and the stunned feeling of being directionless provide the basis of consciousness in Corbière's poems. Nevertheless, his poetry is not unrelievedly bleak; on the contrary, it is filled with a delight in plays on words, allusions, and odd linguistic inventions. Language has a potential of liveliness which experience often lacks. Set expressions, literary and colloquial, are twisted around to show how mindless and arbitrary language is: "Non, petit, il faut commencer par être grand," "Jette le vin, garde la lie." There are extraordinary naturalistic street scenes like "Idylle coupée" written in an argot-colored narrative language several years before Zola tried such a style in *L'Assommoir*. The whole "Gens de mer" section of *Les Amours jaunes*, with its contrast between banal poetic notions of the sea and the precise vocabulary of maritime life, can be interpreted as a study of the relationship between language and reality.

Sometimes the interpretation of Corbière's odd diction is not perfectly obvious. Such is the case of one of his best known poems, the elaborate, ambiguous "Poète contumace," which is a letter written by a poet existing in a limbo between life and death; he is living *par con-*

tumace, that is, he has not shown up in court for judgment to be passed on him. (This is one of Corbière's most striking metaphors for the ambiguous feeling of death in life, with no sense of an ending.) The letter is addressed to *l'Absente* and consitutes the principal poem of love and memory in the collection. ("Steamboat," also about recollections and love, deals with the erosion of memory.) The letter is actually a very free monologue, full of dashes and suspension points, and shows so little concern for rhetorical development that it is impossible to quote from it: the impression of the whole is necessary in the absence of argument, as is usually the case in styles trying to render a stream-of-consciousness. Jokes, funny and not funny, pathos, allusions to romantic literature, which give a certain richness of reference to the speaking voice, and a great deal of fantasy mingle in a rather irregularly versified language; we have, in short, an example of romantic irony. At the end of the poem, the poet tears up his letter, and we may ask why. The most obvious answer is that it is merely a last gesture of romantic irony, the fondness for a sweet-and-tart effect. But other poems lead us to believe that Corbière was a more complex artist, and, if we observe the place of "Le Poète contumace" in the volume, we see it concludes a section at the beginning of which stands "Paris," a series of sonnets on the personae and disguises of poets; we realize that the monologue of "Le Poète contumace" is an example of these personae and suspect of charlatanism in so far as it is one. This poem, apparently romantic in the banal sense, about a man who "avait trop aimé les beaux pays malsains," actually deals with the inauthenticity of poetic expression, a problem that would obviously be acute for a writer so suspicious of abstraction and generalization as Corbière. "Ce fut un vrai poète: il n'avait pas de chant"; the temptation for someone like Corbière is to deny absolutely the possibility of genuine expression.

Concerned over the value of language, Corbière generally avoids the evocative image. He favors a dry suggestiveness, with few adjectives, over the traditionally poetic. His witty figures often lack evocativeness because of the simultaneous presence of concrete and general meanings. The tendency to avoid abstractions of the larger, philosophical sort shows up in the fondness for expressions like "ce crampon est au clou'': the boring person (clamp) is gotten rid of (or pawned, on the nail). A word like bore is not completely an abstraction, but it denotes a class, and Corbière chooses a more vivid familiar expression. The concrete meanings are intensified by juxtaposition of expressions, with results that are arresting but quite different from the traditional conception of concreteness and vividness in poetry. The poems in which there is an extensive development of one image —the painting-corpse in "Le Convoi du pauvre," food and drink in "Paris"—are less numerous than those in which there is a constant tangential movement and shifting of metaphor. All of these effects depend on the semantics of familiar language, which is a function of the creation of personae in Corbière's verse.

At the very end of *Les Amours jaunes* Corbière placed six "Rondels pour après" (which are not all rondeaux). These poems on death are arranged in a subtle pattern: the picture of a child sleeping fades gradually, in the course of the series, into that of the dead poet and his grave. The metamorphosis is aided by a certain cryptic fantasy in the imagery: death is represented as a half-conscious dreaming state, for which Corbière invented a different, more lyric kind of imagery of lights in the dark (stars, sparks, candles, comets) and cemetery flowers. This use of lyrical expansion and suggestiveness, which has occupied such a small place in the depiction of life, is the last and most brilliant example of juxtaposition of styles in *Les Amours jaunes*, certainly one of the most interesting modernist ideas in poetic structure. If we look at the book as a fictional whole, this representation of the annihilated consciousness is a striking novelistic notion.

Before making any conclusion about the novelistic character of *Les Amours jaunes*, one word must be said against simplistic autobiographical readings. First, many poems deal with a figure obviously older than Corbière was at his early death, and, secondly, the whole depiction of penniless bohemianism has little to do with the life of this *fils à papa*. As an example of the transmutation of reality, we might take "A mon cotre le Négrier," dealing with a boat the poet is obliged to sell because of his poverty. Le Négrier was indeed a boat of Corbière's and was indeed sold, but only because Corbière's father was buying him a yacht instead. Corbière had a powerful imagination for realistic situations, and few nineteenth-century poets could equal him in creating events in all their emotional color.

Corbière understood, as French novelists were not to do until quite recently, that the play of consciousness around events and the distinction of points of view among characters can be considered the essential elements in fiction and that the concatenation of events into a plot or the presence of a generalized guiding theme, like the conflict of dream and reality in Emma Bovary's mind, is superfluous, agreeable perhaps, but not strictly *romanesque*. Even the unity of character, if we conceive of it as a sequence of realistic actions in life, can be dispensed with. Thus Corbière is able, and most of all in the Paris sections of *Les Amours jaunes*, to create a poet figure for whom we could not perhaps construct a factual biography, but whose novelistic existence is intensely real. He cannot be summed up as an illustration of three or four "themes"; his consciousness is nearly always of particulars and, yet, artistically coherent from poem to poem. His mistress' thoughts in "Pauvre Garçon" or "Femme," and the intermittent commenting voice, sometimes identical with that of the poet, sometimes more distant, give an effect of shifting perspectives on the same character, as does the aging, barely stated but unmistakable, which he undergoes. The suppression of schematic, overintellectualized causality, of transcendental concepts, and the avoidance of lyrical evocations, which constitute an escape from the time-bound, make *Les Amours jaunes* a book truly in advance of its time. Its nineteenth-century qualities, the anecdotes, the romantic satire, are to a surprising degree modified in their effect by the juxtaposition of what is genuinely new in Corbière's art.

While Corbière's evolution toward the use of a dramatic speaker in his poems seems to come from a rather simple nineteenth-century conception of poetry as the expression of personality—a conception one can derive from Hugo and Baudelaire even though they held more elaborate theories of poetry—Laforgue arrived at dramatic monologue in a more devious way. Laforgue's early collection, *Le Sanglot de la terre*, which he did not publish, shows a primary concern for philosophical poetry; the "philosophy" is a mixture of ideas on the evolution of the universe derived from contemporary astronomy and elements of Hinduism and Buddhism, which came perhaps from the work of Mallarmé's friend Cazalis and, in any case, had found some expression in Leconte de Lisle's early work. The unifying bond between science and oriental thought is pessimism, and this is emphasized by the fact that Laforgue's poems are mostly first person ones expressing a certain anguish: this is *felt* philosophy. The poems are not more—nor less—close to dramatic monologue than is the traditional kind of first person portrait of a mind such as Mallarmé's "L'Azur"; that is to say, a strongly logical organization prevails in the poem.

Laforgue stated in a letter that the idea of writing *complaintes,* which was to be the title of his first published volume, came to him on September 2, 1880, as he moved among the crowd at the inauguration of the Lion de Belfort statue on the Place Denfert-Rochereau. A *complainte* is a sad popular song, and while Laforgue did write two pieces in that vein ("Complainte du pauvre jeune homme," "Complainte de l'époux outragé"), what he hit upon while listening to street singers entertain the crowd was not really the idea of writing melancholy ballads. Rather, it was the fact of a character ruminating in particular circumstances that struck him in the songs. Songs often begin abruptly in the middle of a plot without preliminaries; ellipsis rather than exposition and explanation is common. Laforgue said the genre of his *complaintes* was "empirical," by which he seems to have meant that their only constant was the notion of a speaker and that everything else—subject matter, diction—varied.

Ellipsis in presentation of a subject was something Laforgue thought about a good deal and not only in connection with the songs he heard on the Place Denfert-Rochereau. In 1881 he wrote about his idea of poetry as "psychologie dans une forme de rêve." Elsewhere he conceives of poetry "sans sujet appréciable," poetry which says nothing but consists of "bouts de rêverie sans suite." In diction there would be words joined which in reality are impossible pairs but would form a "dream harmony."[17] These expressions suggest to us perhaps something more surrealistic than Laforgue had in mind; nineteenth-century French poets were often hampered in their attempt to describe the alogical by lack of an adequate terminology. Poets as different as Hugo and Mallarmé used *rêve* rather freely in talking about poetry, and the sense ranges from the literal meaning of dream through irrationality, reverie, and vision. By dream Laforgue designated associative or elliptic movement in verse, which occasionally includes unconscious activity.

We might expect a poem consisting of "bouts de rêverie" to employ some relatively straightforward verse form like alexandrine couplets in order to allow free play to associative movement and its peculiar syntax. Laforgue, however, was a great student of prosody, and worked out extraordinarily expressive uses of rare verse forms in combination with inner monologue. Here are stanzas unprecedented in themselves and in their combination:

> Plages, chemins de fer, ciels, bois morts,
> Bateaux croupis dans les feuilles d'or,
>   Le quart aux étoiles,
> Paris grasseyant par chic aux prises de voiles:
>   De trop poignants cors
> M'ont hallalisé ces chers décors.

>   Meurtres, alertes,
>   Rêves ingrats!
>   En croix, les bras;
>   Roses ouvertes,
>   Divines pertes!

Beaches, railroads, skies, dead woods, boats sunk in gold leaves, the watch under the stars, Paris making smart crude remarks as novices take the veil: too poignant horns have sounded their call in these dear settings. Murders, alerts, unrewarding dreams! Crossed arms; open roses, divine losses! ("Complaint of Monotonous Autumn")

In this "Complainte de l'automne monotone" the longer stanza suggests the speaker's impression of the landscape and city; he sees images of infinity in the sunset on the sea and the night sky and thinks of the melancholy of hunting horns, while the crowd profanes the nostalgia of the nun's vocation. The outside world is dying, however; the short stanza represents his taking refuge in dreams of a life filled with drama and love, but he realizes immediately that dreams disappoint and stoically resigns himself to his loss of what never existed. As the sun is covered by clouds, the disparity between the imagery of the two stanza forms grows more pronounced, a characteristic kind of dynamic structure in Laforgue's prosody:

> Le soleil mort, tout nous abandonne.
> Il se crut incompris. Qu'il est loin!
> Vent pauvre, aiguillonne
> Ces convois de martyrs se prenant à témoins!
> La terre, si bonne
> S'en va, pour sûr, passer cet automne.

> Nuits sous-marines!
> Pourpres forêts,
> Torrents de frais,
> Bancs en gésines,
> Tout s'illumine!

The sun once dead, everything abandons us. It thought itself misunderstood. How far away it is! Weak wind, spur on these funeral processions of martyred clouds calling on each other to bear witness! The earth, so good, is surely going to pass away this autumn. Submarine nights! Purple forests, torrents of coolness, parturient fish schools, all lights up!

The death of the world is contrasted with the life force or unconscious surviving in the speaker. The ambiguity of the submarine imagery is of a kind we often find in Laforgue's inner monologues: it might be a vision or else a representation of something the speaker could not even put into words. Laforgue carries the depiction of mental life far beneath the surface of consciousness at times. The conclusion of the poem shifts tone to the colloquial:

> —Allons, fumons une pipette de tabac,
> En feuilletant un de ces si vieux almanachs,

> En rêvant de la petite qui unirait
> Aux charmes de l'oeillet ceux du chardonneret.

Enough. Let's smoke a pipe, while we look through one of these so ancient almanacs and dream of the girl who unites the charms of the carnation with those of the finch.

The unconscious has risen to affirm itself in the form of a reflection on mating and spring.

Laforgue used the combination of short and long stanzas in various ways. Here an adolescent dreams of sanctity and asceticism; the shorter lines represent ironic reflections on the longer ones:

> Mon Dieu, que tout fait signe de se taire!
> Mon Dieu, qu'on est follement solitaire!
> Où sont tes yeux, premier dieu de la Terre
> Qui ravala ce cri:
> "Têtue Eternité! je m'en vais incompris...?"
>
> Pauvre histoire!
> Transitoire
> Passeport? ("Complainte de la fin des journées")

My God, how everything signals to be silent! My God, how terribly lonely I am! Where are your eyes, first god of Earth, who swallowed the cry, "Stubborn eternity, I am leaving misunderstood?" Poor story! A transitory passport? ("Complaint of the Days' End")

The syntax and rhyme of the shorter lines give them a tone that is distinct, but best understood as a modulation in the one voice, rather than as an authorial comment, although sometimes with Laforgue's romantic irony the distinction is difficult to make. The crucifixion as passport to eternity is unsatisfactory to the speaker's scientific sense; having buffoonishly adapted "My God, why hast thou forsaken me," he deforms another line of the Gospel:

> J'ai dit: mon Dieu. La terre est orpheline
> Aux ciels, parmi les séminaires des Routines.
> Va, suis quelque robe de mousseline...
> —Inconsciente Loi,
> Faites que ce crachoir s'éloigne un peu de moi!
>
> Vomitoire
> De la Foire,
> C'est la mort.

I said: My God. The earth is an orphan in the skies, amid the seminaries of Routines. Come, follow some muslin dress. Unconscious Law, let this spitoon pass from me! Vomitorium of the Carnival, Death.

The pun on *vomitoire*, which is not a vessel into which one vomits and therefore connected with *crachoir*, but rather the exit in a Roman amphitheater, is characteristic of Laforgue's monologues, and the *crachoir* itself is probably brought in partly as a play on the expression *tenir le crachoir*, talk interminably, which is what the speaker has been doing. The unconscious law which impels one toward muslin dresses is the force behind the carnival of life, which Christ supposedly rejected.

The disparity between short and long stanzas in *Les Complaintes* ranges from the slight one between statement and ironic comment to the contrast between two or more speakers. The relations between their lines, in the latter case, are sometimes complex and represent several kinds of consciousness. In the "Complainte des pianos qu'on entend dans les quartiers aisés" the adolescent poet wonders about the girls whose voices, singing a *complainte*, drift with the sound of the piano through the windows in early spring:

> Jolie ou vague? triste ou sage? encore pure?
> O jours, tout m'est égal? ou, monde, moi je veux?
> Et si vierge, du moins, de la bonne blessure,
> Sachant quels gras couchants ont les plus blancs aveux?
>
> > Mon Dieu, à quoi donc rêvent-elles?
> > A des Roland, à des dentelles?

Pretty or vague? Sad or well-behaved? Still pure? "O days, it's all the same," or "World, *I* want"? And if virgin at least of the good wound, knowing what luxuriant sunsets suit the most virginal confessions? My God, what are they dreaming of? Rolands? Lace trimmings? ("Complaint of the Pianos")

The recurrent alexandrine quatrain is always cast in extremely elliptical syntax, representing emergence of thought, while the octosyllabic couplet consists of a clearly formulated question or comment. In the girls' lines, a short impression of their life is followed by two verses of the *complainte*, trailing off into a parodic image which expresses their feelings but which they would hardly choose:

> —"Coeurs en prison,
> Lentes saisons!
>
> "Tu t'en vas et tu nous quittes,

> Tu nous quitt's et tu t'en vas!
> Couvents gris, choeurs de Sulamites,
> Sur nos seins nuls croisons nos bras."

"Hearts in prison, slow seasons! You're going off and leaving us, you're leaving us and going off! Gray convents, choir of Shulamites, over our nonexistent breasts let us cross our arms."

The third occurrence of the *complainte* ends with the silent words "Et lui qui ne vient pas," which the poet picks up immediately: "Il viendra!" In other words, his thoughts are completely enmeshed with the girls', so that from the mere two lines of the *complainte* a whole series of contrasting yet complementary reflections arise.

Laforgue's handling of consciousness in the "Complainte des pianos" compresses into a relatively short poem a quite elaborate scene of overheard words, conjectures, divagations, imagistically stylized thoughts and colloquially worded ones. At times Laforgue abandons the extreme realism of the representation of interreacting characters for more imaginative patterns. The "Complainte des grands pins dans une villa abandonnée" tells us from the title that pines are speaking and that someone is no longer living with a certain elegance. The opening imagery is of a sky covered with "packets of asphalt" (clouds) driven by "black Misereres." Then:

> —Oh! ces quintes de toux d'un chaos bien posthume!
> Chantons comme Memnon, le soleil a filtré,
>
> > —Et moi, je suis dans ce lit cru
> > De chambre d'hôtel, fade chambre,
> > Seul, battu dans les vents bourrus
> > De novembre.
>
> —Qui, consolant des vents les noirs Misérérés,
> Des nuages en fuite éponge au loin l'écume.

Oh, these coughing fits of a quite posthumous chaos! Let us sing like Memnon, the sun has filtered through, (and *I* am in this rough hotel room bed, a dreary hotel room, alone, beaten by the cross November winds) which, consoling the black Misereres of the winds, wipes off in the distance the foam of fleeing clouds. ("Complaint of the Great Pines")

The long lines are grammatically continuous and employ diction of great pomp—comparing the sun to a resurrection after the Mass for the dead—to suggest the magnificent expanse of the landscape. The pines' former owner feels his existence withering, as they rejoice:

> —Memnons, ventriloquons! le cher astre a filtré
> Et le voilà qui tout authentique s'exhume!

> —Oh! quel vent! adieu tout sommeil;
> Mon Dieu, que je suis bien malade!
> Oh! notre croisée au soleil
>   Bon, à Bade.

> —Il rompt ses digues! vers les grands labours qui fument!
> Saint Sacrement! et *Labarum* des *Nox irae!*

> —Et bientôt, seul, je m'en irai,
> A Montmartre, en cinquième classe,
> Loin de père et mère, enterrés
>   En Alsace.

Let us Memnonize, ventriloquize! The dear heavenly body has filtered through and there it is, authentic and exhumed! (Oh, what wind! Farewell all sleep; my God, how sick I am! Oh, our window in the good sun in Baden!) It has broken through the dikes, toward the great misty fields! Blessed Sacrament and *Labarum* of the *Nox irae!* (And soon, alone, I will go off to Montmartre, in my fifth-class funeral, far from my father and mother buried in Alsace.)

The golden statue of Memnon, which sang as the sun hit it, the Host displayed in a monstrance shaped like a sunburst, and Constantine's imperial standard with a cross are the elements from which the grandiose imagery of the pines' speech is made. They represent vigor and strength amid the turmoil of the weather, while life ebbs for the impoverished speaker, who will never again take the waters or enjoy similar luxuries. His death is juxtaposed to the resurrection of nature. The fragmented references to the speaker's life form a kind of covert plot, of which there are other examples in *Les Complaintes:* Laforgue discovered in this device a concise means of heightening the quality of situations by exploiting the reader's capacity for inventing what the poet omitted. The hints of plot suggest to us merely the essence, that is, the mood of the situation; the pines' speech functions also as a way of creating mood, a contrasting one, and the point of this *complainte,* like that of some others, is the building of an emotional ambience, free from the commonplaces of thought traditional in poetry. If the "Complainte des grands pins" resembles a mood poem, other *complaintes* belong to various genres; while they are all characterized by the use of distinctive voices, there is a considerable variety among them. One kind of voice that occurs in certain poems has a mingling of the pretentiously literary and the colloquial; it expresses the clichés of instinct and emotion, as in this invitation to a walk in spring:

> Permettez, ô sirène,
> Voici que votre haleine
> Embaume la verveine;
> C'est l'printemps qui s'amène!

—Ce système, en effet, ramène le printemps,
Avec son impudent cortège d'excitants. ("Complainte des printemps")

Allow me, O siren; now your breath has whiffs of verbena; spring is coming along!—This system, indeed, brings along spring, with its impudent entourage of stimulants. ("Lament of the Springtime")

This absurd language cannot of course belong to any realistically conceived individual; it is the language Laforgue lends to the life force. The alternating voice in this case represents a kind of rational critical faculty. From these abstractions it is only a step to such oddities as the *complaintes* of the poet's fetus as he is being born, the dialogue of musical instruments at the *comices agricoles,* and the symbolic figures of Lord Pierrot and the King of Thule. These are far from being primarily mood poems; they illustrate the second phase of Laforgue's philosophical poetry and do not concern us here, although the philosophical conceptions involved will be relevant to the analysis of the more realistic dramatic situations of Laforgue's last group of poems, usually known simply as *Derniers Vers.*

Eduard von Hartmann, the author of Laforgue's *livre de chevet, Die Philosophie des Unbewussten* (1869), is usually thought of as a disciple of Schopenhauer's, and the "Unconscious" of the title of his most famous book bears strong resemblance to the older philosopher's Will (and less to the Freudian unconscious): it is an irrational life force opposed to that state of emancipation of the intellect or Idea from the

Will which we call consciousness. Hartmann's Unconscious is less sinister than Schopenhauer's Will; as a matter of fact, it seems to be the source of everything important: art, character, morals, wit, and the idea of God. Another difference is that while Schopenhauer disclaimed having a practical philosophy, Hartmann's book is filled with the most varied illustrations from life and suggests in conclusion that the ends of the Unconscious must be made the ends of consciousness and that optimism and pessimism should be reconciled in the devotion to life. Among Hartmann's most specific discussions are those dealing with sexuality, and here we see an aspect of Hartmann's influence that is pervasive in Laforgue. Sexual impulses are degrading, shameful, and inevitable. Erotic pleasure is no greater than any other; despite repeated disappointments of a conscious nature, however, the Idea and Will impel one into coitus. Before marriage, which occurs at the age of twenty-five in the more civilized classes, either abstinence or vice results in more pain than the total of subsequent coital pleasure. Of two people in love, one usually loves more than the other with resultant misfortune. Adultery in marriage is almost inevitable and invariably unpleasant. The sexes are extremely different from each other and exert their attraction, as do gorillas, through size and beauty, although it is possible that in advanced human societies intelligence could replace these allurements.

What Hartmann's views on sexuality gave Laforgue was an elaborate theoretical justification, based on the Unconscious, for portraying awkwardness and maladjustment in the relations between the sexes. The failure of these rapports is not local, contingent, or remediable; it is inherent in the structure of the mind. Trivial misunderstandings are symbolic of the human condition, which is sexual frustration and profound unhappiness. The adolescent poet of the "Complainte des pianos" is discovering a world of conflicts that can only be avoided by the asceticism and renunciation envisaged in the "Complainte de la fin des journées." The symbolic figures in *Les Complaintes* like Lord Pierrot and the King of Thule all illustrate aspects of Hartmann's thoughts on sexuality and the unconscious. In the *Derniers Vers*, however, Laforgue moved away from such fanciful figures and embodied Hartmann's philosophy—or what parts of it he found valid and relevant—in a kind of loose fictional form, a series of inner monologues through which we can perceive a realistic point of departure for the speaker's fantasies.

The first of the *Derniers Vers*, "L'Hiver qui vient," is a mood poem describing the gradual desertion of the landscape in autumn and the huddling city in winter. "Every year, like a chorus, I will try to give its note." The image of the sun which lies on the hill "like a gland torn from a throat," "like spittle on a tavern floor," specifically suggests the solitary death from tuberculosis mentioned at the end of the poem. In later parts of *Derniers Vers* sickness and death will be alluded to succinctly, and we are intended to understand them as coming from this common urban disease (of which Laforgue died). "L'Hiver qui vient" supplies us with the atmosphere presupposed in the much less descriptive poems that follow; it is a general introduction and not an inner monologue on specific events. The same is true of the fable of the three horns placed immediately after; their suicide-death from love at sunset suggests the kind of imagery lurking in the mind of the speaker of the later poems. Sunset will always inspire feelings of loneliness and longing.

The first of the two "Dimanches," sections three and four, opens on the anniversary of the break with the narrator's fiancée and goes on to the contemplation of a young girl on Sunday after Mass. This double plane of present and past is characteristic of Laforgue's way of giving a certain depth of memory and experience to the inner monologue and of avoiding a straight-line narration. A silent, inner address—of which there are many in *Derniers Vers*, to be carefully distinguished from the rare cases of true address—directed to the young girl joins the anniversary night wind theme of the Valkyries (in moments of frustration the narrator tends to turn to the elements), with another one:

> Oh! voilà que ton piano
> Me recommence, si natal maintenant!
> Et ton coeur qui s'ignore s'y ânonne
> En ritournelles de bastringues à tout venant,
> Et ta pauvre chair s'y fait mal!...
> A moi, Walkyries!
> Walkyries des hypocondries et des tueries!

Oh, now your piano is beginning on me again, so instinctive now! And your heart, which hardly knows itself, is droning in tavern songs addressed to any passerby, and your poor flesh is suffering. Come, Valkyries of hypocondria and massacres!

He imagines the very virginal girl with the "reblanchi" body to be a prey to promiscuous instincts. This morbid fantasy is connected ultimately in the *Derniers Vers* with *Hamlet*, which, quite subtly, serves as an archetypical reference for the poet. As it was finally worked out, *Derniers Vers* has one general epigraph from *Hamlet* and one applying specifically to the last section; in the *Fleurs de bonne volonté*, however, a collection Laforgue never published and which is both a source and a prefiguration of *Derniers Vers*, Laforgue used more abundant quotes from *Hamlet*, showing how much it was relevant to his themes, and the point these quotes mostly tend toward is worth observing:

OPHELIA: 'Tis brief, my lord.
HAMLET: As woman's love.

HAMLET: Let her not walk in the sun: conception is a blessing; but not as your daughter may conceive.

HAMLET: I have heard of your paintings too, well enough. God hath given you one face, and you make yourself another, you jig, you amble . . .

LAERTES: The chariest maid is prodigal enough/If she unmask her beauty to the moon.

The "Get thee to a nunnery" passage serves more than once. Hamlet's obsession with woman's depravity has its counterpart in the mind of the narrator; in terms of Hartmann's thought, he fears the completely unknown quantity which is the unconscious of the opposite sex and with which his can never mesh. The general epigraph to *Derniers Vers*, which may seem obscure at first, is the speech where Ophelia describes Hamlet's taking her hand, studying her face, sighing, and departing as if in a trance. "The very ecstasy of love," comments Polonius, which it may be, but Laforgue also took the episode to symbolize the impossibility of Hamlet's ever coming to terms with Ophelia as a woman.

The narrator suddenly ceases to think of the young girl's depraved heart, and the quick succession of thoughts and attitudes that pass through his mind are characteristic of the elliptical texture of *Derniers Vers*:

> Non, non! C'est sucer la chair d'un coeur élu
> ....
> Mais quoi! s'en aller faire les fous
> Dans des histoires fraternelles!
> ....
> L'âme et la chair, la chair et l'âme,
> C'est l'esprit édénique et fier
> ....
> En attendant, oh! garde-toi des coups de tête

No, no, it would be sucking the flesh of one of the Elect . . . Come now, to think of foolishly trying fraternal relations . . . The soul and the flesh, the flesh and the soul is the proud Edenic spirit . . . Meanwhile, oh, watch out for impulsive actions

The first line despite its present tense is a hypothetical fantasy: she is too spiritual for her flesh to be touched. On the other hand, nonerotic relations, relations of equality are impossible between the sexes, because of the very structure of the unconscious. For a moment, the narrator envisages a reconciliation between flesh and spirit, which again is impossible thanks to the difficulty of uniting the unconscious with consciousness. The retreat from the idea of marriage, renunciation, is the only reasonable conclusion, and the narrator offers Hamlet-like advice to the girl to remain chaste. This sequence of reactions and variations on it constitute an essential pattern of movement in *Derniers Vers*, and the logic of it lies in Hartmann's analyses.

Another fantasy encounter with a young girl leads, in the second "Dimanches," to a love-death-Mass-renunciation, alluded to but not overtly put until the end, which would break the cycle of sexuality and reproduction. In a complete reversal, the following poem, "Pétition," imagines the divine rose window of renunciation faded and darkened; now the narrator finds himself, still in imagination, involved in a compromise marriage with a girl full of a sentimental, idealized vision of herself which the narrator has helped create and cannot endure. (This ambivalent monologue is one of the most difficult to follow, unless one has the general underlying theme in mind.) The first of the two summer poems placed in the center of *Derniers Vers* contains a vision of social upheaval, whose relation to what precedes may seem obscure, unless we remember that the narrator tends to contemplate violence, though usually in the form of the elements, when frustrated. The second summer poem is one of memory of a parting and anguish at the bad health and promiscuity of the abandoned woman; its themes are recurrent from earlier sections, and its function is to give temporal depth to the whole.

With sections eight, nine, and ten we return to the encounter and retreat pattern of part four. It is varied, however; with such basic sameness in the movement of the unconscious as it impinges on consciousness, Laforgue is obliged to rely on the element of daydream detail to diversify it. "Légende," part eight, is a scene by the seashore, which appears to involve real conversation—or perhaps it is only a very precise fantasy. Jealousy of a past love is the new variation involved. Parts nine and ten belong together: in them one of the young girls who go to mass on Sunday (parts three, four) comes to offer herself. The marriage section is one of the most elaborate examples of Laforgue's imagery in *Derniers Vers:*

> O géraniums diaphanes, guerroyeurs sortilèges,
> Sacrilèges monomanes!
> Emballages, dévergondages, douches! O pressoirs
> Des vendanges des grands soirs!
> Layettes aux abois,
> Thyrses au fond des bois!
> Transfusions, représailles,
> Relevailles, compresses et l'éternelle potion,
> *Angelus!* n'en pouvoir plus
> De débâcles nuptiales! de débâcles nuptiales!

Oh diaphanous geraniums, enchanted warriors, sacrilegious monomaniacs! Enthusiasms, depravities, disillusions! Oh presses of the great evening vintages! Linen at bay, thyrsi in the woods! Transfusions, reprisals, churching, compresses and the eternal potion! Angelus! Unable to take more of nuptial collapses!

This passage, which T. S. Eliot quoted with admiration, is a crucial example of how we should read Laforgue: I take this not as sheer mood imagery but as a highly metaphorical account of an event in which the nouns can ultimately be translated—and must be ultimately—into quite physical terms. The mingling of the traditionally poetic, the erotic, and the medical conveys with ineffable deftness the deflowering of a Victorian virgin full of sensibility and vapors. Fantasies of abandoning her follow, as she becomes a dull *petite quotidienne*, and at the end the narrator, suddenly speaking soberly in the present and nonhypothetical, says that he will have spent his life *almost* departing on disastrous adventures. After this prolonged bout of imagination, the element of daydream diminishes in *Derniers Vers*. "Sur une défunte," the penultimate section, seems to deal with an actual fit of jealousy in the past—the *défunte*, however, may be so only figuratively and thus called because she no longer exists save as a subject of painful memories. The theme of jealousy occurs already in part eight and is adumbrated in part three.

In the twelfth and last section of *Derniers Vers* there is a striking recurrence and intensification of earlier motifs. The encounter-retreat pattern vanishes, and the epigraph from *Hamlet* sets the tone: "Get thee to a nunnery: why wouldst thou be a breeder of sinners." A vision of a city at night in winter and of a man picking up a prostitute repeats the city imagery of "L'Hiver qui vient"—instead of the usual autumn we are now firmly into winter—and finally makes explicit the prostitute theme from part three; the narrator focuses his thoughts on a woman he has broken with and whose instincts may be driving her into "histoires trop humaines." The interesting thing in this passage is that it appears not to be a fantasy but about a real woman, just as the one abandoned and remembered in part seven seems real. In contrast, the girl in the village convent, whom he thinks of next, is evidently hypothetical, one of the young girls spotted on Sunday after mass in earlier sections. The transition between the two drifts of thought is made by means of Hamlet's words, "To a nunnery, go!": "Nuit noire, maisons closes, grand vent/Oh! dans un couvent, dans un couvent!" The convent girl is likewise a prey to her unconscious drives; the narrator begs her to stay away from the window (a soliciting situation) and the sight of the setting sun, the erotic and solitary associations of which are finally clarified. The renunciation of marriage is the theme of a long silent address to the girl. The full emergence of the Hamlet theme clarifies in retrospect all the preceding sections of *Derniers Vers*, and it seems as if renunciation is the burden of the whole work. Suddenly, however, at the very end, the narrator is reconciled to the girl and her unconscious as symbolized by her eyes (a motif from an earlier section):

> Eh bien, pour aimer ce qu'il y a d'histoires
> Derrière ces beaux yeux d'orpheline héroïne,
> O Nature, donne-moi la force et le courage
> De me croire en âge,
> O Nature relève-moi le front!
> Puisque, tôt ou tard, nous mourrons.

Finally, to love the toubles behind the beautiful, heroic orphan's eyes, O Nature, give me the strength and the courage to think myself old enough; O Nature, raise my brow! since sooner or later we shall die.

The "O Nature" is an echo of Baudelaire's prayer to be able to contemplate his heart and body without disgust ("Un Voyage à Cythère"). This resolution in the face of death (the inevitability of "L'Hiver qui vient") represents Hartmann's devotion to life, the practical outcome of the philosophy of the Unconscious.

The monologue created by Laforgue is largely an inner one, and if the analogy with drama is appropriate to the monologue invented by Browning, that with the stream-of-consciousness novel is more so in this case. The actual prototype of the stream-of-consciousness novel, Dujardin's *Les Lauriers sont coupés* is contemporaneous with *Derniers Vers*, but of the two Laforgue's work is the more supple in technique and exploits more interestingly the play of imagination. It is not, of course, cast in the strict time and event pattern Dujardin's novel is, but its relevance to the future of inner monologue fiction is as great. Both owe their origin in part to the idea widespread in late nineteenth-century France that modern urban man has a particularly nervous, exacerbated sensibility and reacts intensely to slight stimuli. This theory of the nerves is a justification for breaking the more rational configurations of the rhetorical tradition. Many mood poems owe something to this conception of *homo nervosus*, as does the exploration of sensations in portraits such as Rimbaud's. It is, of course, more than plausible to maintain that man's nerves do not change and that the innovations of Laforgue's or Rimbaud's style derive from a new inquiry into the possibilities of language and expression. This seems to me a more adequate explanation of the phenomenon, and it is one to which we shall return in connection with the general problem of style.

Derniers Vers is the first lengthy poetic structure to rely primarily on the recurrence of motifs for its organizing principle (and there are far more of these than I have noted). The fact that much of it is associative fantasy, and therefore free from traditional rhetorical development or the rigor of a plot line, facilitates a freer use of patterns of recurrence than the imagistic repetitions of Shakespeare's plays or *Madame Bovary*. This purely literary phenomenon was constantly compared with music by those who had an inadequate idea of musical structures or who felt for some reason that poetry had a lesser prestige and must be enhanced by such analogies. Naturally, in an age of music drama and program music, when musicians were given to modish literary impressionism in their writings, it is not surprising that this counterpart should have arisen.

Taken together, *Les Complaintes* and *Derniers Vers* offer an extraordinarily rich array of poetic structures using distinctive voices. While the relevance of the monologue in *Derniers Vers* to a new kind of presentation of characters is obvious, the more unusual forms in *Les Complaintes* suggest subtle technical possibilities for narration: the use of two voices for one speaker, an intervening impersonal voice in a remote style, the intertwining and interrelationship of a character's thoughts with another's, the use of fragments of plot, the exploitation of the ambiguity of words that could be either spoken or solely thought, the creation of an imaginary voice like that of a fetus. The many powerful ideas in fictional technique that are embodied in Laforgue's poetry give it a richness beyond the somewhat repetitive content of Hartmann-like situations and dilemmas. No other poet has a really comparable place in the history of modern narration. The two most famous long poetic works of the twentieth century in English, *The Wasteland* and the *Cantos*, both make use of the monologue as a basis for elaboration. Eliot comments in his notes to his poem on the role of Tiresias, who, in his metamorphoses, sees the whole action of the work. The techniques of disguises and shifting of role are already present in two of Eliot's French poems, "Dans le restaurant" and "Mélange adultère de tout," and even in the fantasies of Prufrock. As for Pound, he insisted even more in the original form of the first cantos than in the ultimate version on the role of Browning as inspirer of his monologue, but the monologue in its elliptic final form resembles to a greater extent passages in Laforgue or James Joyce, if anything. Questions of influence are always obscure, but in the history of forms it appears that Laforgue is the first to have created the highly flexible technique of the fragmented first person poem.

7. Rilke, Guillén, and Epiphanies

It is often said that the stream-of-consciousness monologue and the presentation of epiphanies or *moments privilégiés*, to use Joyce's and Marcel Proust's terms, are the distinguishing characteristics of modern fiction and that the second of these corresponds to a poetic device as old as Wordsworth's "spots of time." The monologue, we have seen, existed in poetry at least as early as Laforgue; as for the privileged moment, certainly nineteenth-century poetry contains many of them, varying in degree of stylization, succinctness, and emphasis on their temporal and irrational aspects. The list could be long indeed if we were to use Joyce's notion of epiphany, which includes more kinds of material than Proust's privileged moment of involuntary memory. However, many of these epiphanic moments in poetry do not resemble their intrusion into the sobriety of prose narration, where their contrastive quality and suddenness, keeping withal a certain unity of style, gives their use in fiction an extraordinary power. There are two poets, Rainer Maria Rilke and Jorge Guillén, who succeeded, by virtue of extreme discipline of style, in conveying this novelistic feeling of the irruption of a kind of spiritual heightening into the prosaic texture of life.

There are many things to admire in Rilke's *Neue Gedichte* (1907) and *Der neuen Gedichte anderer Teil* (1908). Each volume opens with an eloquent series of poems on biblical, Greco-Roman, and medieval subjects. These historical narratives, speeches, scenes, and portraits had become very characteristic of French poetry after Leconte de Lisle—countless ones are scattered through the works of late nineteenth-century poets whom we may not even think of in this connection; Rilke's poems, however, surpass their French prototypes, by and large, in beauty of dramatic conception and diction. Alongside such historical poems by French poets we usually find descriptive ones: the line between the two is often not sharp, and, in any case, the same cast of style informs the two. This is also the case of *Neue Gedichte*. Whether or not we think that all the poems really belong to the same aesthetic category, Rilke had ample precedent for yoking the historical and the descriptive together; like the French poets, he imposed on them a unity of style, with the result that *Neue Gedichte* forms a coherent phase in Rilke's production, his first masterfully sustained work after much rather uneven earlier poetry.

The outlines of the history of this phase of Rilke's poetry are well-known. Under the influence of Auguste Rodin, whose secretary he became for a while, Rilke grew increasingly concerned with what he called the *things* of poetry: art objects, animals and natural objects, and men's gestures in situations present and past. This is, of course, related to the ideas that had emerged in France about the impersonal, imagistic poem: things must be objectively presented, that is, without interpretive commentary; if they are left alone, so to speak, a momentary special impression may emanate from them. The filiation of this characteristically French aesthetic is unimportant; Rilke may have arrived at such considerations completely on his own. The poems themselves are more varied and interesting than the theory may imply. In fact, the peculiar kind of impersonal discipline he achieved in rendering realistic modern contexts and the extraordinary quality of impressions he created make a large part of the *Neue Gedichte* seem to belong to a quite new kind of poetry altogether, despite the stylistic affinity with the other, more conventionally Parnassian impersonal strain. There are a great many anonymous he's and she's undergoing experiences in *Neue Gedichte:*

Ihm ward des Eingangs grüne Dunkelheit
kühl wie ein Seidenmantel umgegeben
den er noch nahm und ordnete: als eben
am andern transparenten Ende, weit,

aus grüner Sonne, wie aus grünen Scheiben,
weiss eine einzelne Gestalt
aufleuchtete, um lange fern zu bleiben
und schliesslich, von dem Lichterniedertreiben
bei jedem Schritte überwallt,

ein helles Wechseln auf sich herzutragen,
das scheu im Blond nach hinten lief. ("Begegnung in der Kastanien-Allee")

Entering the green darkness was cool to him like an enfolding silk cloak, which he put on and arranged, when, at the same moment, at the other transparent end of the darkness, far away, out of the green sun and out of the green disks, white, a single face shone, which long remained distant and, finally, covered in a wave by spots of light falling at every step, approached in a brightly transformed state that shyly stretched to the flowing blond hair. ("Meeting in the Chestnut Walk")

The construction of the sentence with its slow unwinding quality belongs to a group of devices, such as the use in other poems of terms like "perhaps," "something," "almost," "yet," "to be sure," "except that," and "even," which render the gradual, groping way the language slowly expands and builds a mental scene. Rilke's elaborate syntax is not a way of indicating multiple logical relations but rather of reaching out to encompass many imagistic details and make of them a whole. It is the movement of consciousness trying to grasp the totality of experience. As such, the use of complex sentence structures is quite unlike their function in prose (except for Proust's), where grammatical development means distinctions as much as comprehension of particulars. Although the style is generally not obscure, Rilke here uses the metaphoric *Scheiben* for leaves, and *Lichter* for the chestnut blossoms in order to convey their mere outlines as perceptions without their being quite rationally identified. Temporal words are important in this kind of poem:

Aber auf einmal war der Schatten tief,
und nahe Augen lagen aufgeschlagen

in einem neuen deutlichen Gesicht,
das wie in einem Bildnis verweilte
in dem Moment, da man sich wieder teilte:
erst war es immer, und dann war es nicht.

But suddenly the shadow was deep, and eyes were near and open in a new distinct face, that, as if in a portrait, lingered in the moment they were passing each other: first it was eternal, and then it did not exist.

The paradox of the final line renders the irrational character of the stream-of-consciousness, which is only aware of being and its absence. The poet thus conveys an elemental level of perception free of causal-spatial relations. This is a poem of epiphany, of giving significance, in that the banal experience of passing someone is transformed into something memorable and with a heightened feeling of reality. That the context is one of ordinary activity contributes immeasurably to the effect.

"Begegnung in der Kastanien-Allee" contains only three local cases of figurative language; in this it is perhaps not typical of *Neue Gedichte*, in which metaphor and, above all, simile (including many *as if* constructions) are constantly encountered. Rilke also uses intricate and sustained metaphors:

> Wie in einem Schlaftrunk Spezerein
> löst sie leise in dem flüssigklaren
> Spiegel ihr ermüdetes Gebaren;
> und sie tut ihr Lächeln ganz hinein.
>
> Und sie wartet, dass die Flüssigkeit
> davon steigt; dann giesst sie ihre Haare
> in den Spiegel und, die wunderbare
> Schulter hebend aus dem Abendkleid,
>
> trinkt sie still aus ihrem Bild. Sie trinkt,
> was wie Liebender im Taumel tränke,
> prüfend, voller Misstraun; und sie winkt
>
> erst der Zofe, wenn sie auf dem Grund
> ihres Spiegels Lichter findet, Schränke
> und das Trübe einer späten Stunde. ("Dame vor dem Spiegel")

As in a sleeping potion spices dissolve, so she dissolves her wearied gestures in the fluid-bright mirror, and her smile occurs wholly in it. And she waits until the liquidity of it increases; then she pours her hair into the mirror, and, lifting her wonderful shoulders out of the evening gown, she drinks silently from her image. She drinks rather like a lover drinking in a daze, testing, full of mistrust, and she only nods at the maid when she finds in the depths of her mirror lights, armoires, and the dismalness of a late hour. ("Lady before the Mirror")

As in "Begegnung in der Kastanien-Allee," a very simple situation such as might be found in the texture of a novel is narrated in such a way that it seems to acquire great resonance and depth. Proust's observation that metaphor gives a kind of eternity to style is relevant here: the water image isolates the moment and gives the experience a wholeness, as if it were lifted out of time; then the recognition of the maid reestablishes temporal continuity.

One of Rilke's favorite kinds of epiphanies is the impossible perception, a sight too fine for the eye to observe or some kind of awareness for which the senses do not suffice. A very large number of pieces in *Neue Gedichte* contain such perceptions, stated sometimes with contrary-to-fact *as if*-clauses, sometimes with *seems*, sometimes as mere fact. Here a combination of all three is used:

> So wie das letzte Grün in Farbentiegeln
> sind diese Blätter, trocken, stumpf und rauh,
> hinter den Blütendolden, die ein Blau
> nicht auf sich tragen, nur von ferne spiegeln.
>
> Sie spiegeln es verweint und ungenau,
> als wolten sie es wiederum verlieren,
> und wie in alten blauen Briefpapieren
> ist Gelb in ihnen, Violett und Grau;
>
> Verwaschnes wie an einer Kinderschürze,
> Nichtmehrgetragnes, dem nichts mehr geschieht:
> wie fühlt man eines kleinen Lebens Kürze.
>
> Doch plötzlich scheint das Blau sich zu verneuen
> in einer von den Dolden, und man sieht
> ein rührend Blaues sich vor Grünem freuen. ("Blaue Hortensie")

Like the last green when colors are melted are these leaves, dry, blunt, and rough—behind the flower umbels, which no longer contain blue but reflect it from a distance. They reflect it, wept out, imprecise, and as if they again wanted to lose it, and just as in old blue letterpaper, there is yellow, lavender, and gray—washed out like a child's school smock, something out of style, something nothing more will happen to: as one might feel of the brevity of a small life. Yet suddenly the blue seems to renew itself in one umbel, and you see something movingly blue rejoice against a green. ("Blue Hydrangea")

It is characteristic that the more than real perception of the last tercet be ushered in by the homely and realistic comparisons with letterpaper and school smocks: this is the irruption of a mythopoeic event into a world of daily objects. The movement of the blue is all the starker in that the poem is not presented as something unfolding in a third person consciousness or colored by such a consciousness, as is the case in the preceding two poems. Here, of course, there is an implied speaker who includes himself in the pronoun *man*, but there is no implication of a distorted point of view; the epiphany is absolute and impersonal.

In the *Duineser Elegien* Rilke occasionally speaks of something having *Dasein*, for which "existence" is a less than rich translation. Reference to philosophy is not especially relevant here: *Dasein* is what, in a myth-suffused world, separates one hydrangea umbel from the others, one object instinct with life from its surroundings. Here objects glow with time; the slow minutes of life are amassed into a moment of intense *Dasein:*

> Selten reicht ein Schauer feuchter Fäule
> aus dem Gartenschatten, wo einander
> Tropfen fallen hören und ein Wander-
> vogel lautet, zu der Säule,
> die in Majoran und Koriander
> steht und Sommerstunden zeigt;
>
> nur sobald die Dame (der ein Diener
> nachfolgt) in dem hellen Florentiner
> über ihren Rand sich neigt,
> wird sie schattig und verschweigt—.
>
> Oder wenn ein sommerlicher Regen
> aufkommt aus dem wogenden Bewegen
> hoher Kronen, hat sie eine Pause;
> denn sie weiss die Zeit nicht auszudrücken
> die dann in den Frucht- und Blumenstücken
> plötzlich glüht im weissen Gartenhause. ("Die Sonneuhr")

Seldom does a shower of moist rot from the garden shadow, where drops hear each other fall and a bird of passage makes its sound, reach the pedestal which amid marjoram and coriander stands and shows the summer hours; only when the lady, followed by a servant, in the bright Florentine sunhat leans over the edge of it, does it become shadowy and silent—or else when a summer rain comes up from the waving motion of the tree tops, does it pause; for it cannot express the time which then in fruit and flowers suddenly glows in the white garden house. ("The Sundial")

The syntax, as everywhere in *Neue Gedichte*, is masterful: the slow, groping suspense of the one long sentence, with its many adverb and adverbial clause articulations, gives a great feeling of attainment and release to the last clause.

Studies of *Neue Gedichte* have tended to drift into a maze of tendentious symbolic interpretations about man and God or the artist and his work. These interpretations are often anodyne but unnecessary, as when "Der Panther" is called a poem about "modern man." A small number of pieces in *Neue Gedichte* make more or less explicit analogies, such as "Das Karussell" with life and "Der Schwan" with death. Nor are poems containing a paraphrasable argument like "Die Spitze" especially abundant. In other words, while the two parts of *Neue Gedichte* do not by any means exclude the discursive or the symbolic, which are essentially traditional rhetorical patterns, the new kinds of epiphanic poems lend the work a special significance in the history of poetic forms. Anthologists tend to choose pieces that might conceivably be reduced to little nuggets of wisdom, but the study of the whole of these two very substantial volumes reveals that such poems do not dominate. Of course, the distinctions among the poems of *Neue Gedichte* that I am making are useful primarily in the context of this study, for the general impression the work gives is of a unifying polish of style, whatever the technique or import of the specific poem may be.

The epiphanies of *Cántico*, Jorge Guillén's first book, make perhaps less use of the imagery of everyday objects than do Rilke's, but many are still grounded in the sights of ordinary life: the look of the world upon awakening, walking on a street in the morning, gazing out the window, closing one's eyes, watching the fire. While there are attempts at stream-of-consciousness representation ("La Rendición al sueño," "Sueño abajo," "Despertar"), the syntactic signs of monologue are usually confined to questions addressed to the self. This self is always a quite impersonal one like that of "Blaue Hortensie" and may, as in "Die Sonneuhr," not even identify himself by so much as a pronoun.

Guillén's critics are fond of quoting the longer, more discursive poems in *Cántico*. Although they are not his most perfect work, they do contain a certain amount of abstract vocabulary and can serve as a springboard for talking of Guillén's "thought." Actually, nothing is more misleading than to try to synthesize thought from *Cántico:* we need in reading it to have only one general notion in mind, that of wholeness, which will be represented in various ways. The abstract vocabulary occurs also in some short poems; there it is used fitfully, at times cryptically, at other times with great clarity. One example will provide us with both the basic notion and spatial forms suggesting it:

> Queda curvo el firmamento,
> Compacto azul, sobre el día.
> Es el redondeamiento
> Del esplendor: mediodía.
> Todo es cúpula. Reposa,
> Central sin querer, la rosa,
> A un sol en cenit sujeta.
> Y tanto se da el presente
> Que el pie caminante siente
> La integridad del planeta. ("Perfección")

The firmament, compact blue, remains curved over the day. It is the rounding of splendor: noon. All is a cupola. There rests, in the center without desiring it, the rose, subject to the sun at zenith. And the present is so strong that the walking foot feels the wholeness of the planet. ("Perfection")

There are four essential images here: the dome or half-circle, the firm roundness of the earth, and the highpoint of the sun, from which a sensible if invisible straight line is drawn down to the rose. Guillén, in "Ciudad de los estíos," speaks of "la ciudad . . . loca de geometría,/Oh, muy elemental"; his poetry is in general mad with basic geometry: "Amor a la línea!" ("El Otoño: Isla"). Circles are everywhere in *Cántico,* sometimes in the form of the vault of the sky, often in the form of a ring around the speaker: "Todas las consistencias . . . me limitan, me centran" ("Más allá"); "Con su creación el aire/Me cerca, divino cerco!" ("El Aire"). Images of water commonly provide horizontal circles, often with a line rising from them:

> Tras de las persianas
> Verdes, el verdor

De aquella enramada
Toda tornasol

Multiplica en pintas,
Rubias del vaivén
De lumbre del día,
Una vaga red

Varia que, al trasluz
Trémulo de estío
Hacia el sol azul
Ondea los visos

Informes de un mar
Con ansia de lago
Quieto, claridad
En un solo plano,

Donde esté presente
—Como un firme sí
Que responda siempre
Total—el confín. ("Tornasol")

Through the green blinds the green of that grove all of sunflowers multiplies in spots, golden with the movement of daylight, a wavering, various network, which, in the quivering filtered light of summer, undulates with the gleams of a sea which wishes to be a quiet lake, a brightness in a single plane where—like a firm "yes" always completely replying—there would be present the boundary. ("Sunflower")

Here there are the horizontal lines of the blind slats, the flat lake the sea aspires to be, and a kind of bulbous shape of spots, the bright sunflowers. In "Tornasol" the positive, epiphanic connotation of circular lines becomes clear: limit means concentration of energy or being—*ser*, a favorite word of Guillén's. The interesting thing, however, about Guillén's imagery of focus and "vigor inmóvil" ("Naturaleza viva") is that what surrounds the point the eye rests on is not dead and meaningless, though it is occasionally described as chaos: unlike Rilke's *Dasein*-filled forms, the centers of energy in Guillén are points of irradiation and what lies beyond them also participates in being. This explains an extraordinary class of images in *Cántico*, in which invisible forms appear: "El ventarrón de marzo/Tan duro que se ve ("Impaciente vivir"); "Todo el aire en realce:/Desnudez de su luz"

("Presencia del aire"); "El agua desnuda/Se desnuda más" ("El Manantial"); "Los muertos más profundos,/Aire en el aire, van" ("Noche de luna"). The whole air is filled with presence. Not only are the ghostly flickers of the invisible shapes full of being; the manifestation of time, often appearing in the paradox of momentary eternity, can have a similar spatialization: "Qué trasparencia/De muchas tardes, para siempre juntas!" "Tiempo en profundidad" ("Los Jardines").

The depth of time represents another aspect of Guillén's imagery of privileged moments; down is as essential as up, being part of wholeness:

> Ya madura
> La hoja para su tranquila caída justa,
>
> Cae. Cae
> Dentro del cielo, verdor perenne, del estanque.
>
> En reposo,
> Molicie de lo último, se ensimisma el otoño.
>
> Dulcemente
> A la pureza de lo frío la hoja cede.
>
> Agua abajo,
> Con follaje incesante busca a su dios el árbol. ("Arbol del otoño")

Now the leaf, ripe for its ordained fall, falls. It falls into the sky, a perennial green, of the pond. At rest, a softness of ultimate things, autumn sinks into itself. Gently the leaf yields to the purity of cold. Down through the water, with never ceasing foliage the tree searches for its god. ("Autumn Tree")

As the leaf falls in the reflected heaven of the pond, its god and the direction to which the tree aspires is ambiguously up or down. It is important for the idea of wholeness, which is a major characteristic of epiphany in Guillén, that he include imagery of what is beneath, for it is associated with firmness, roots. Nor is the vertical more pleasurable than the horizontal:

> Un resto de crepúsculo resbala,
> Gris de un azul que fue feliz. ¿Ceniza
> Nuestra? La claridad final, melliza
> Del filo, hiere al bosque: fronda rala.

Cae talando el sol. ¡Cruel la tala,
Cruel! No queda tronco. Se encarniza
La lumbre en la hermosura quebradiza,
Y ante el cielo el país se descabala.

¿Todo a la vez? Ahora van despacio
Los juntos por su ruta de regreso.
Ya es íntimo, ya es dulce el día lacio.

Todo a la vez. Se encienden las primeras
Luces humanas. ¡Ah, con qué embeleso
Ven al sol las nocturnas mensajeras! ("Electra frente al sol")

A remnant of twilight slips by, the gray of a blue that was happy. Our ashes? The final brightness, akin to the cutting edge, wounds the wood: sparse branches. The sun falls, laying waste. Cruel, the felling of the trees, cruel! No trunk remains. The light grows violent in the brittle beauty, and the landscape lies maimed before the sky. All at once? Now those walking together go slowly back. Now the daylight is intimate, now sweet the faded light. All at once. The first human lights are lit. Ah, with what enchantment the messengers of night see the sun! ("Electra opposite the Sun")

Here, as often in Guillén's poetry the spatial dominant, which is established after chaos, is the invisible horizontal sight line, running from the houses to the setting sun. As we have already seen, perfect invisible forms are quite as real in *Cántico* as hard objects: after all, geometry consists of imaginary lines. Sometimes Guillén represents stylized movement in the form of a wavy line ("Primavera delgada") or the actual undulating motion of flames ("Las Llamas") or the regular pitching of waves ("El Durmiente"), which in their periodicity resemble stasis.

Sometimes it is texture as much as shape that fixes the attention in Guillén's poetry. Clouds ("Tres nubes") or hills have an enchantingly untouchable surface:

¿Pureza, soledad? Allí. Son grises.
Grises intactos que ni el pie perdido
Sorprendió, soberanamente leves.
Grises junto a la Nada melancólica,
Bella, que el aire acoge como un alma,
Visible de tan fiel a un fin: la espera.
Ser, ser, y aun más remota, para el humo,

> Para los ojos de los más absortos,
> Una Nada amparada: gris intacto
> Sobre tierna aridez, gris de esos cerros. ("Esos Cerros")

Purity, solitude? There. They are gray. Intact grays that the wandering foot never came across, sovereignly light. Grays next to the beautiful melancholy Nothingness that the air shelters like a soul, visible because it is so true to its object: waiting. Being, being, and even more remote, for the smoke, for the eyes of the most distracted, a sheltered Nothingness: an intact gray over tender aridity, the gray of those hills. ("Those Hills")

"Ser," the word corresponding to Rilke's *Dasein,* is prominent in this epiphany of the most subtle visual and emotive quality: the half-dome of gray above nothingness, instinct with being and futurity, expresses that quality basic shapes have of making one feel one's own existence as well as that of the object.

While he occasionally uses his imagery in an overt analogy with poetic creation, Guillén's poetry is by and large not symbolic save in the ordinary, synecdochic sense in which a tree can be said to symbolize life. His poetry has consciousness as its subject, consciousness sometimes of self, more often of the surrounding world, and, at the height of consciousness, of the invisible spatialized. The occasional use of words like *verdad, realidad* and their adjectives should not distract one by their philosophical air: they do not add up to any consistent metaphysical doctrine that can be extracted from *Cántico.* More pertinent is the old mythic notion of the center: paradise was once the center of the earth, and any spot which is felt to be a center—the North Pole, the navel of the sea, Guillén's "central rose" in "Perfección," the tree of life in "Arbol del otoño," or the focal point of attention in other poems—conveys a more intense feeling of reality than ordinary space. The center can be said to correspond in spatial terms to the timeless moment of epiphany: it too is lifted out of the context of banal perception. Whereas Rilke chooses to emphasize temporal references in *Neue Gedichte,* Guillén uses geometry to make us feel freedom from time.

The heightened moments of Guillén's poetry vary somewhat in presentation, so that the spiritual revelation or epiphany may seem to come at times from without, at times from within, an ambiguity also found in Rilke. If we were trying to reduce poetry to a metaphysical system, this difference would be important, but, since, in a nonreligious sense—as Joyce meant the term epiphany—the revelation is dependent on its perceiver, not on an external source, the degree to which the experience seems determined from without is merely part of its psychological character and has no absolute meaning. Essentially it is a matter of technique and of the effect desired. Again, we must put philosophy out of our minds if we wish to read *Cántico*—and *Neue Gedichte*—correctly.

The developing idea of the work of art as autonomous, objective, and free of the traditional rhetorical framework does not lead inevitably to one kind of emotive content, however frequently melancholy seemed to be its burden in our earlier examples. The contemplation of pure beauty, the cityscape, the portrait, the scene of reflection, the hallucination, and the coming awareness of a significant event in the surroundings can encompass a great range of affective values. But the quality of emotion or feeling is less important as we move toward the inner monologue or epiphany than the rendering of the actual process of becoming conscious, which in often manifold detail comes to be a concern of poetry. From the time that Flaubert drew on poetic imagery for rendering Emma Bovary's states of mind, it was equally a major aspect of the novel, and certain technical rapprochements are possible. However, the new phenomenological content of literature was not very clearly isolated in critical writings by and large; they tend, when seeking large generalizations, to use ideas borrowed from philosophy like solipsism or idealism, which are loosely, if at all, connected with aesthetic facts.

One of the signs of a new phase of literature is the stylistic peculiarities—with reference to previous poetry—that can be observed in poems of consciousness. Verhaeren's verbless constructions, Verlaine and Maeterlinck's parataxis, Bataille and Rimbaud's prosaic realism, Cendrars' free verse, Laforgue's fragmentary syntax, Corbière's avoidance of logical connection, the confusions of Mallarmé's faun, Pound's representation of mental drifting, and the elaborate reaching out after detail in Rilke's syntax all involve some perturbation of logical, lexical, or grammatical conventions. I shall now envisage poetic developments of the late nineteenth and early twentieth centuries as stylistic configurations.

II
Style

1. *Prose Grammar and Verlaine*

There have been a number of attempts in the nineteenth and twentieth centuries to reject "poetic" language, meaning the habits in diction of the preceding generation or two. Wordsworth's reform in that direction is well-known in the English-speaking world, as is that of Pound, Eliot, Williams, and others near the beginning of the twentieth century. Montale and Ungaretti did away with the stylistic example of Gabriele D'Annunzio. In French literature the situation is double: romantic poets created a new diction, drawing on some prosaic elements, as did Apollinaire, Cendrars, and the surrealists in the early twentieth century with a different kind of prose inspiration. In between, however, two generations of poets were occupied with rebuilding a new, very antiprosaic diction. These poets, Mallarmé, Verlaine, Rimbaud, and the younger ones of the 1880s and 1890s are exemplary for twentieth-century poets like Pound, Eliot, Ungaretti, and Perse, whose early experiments in the prosaic were followed by the invention of intricate, new kinds of distinctly poetic language. (It is noteworthy that the principal German poets did not formulate the idea of remaking diction in terms of prose, although there are examples of it.) I shall begin by examining the conceptions of poetic language in mid-nineteenth-century France and gradually study successive innovations and their relationship to other literatures.

While neoclassical French writers generally held French verse to be very much like prose, which it perhaps was in comparison with English or Italian poetry, Hugo and other romantics found it necessary to move even further in the direction of prose, by discarding the periphrasis in diction and, in syntax, the inversion. The elimination of the latter involved the habit of ignoring the convention of end-stopped lines and allowing the sentence form to begin or end wherever necessary in the line, providing prose word order was observed:

> C'est nous que vous nommez démons; homme, tu sens
> Sous des souffles confus tes cheveux frémissants,
> C'est nous. Nous versons l'ombre aux jours que tu consommes;
> Nous jetons des lueurs dans ton sommeil; nous sommes
> Pris dans l'obscurité comme vous dans la chair.
> Nous sommes les passants sinistres de l'éclair,
> Les méduses du rêve aux robes dénouées,
> Les visages d'abîme épars dans les nuées. (Hugo, *Dieu*, "Dixième Voix")

We are the ones you call demons; Man, you feel your hair quiver under vague breaths; it is we. We pour shadow into the days you use up; we cast glimmers into your sleep; we are caught in darkness as you are in flesh. We are the sinister passersby of the lightning flash, the dream medusas with loosened robes, the faces of the abyss scattered in the storm clouds. (Hugo, *God*, "Tenth Voice")

We observe in this passage not only the lack of coincidence of sentence and verse line but also a tendency to parataxis and, in the last three lines, the device of lengthening the sentence through reduplication of one of its elements (here the predicate nominative) rather than through varied or complex constructions. This is a common phenomenon in romantic poetic syntax. Quite elaborate passages from the imagistic point of view often contain at most a simple relative clause in the way of subordination. Plainness in sentence form is even commonly reinforced by using short sentences with anaphora, as with the "nous sommes" clauses above. Within this preference for syntactic simplicity, however, two innovations are found, both inventions of Hugo. Image-appositions become numerous, as well as other adjectival elements:

> Oui, ces spectres, de feux rougis, d'aube dorés,
> Ces aspects vains, voilà ce que vous adorez;
> Oui, vos religions naissent de ces passages
> De vents et de brouillards dans l'esprit de vos sages;
> Oui, ces arrachements du nuage sacré,
> Ces fragments monstrueux du grand Tout ignoré,

Qui dans le crépuscule errent, et se déforment,
Sinistres, sur le front des hommes qui s'endorment,
Ces haillons d'infini, vus des pâles mortels,
Sont rêves dans vos nuits et dieux sur vos autels. (Hugo, *Dieu*, "Neuvième Voix")

Yes, these specters, red with fire, golden with dawn, these vain appearances are
what you worship; yes, your religions are born from the passing of wind and fogs in
the minds of your wise men; yes, these bits snatched from the sacred cloud, these
monstrous fragments of the great unknown all, which wander in the twilight and
take on sinister deformations over the brows of sleeping men, these tatters of the
infinite, seen by pale mortals, are dreams in your nights and gods on your altars.
(Hugo, *God*, "Ninth Voice")

The other new kind of noun-modifier relationship comes from the
displacement of the adjective *sinistre*, which has an expressive position as it might have in Latin. We do note still another example of
anastrophe, the position of *d'aube* and *dans le crépuscule;* although
in principle they avoided transposition of prepositional phrases,
Hugo, Baudelaire, Gautier, Leconte de Lisle, and others found it impossible to do entirely without this handy device of neoclassical poetic
syntax: *de*-phrases in particular sometimes form an exception to the
rule of prose word order. Substantial passages of romantic poetry,
however, conform to normal syntax, such as the bulk of Leconte de
Lisle's most famous poem "Midi"; in the latter, as is often the case,
the only unusual and poetic grammar is that necessitated by the apostrophe and the second person. Complex and elaborate syntax is not
absolutely excluded, of course, but it is saved for heightened effect;
we have seen in Rimbaud's "Les Poètes de sept ans" and "Les Premières Communions" fine examples of this alternation between prosaic grammar and syntactic elaboration.

Basing poetic language on prose grammar—though with more
use of exclamation and apostrophe than is found in most prose—
inevitably results, at times, in the other elements of poetic diction
falling into line, and there are cases where little difference can be felt
between the two except for the presence of meter and rhyme. In his
myriad experiments with style, Baudelaire sometimes chose a prosaic
effect in vocabulary, as in the beginning of "J'ai plus de souvenirs que

si j'avais mille ans" and much of "Le Voyage." (We should note, however, that the prosaic and the colloquial may be quite different; Corbière and Laforgue are often colloquial but never prosaic, there being a considerable discrepancy between the familiar or slang expression and sustained prose discourse.) To be sure, heightened prose had undergone the influence of poetry, but we may still distinguish between the two of them insofar as extensive metaphor and metaphoric apposition generally remained the province of verse. Verse which eschews elaborate figurative language, however, as Baudelaire's does only intermittently, is a special case, that of Parnassian poets.

Gautier, Théodore de Banville, José-Maria de Heredia, and others, and above all Leconte de Lisle, evolved a predominantly descriptive style (to be found in "Paysage polaire," quoted earlier) which differs from Hugo's verse, its principal source, in the subdued role metaphor and comparison play in it and in the concern not merely for the visual in an approximate sense but for consistent rendering of line and color in an almost pictorial way. For Mallarmé, it was the poetic counterpart to realist fiction, which, in Flaubert's followers, focused constantly on things and scenes; for Rimbaud (after he had exploited the style and finished with it), this descriptive style was essentially alien to the imagination. On the other hand, Rilke and George both found inspiration in the *plastique* obsession of French poets; Pound thought that Baudelaire had nothing to teach a poet writing in English but held Gautier essential. Obviously this line of poetry represents a very ambiguous achievement. For poets who were repelled by feeble visual and auditive imagery or by jejune poetic terms, the descriptive style with its well-defined, if limited vocabulary, and normality of word order, often differing from prose only by its frequency of epithets, meant firmness, clarity, and concreteness. Furthermore, the general characteristics of this style could, with slight modifications, be used for descriptions of a kind Leconte de Lisle would not have thought of:

> La blême lune allume en la mare qui luit,
> Miroir des gloires d'or, un émoi d'incendie.
> Tout dort. Seul, à mi-mort, un rossignol de nuit
> Module en mal d'amour sa molle mélodie.

Plus ne vibrent les vents en le mystère vert
Des ramures. La lune a tu leurs voix nocturnes:
Mais à travers le deuil du feuillage entr'ouvert
Pleuvent les bleus baisers des astres taciturnes. (Merrill, "Nocturne," *Les Gammes*)

The pallid moon lights in the gleaming pond, the mirror of golden glories, an agitated fire. Everything sleeps. Alone, half-dead, a nightingale modulates in love pangs its soft melody. The winds no longer tremble in the green mystery of the boughs. The moon has silenced their night voices: but through the mourning of the gaping foliage the blue kisses of the silent stars rain. ("Nocturne," *Scales*)

These lines are by Stuart Merrill and they belong to the poetry of the 1880s and 1890s, as can be seen from the affected use of *en* for *dans*, from the alliterations and assonances, which are more obtrusive than Leconte de Lisle's, and the slightly archaic word order in the fifth line. Nevertheless, the choice of words denoting color and sound, the general plotting of the sentence structure, and its relationship to the alexandrine quatrain observe the lesson of Leconte de Lisle. Certainly Leconte de Lisle was very much a living influence when these lines were published (1887); he brought out a major collection, *Poèmes tragiques* (1884), just when poets like Merrill, who were to be known as *symbolistes*, were writing their first verse. The work of Mikhaël, Pierre Quillard, André-Ferdinand Hérold, Jean Lorrain, Samain, Henri de Régnier, Louÿs, and others demonstrates how, with a somewhat greater use of metaphor, the older poet's working out of the general problem of verse style could still be to some extent valid. And it must be remembered that, until the late 1880s, much of Mallarmé, Verlaine, and Rimbaud was either unpublished or difficult to procure, so that their answers to the question of style were only partially known.

As might be expected, Verlaine mastered the Parnassian style, of which there are examples in his first volume, *Poèmes saturniens* (1866), but the essential direction of his imagination was completely away from anything resembling Leconte de Lisle's manner. The syntax Verlaine evolved for the alexandrine bears no relation to prose sentence structure:

Je fais souvent ce rêve étrange et pénétrant
D'une femme inconnue, et que j'aime, et qui m'aime,
Et qui n'est, chaque fois, ni tout à fait la même
Ni tout à fait une autre, et m'aime et me comprend.

Car elle me comprend, et mon coeur, transparent
Pour elle seule, hélas! cesse d'être un problème
Pour elle seule, et les moiteurs de mon front blême,
Elle seule les sait rafraîchir, en pleurant. ("Mon Rêve familier")

I often have the strange and penetrating dream of an unknown woman, whom I love
and who loves me and who, each time, is not quite the same nor quite another, and
loves me and understands me. For she understands me, and my heart, clear for her
alone, alas, ceases to be a problem for her alone, and the dampness of my pallid
brow she alone knows how to cool with her tears. ("My Recurrent Dream")

When this is written out in linear fashion, it is considerably more difficult to follow than in verse form, so meandering is the movement. The casual protraction of the sentence through multiplication of *et*'s in polysyndeton is of a kind avoided in prose and not really usual in verse: the reprise pronoun in the last line creates an asymmetrical construction, and, finally, the abundant repetition of words and sounds other than at the rhyme has the effect of slightly obscuring the phonetic structure of the basically regular alexandrine. Comparable stylistic devices are to be found elsewhere in the group of sonnets that opens *Poèmes saturniens*, and, as his style matured, Verlaine was to expand the techniques aiming at irregular, antiprosaic syntax and kinds of plays with sound largely unknown since the Middle Ages.

Verlaine's principal work is less associated with the alexandrine than that of other poets, and the best of what he wrote in alexandrines tends to be idiosyncratic. The basically symmetrical structure the line has in Leconte de Lisle, despite limited variations through enjambment, inner pauses, and exceptional divisions like 4/4/4, often yields in Verlaine to patterns in which only the variations and none of the regularity persist: "Langueur" in *Jadis et Naguère*, for example, consists almost exclusively of tripartite alexandrines. When the alexandrine is less violently dislocated, Verlaine tends to use his uncertain, wandering, antiprosaic syntax in order to mute the regular pattern of the line. But the eleven- and thirteen-syllable lines, the latter of which we have seen in "Sonnet boiteux," realize Verlaine's ideal of asymmetry without any particular grammatical effort; they are by nature so unstable and drifting that almost no examples of them are to be found before Verlaine and Rimbaud's work of 1872–1873. The unusual nine-syllable line and all the more common shorter ones do not have traditionally fixed rhythmic patterns, so that they also fit Verlaine's purpose of creating irregular movement. No previous French poet had such an aesthetic of prosody, which extends even to choosing oddities in line endings (lack of alternance of masculine and feminine rhymes, monorhyme, blank lines, and coupling masculine with feminine rhymes). To this array of irregularities Rimbaud, during the period he and Verlaine worked together, contributed the use of assonance rather than rhyme and the juxtaposition of lines of similar length such as seven and eight syllables.

Verlaine's prosody is reflected in the work of Laforgue and Gustave Kahn just before they moved into free verse (*Les Complaintes* and the early sections of *Les Palais nomades*). His *vers libéré*, as Kahn called it, seems, in conjunction with the neoclassical *vers libre*, to have suggested the early form of Symbolist free verse, as it was practiced by Laforgue and Kahn. In this, much use is made of alexandrines and shorter lines; anything longer than the fourteen-syllable line—which poets of the 1880s and 1890s now and then employed for whole poems—is rare. (Later free verse, as we shall see, follows a different aesthetic.) Verlaine and Rimbaud's innovations together inform some of the most elegant *vers libérés*, in Régnier's *Poèmes anciens et romanesques* (1890) and Apollinaire's *Alcools* (1913). The repetitions of sounds which occur frequently in late nineteenth-century poems—as in the lines of Merrill quoted earlier or Rodenbach's poem on hands—derive from Verlaine's example; they serve as an element of irregularity in that they usurp some of the effect of the rhyme scheme. The significance of Verlaine's prosody for later poets does not, of course, merely consist in their adaptation of this or that detail, but in a whole aesthetic of asymmetry, which his *vers libéré* embodies quite as much as does the Symbolist *vers libre*. And Verlaine's syntax is not to be separated artifically from his versification; his grammar is not precisely the same as what we have seen in Laforgue's verse, but they have in common the tendency to abandon prose sentence structure, whether by resorting to fragments, colloquialisms, meandering syntax or whatever. The savant combination of regularity with small variation, on which the traditional rhetorical criteria for style are based, vanishes.

Verlaine wrote a beautiful "Art poétique" in which he prescribes and describes, but offers no theoretical self-justification. He did not theorize and did not, in his later years, at least, like people who did. Verlaine summarizes his practice in diction and imagery quite memorably, however: there should be "carelessness" in choice of words (a studied carelessness, to be sure) and the mingling of the indeterminate and the precise in imagery. "Il faut aussi que tu n'ailles point/Choisir tes mots sans quelque méprise," a sentence whose odd grammar exemplifies *méprise*. Verlaine's examples of imagery are equally apt, this one mingling not only the precise (*crispé*) with the less precise, but also using uncertain echoes of *dire la bonne aventure* and English "crisp": "Que ton vers soit la bonne aventure/Eparse au vent crispé du matin." What generally characterizes Verlaine's notions of diction is their complete opposition to Leconte de Lisle's idea of style with its exact vocabulary and sharply defined imagery. If we were to supply the theory of style that Verlaine does not, we might say that his language represents the result of a highly deforming point of view, whereas Leconte de Lisle's pretends to a pseudo-objectivity. However, it would be wrong to suggest that there is any trace of a philosophical conception behind Verlaine's innovations. His motivation is primarily aesthetic. To the extent that he intended to create an individual voice distinct from the common, generally valid style Leconte de Lisle envisaged, we are justified, nevertheless, in considering that Verlaine's verse embodies a point of view chosen for artistic reasons and a certain kind of psychological representation. The latter shows up in favorite words and roots: *monotone, bercer, endormir, languir, sommeiller, rêver*. Many of Verlaine's best-known poems deal with either dream or a feeling of unreality; here is a less familiar passage in which the poet meditates on his potentially criminal hands:

> J'ai peur à les voir sur la table
> Préméditer là, sous mes yeux,

Quelque chose de redoutable,
D'inflexible et de furieux.

La main droite est bien à ma droite,
L'autre à ma gauche, je suis seul.
Les linges dans la chambre étroite
Prennent des aspects de linceul,

Dehors le vent hurle sans trêve,
Le soir descend insidieux . . .
Ah! si ce sont des mains de rêve,
Tant mieux,—ou tant pis,—ou tant mieux. ("Mains")

I am afraid, seeing them on the table premeditating there, before my eyes, something dreadful, inflexible, and furious. The right hand is indeed to my right, the left one to my left; I am alone. The linen in the narrow room assumes the look of a winding sheet. Outside the wind roars without respite; the evening comes down insidiously. Ah, if these are dream hands, so much the better—or worse—or better. ("Hands")

Here Verlaine's fondness for juxtaposition of the precise (the hands in their place) and the blurred outline (dream hands) shows how his reaction against Parnassian imagery goes farther toward creating special states of mind than anything in "Art poétique" would suggest.

Familiarity and a certain thinness in even his best poetry should not be allowed to conceal the vast technical importance of Verlaine's discoveries—quite apart from his other fine qualities as a poet, some of which we shall return to in connection with symbolic structures. He had, very early, a completely new vision of what French poetry could be, and his verse, far from displaying monotony and sameness, shows an extraordinary deployment of stylistic means. In his later years, worn out and distrustful of the young, he created his *faux naïf* posture, which was assimilated to his poetry by those whose ear was too poor to understand its intricacy or too blunted by gaudier recent innovations to appreciate its subtlety. The complexity of his gift, however, is apparent when it is examined in the light of the rejection of prose standards in French verse in the later nineteenth century.

2. Mallarmé and Imagery

Unlike Verlaine, Mallarmé clearly formulated a theory of style as psychological representation. We have seen how syntax and vocabulary convey the waking faun's consciousness; Mallarmé envisaged an even broader relationship between style and depicting perceptions. When he began to work on *Hérodiade* in 1864, he realized that a new technique was needed that would separate his future work from his early poetry: "Peindre non la chose mais l'effet qu'elle produit." The extent to which this principle is a criticism of Leconte de Lisle's imagery is obvious. However, there are all kinds of ways of depicting effects on one, and Mallarmé's theory needs to be supplemented with an example. What follows is later Mallarmé, but the principle of painting not the thing but the effect he repeated toward the end of his life, so that we may take the following lines from 1887 as merely a denser example of effect than what we find in *Hérodiade*:

> La chevelure vol d'une flamme à l'extrême
> Occident de désirs pour la tout déployer
> Se pose (je dirais mourir un diadème)
> Vers le front couronné son ancien foyer
>
> Mais sans or soupirer que cette vive nue
> L'ignition du feu toujours intérieur
> Originellement la seule continue
> Dans le joyau de l'oeil véridique ou rieur
>
> Une nudité de héros tendre diffame
> Celle qui ne mouvant astre ni feux au doigt
> Rien qu'à simplifier avec gloire la femme
> Accomplit par son chef fulgurante l'exploit
>
> De semer de rubis le doute qu'elle écorche
> Ainsi qu'une joyeuse et tutélaire torche.

The hair, a flight of flame to the farthest west of desire when completely loosened, alights (it looks like a dying diadem) near the crowned head, its former hearth. But how can I hope that, without light, this living cloud will continue, as the burning of the inner fire, originally the only fire, in the truthful or laughing jewel of the eye? A tender, naked hero defames her who, moving neither fire nor star on her finger, solely to simplify Woman gloriously, dazzlingly accomplishes the feat of covering with rubies the doubt she flays, like a joyous, tutelary torch.

The apparent difficulty of these lines is not hard to resolve: after seeing the lady's hair shining in the setting sunlight, the poet wonders whether, with nightfall, she will still glow. The lady, "defamed" by his doubt, proves it groundless by shining like a torch with her inner light. The conceit about the lady's light is a distantly Petrarchan one, and the poem is a compliment, an adaptation of the traditional poem of praise.

A number of details are worth commentary for what they show about Mallarmé's handling in general of syntax and imagery. The principles, let us state them right at the outset, are an emphasis on nouns at the expense of finite verbs and the use of one-word metaphors or metonymies. The flight of the flame, which the hair constitutes in an apposition (a favorite construction), prepares us for the fire-lady images and the cloud-bird-hair ones that follow. The poet and the lady's sexual desires have been satisfied: the setting sun in the west, toward which the hair seems to stream, is analogous with the ending of violent desire. What follows is contemplation of beauty. The lady is not only a fire but a jewel; her fire-hair, like a diadem, dies into her hearth-forehead. (Jewels, of course, have "fire" in ordinary language, so that the fire-jewel conjunction is based on an everyday metaphor.) The second apposition, "hearth," will be followed by a third one after "continue as"; appositions create density of nouns without finite verbs, and the latter are further reduced by the unusual infinitive clause "dirais mourir" and the infinitive exclamation of the second quatrain. Gold is a common metonymy for light, here sunlight, in Mallarmé, and the stars and fires the lady does not have on her finger are jewels, an elegant reversal of the light-matter equivalence. The hero is, of course, the poet, who speaks of himself in the third person for solemnity. By "not moving" and "simplifying" in a present participle and an infinitive construction, Mallarmé again avoids finite verbs in clauses. The glory into which the lady simplifies herself is pure light, a common meaning of the word in poetry, with, of course, its connotation of sacred magnificence. The positioning of the adjective "fulgurante" represents hyberbaton at its most expressive and Latinate (the adjective is placed by a noun of the opposite gender just as in Roman poetry), and, finally, the rubies are light cast by the torch.

This imagery of light as precious matter and precious matter as light may well awaken in the reader recollections of Luis de Góngora and other baroque poets given to jewels, metonymy, and conceits. It is significant, however, that Mallarmé describes his imagery in psychological terms, the effect of things on a consciousness, rather than in rhetorical terms. Even in his three substantial poems where the rhetorical flourishes of questions, exclamations, invocations, and apostrophes dominate (*Hérodiade*, "L'Après-midi d'un faune," and "Toast funèbre"), we can often analyze the figures into forms of subjective impression, especially visual ones, which are quite different from the inventive, witty amplification of the seventeenth century. In "La Chevelure vol" the disordered-seeming syntax, the absence of punctuation, the mysterious causality, and the mythic involvement of the lady in the setting create a kind of peculiar vision, as of something unfolding before one, especially when the metaphors are not analyzed too closely. Such appears to have been the dominant impression made by Mallarmé's poems on his contemporaries, who were not inclined to see in them precise, organized elements.

Nominal, participial, and infinitive constructions, the weakening of the verb to *a* or *est* in lengthy sentences, and elliptic clauses of several kinds characterize Mallarmé's syntax as well as hyperbata, such as the curious *apposition antécédente*, which is one of his most idiosyncratic constructions; there bursts forth (the verb is singular):

> Trompettes tout haut d'or pâmé sur les vélins,
> Le dieu Richard Wagner irradiant un sacre
> Mal tu par l'encre même en sanglots sibyllins. ("Hommage")

The god Richard Wagner irradiating consecration (trumpets loudly of gold swooning on the vellum) ill-silenced by the very ink into sibylline sobs.

"Trompettes" modifies either "dieu" or "sanglots." Such grammar is the signature of Mallarmé, and it is especially suggestive of an effect toward which his sentences often tend: the reader's grasp of the syntax is momentarily enfeebled owing to the complexity of the language, and one has almost the feeling of reading sentence fragments, such as Laforgue might use. In fact, Laforgue actually characterized Mallarmé's language as the "absence de syntaxe ou plutôt de fil de phrase."[1] It is the thread that may seem lacking, even though the syntax is actually coherent and elaborate. There is a sonnet closely related in theme to "La chevelure vol," which shows best the two opposite directions in which Mallarmé's language can move. The opening two lines describe, in periphrases, the sunset, which is the death of the day-god:

> Victorieusement fui le suicide beau
> Tison de gloire, sang par écume, or, tempête!
> O rire si là-bas une pourpre s'apprête
> A ne tendre royal que mon absent tombeau.

Victoriously avoided the magnificent suicide, glorious firebrand, blood through foam, gold, storm! I laugh if in the west a purple glow is getting ready to drape royally the tomb I am absent from.

The poet contrasts his survival with the death of the sun in truly fragmentary syntax. The breaking up of language which marks the demise of the god is followed by grammatical reconstruction, as the poet contemplates the light emanating from his lady:

> Quoi! de tout cet éclat pas même le lambeau
> S'attarde, il est minuit, à l'ombre qui nous fête
> Excepté qu'un trésor présomptueux de tête
> Verse son caressé nonchaloir sans flambeau,
>
> La tienne si toujours le délice! la tienne
> Oui seule qui du ciel évanoui retienne
> Un peu de puéril triomphe en t'en coiffant
>
> Avec clarté quand sur les coussins tu la poses
> Comme un casque guerrier d'impératrice enfant
> Dont pour te figurer il tomberait des roses.

What! From all that brilliance not even a remnant lingers (it is midnight) in the festive shadow, except that a head, a presumptuous treasure, pours forth its caressed unlit languor, your head, so eternally my delight, yours, yes, alone, which from the vanished sky retains a bit of childish triumph by covering you with brightness, when on the pillows you rest your head, as if it were the bellicose helmet of a child-empress from which roses fell to image your body.

Seven finite verbs, three participles, and one infinitive are enmeshed in this elaborate grammatical structure. This supersyntax, which is considerably more elaborate than most prose constructions, demonstrates, in conjunction with the first quatrain, how the accumulation of perceptions lends itself equally well to fragmentary syntax, such as Laforgue uses extensively, or to the hypertrophic grammar we have observed in Rilke as well as in Mallarmé. (In prose there are the comparable alternative solutions of broken stream-of-consciousness language and Proust's supersyntax.) Accompanying such unusual experimentation in sentence structure is, not unexpectedly, a generous use of irregular, tripartite alexandrines, for Mallarmé, while not a bold user of all the recent innovations in prosody, had, from an early point in his poetry, adjusted line rhythm to the idiosyncrasies of his grammar.

Mallarmé's grammatical innovations left their mark on Valéry, but more surprising is the way in which Stefan George adapted them to German, especially in his early work. Different as the structures of French and German are, George found ways either to use similar constructions, such as abundant participles, appositions, ellipses of verbs (and pronouns), somewhat archaic or unusual words or forms, or else to apply the essential spirit of Mallarmé's syntactic idea, inspissation, to his own language in a manner proper to it: new compound words, constructions that dispensed with the monosyllabic particles so characteristic of German, the genitive preceding the noun it modifies (eliminating thereby one article). In his first book, *Hymnen*, George employed periphrases and one-word metaphors in a fashion startlingly reminiscent of Mallarmé, as well as rich and rare rhyme and exact rhythm in a way far more French than consonant with German tradition. Although in his middle period the statistical distribution of nouns, finite verbs, and adjectives is not much different from that of Goethe's lyrics, the impression of density remains, thanks to a continued search for constructions in which articles, pronouns, particles, and auxiliary verbs play a reduced role. The elliptical metaphors, however, vanish.

In discussing Mallarmé's sonnets we have passed back and forth from considerations on grammar to comments on imagery. The two are closely related. Heavily nominal syntax—through image-appositions, fragmentation of the sentence and omission of verbs, accumulation of prepositional phrases bearing nouns, participles and nouns replacing finite verbs, or other devices—is obviously going to offer dense possibilities for metaphor, and the use of the metonymy or one-word metaphor is an especially acute case of this. We are now going to consider primarily the structure of images.

One-word metaphors and periphrases in which the reference is not quickly guessed are perhaps the most characteristic forms of figurative language in modern poetry. Sometimes they are called symbols to distinguish them from the classic, explicit A-is-the-B-of-C type of metaphor, but I prefer to save the term for more elaborate symbolic structures. The peculiar character of these modern figures is not so much that they are difficult to understand, however often that may be the case, as that their interpretation may depend either on a visual or other sensory rapprochement or else on a purely logical analogy, not to mention possible stages in between these extremes as well as degrees of elusive associationism in each category. Which kind we are confronting is not always immediately apparent. The logical analogy tends toward the witty conceit, the sensory comparison toward subjective *données* of experience, but it is the frequency with which they occur in juxtaposition that makes the reading of them problematic. Baroque rhetoric differs from modern tropes, which are often compared to it, in that the metaphoric figures of the seventeenth century were conceived of in a logical scheme of language, whereas the psychological dominates today with its greater range of associative phenomena. Reading Dylan Thomas or Hart Crane is a constant exercise in sorting out the various categories of meaning, and one needs quite as much to identify these classes as actually to isolate the metaphoric equivalence. Rimbaud, Gerard Manley Hopkins, Mallarmé, and Laforgue are the poets in whom these difficulties first obtrude, and of them Laforgue, because of his peculiar mixture of fantasy and irony, is notably hard to analyze definitively or even satisfactorily. We have already seen the most obscure passage in *Derniers Vers*, dealing with defloration. Here is another characteristic one:

> L'Extase du soleil, peuh! La Nature, fade
> Usine de sève aux lymphatiques parfums.
> Mais les lacs éperdus des longs couchants défunts
> Dorlotent mon voilier dans leurs plus riches rades,
> > Comme un ange malade...
> > O Notre-Dame des Soirs,
> > Que je vous aime sans espoir!

Lampes des mers! blancs bizarrants! mots à vertiges!
Axiomes *in articulo mortis* déduits!
Ciels vrais! Lune aux échos dont communient les puits!
Yeux des portraits! Soleil qui, saignant son quadrige,
  Cabré, s'y crucifige!
  O Notre-Dame des Soirs,
  Certes, ils vont haut vos encensoirs!
  ("Complainte à Notre-Dame des Soirs")

The sun's ecstasy, huh! Nature, an insipid factory of lymphatic smelling sap. But the desperate lakes of the long, dead sunsets pamper my sailing ship in their richest harbors like a sick angel. O Our Lady of the Evening, how I love you hopelessly. Lamps of the seas! Estranging whites! Dizzying words! Axioms deduced *in articulo mortis!* True skies! Wells taking communion with moon echoes! Eyes of portraits! Sun bleeding its quadriga, reared up, cruciclotting! O Our Lady of the Evening, indeed your censers rise high! ("Complaint to Our Lady of the Evening")

The poet, as we learn only at the end of the poem, has been rejected by the real eyes of a girl and expresses his distaste for the human and natural world identified with day and the life process. Water is a night and moon element, making the transition between sunset, with its illusion of lakes of colored light, and moonrise. In other words, the lakes' significance is that they are formed by light but are figuratively water. The stars' strange light, alien to nature, brings to mind the philosophical mystery of the cosmos ("mots à vertiges," unless the words are merely the names of the stars), their permanence beside the sun's death ("axiomes . . . déduits"). The artifice-like eyes of the night sky denote a reality beyond nature. The censers could be giving forth the cloud-smoke of the evening sky, or they could be purely figurative. Various other relations between the images and their concrete or abstract meanings are conceivable. What is important is the possibility of ambiguity, when the periphrasis and the one-word metaphor are extensively exploited. While the rhetorical tradition at its most elaborate allowed puns based on this ("Brûlé de plus de feux que je n'en allumai"), difficulties of resolving the question of figurative and concrete reference are more characteristically modern.

In the Mallarmé sonnets we have quoted and in the poem of Laforgue, the metonymies and periphrases tend to create a persona we encounter in other modern poets who share their taste for ostentatious figures: this is the self-conscious poet in an age of prose, whose attitude toward language becomes the subject of the poem. We encounter this persona especially in Wallace Stevens, whose diction in *Harmonium* has marked resemblances to French styles:

> Gloomy grammarians in golden gowns,
> Meekly you keep the mortal rendezvous,
> Eliciting the still sustaining pomps
> Of speech which are like music so profound
> They seem an exaltation without sound.
> Funest philosophers and ponderers,
> Their evocations are the speech of clouds.
> So speech of your processionals returns
> In the casual evocations of your tread
> Across the stale, mysterious seasons. These
> Are the music of meet resignation; these
> The responsive, still sustaining pomps for you
> To magnify, if in that drifting waste
> You are to be accompanied by more
> Than mute bare splendours of the sun and moon.
> ("On the Manner of Addressing Clouds")

Here the play of literal and figurative resembles that in Laforgue: the "gloomy" could mean that these are dark clouds with golden edges, for example. The pomps of speech seem at first to be merely magnificent language; it is only when we see they must be contrasted to "mute" and "bare" that pomp takes on its concrete meaning of an ostentatious procession, here with music. The exaltation is literally high up, on the level of the clouds, and evoking is calling out loud. Finally, the evocation of the tread of clouds could refer to poetry of the process of man's life, time, and death, or be concrete nature poetry, clouds being literally part of nature but here associated with man's funest condition. But it is as much in the tone, at once ironic and grandiose, as in any figure that we find the similarity between Stevens and Mallarmé or Laforgue. What they share is a certain initial relationship to written language and the idea of it rather than any community of themes or inspiration. From this follows the taste for the striking word, the cryptic metaphor, the seeing of Latin roots in ordinary words.

As we have moved beyond Mallarmé in the examination of one-word metaphors and periphrases, the contrast between the abstract and the concrete has obtruded. Actually there are examples of curious abstractions in poems quoted earlier in this chapter: Hugo speaks of the "arrachements du nuage," Merrill of an "émoi d'incendie" being lit and of light passing through the "deuil du feuillage." Even in Leconte de Lisle it would be possible to find an expression like "filling" the "horreur de l'espace." Mallarmé speaks of a "nudité de héros" rather than a naked hero, and "une pourpre" is a purple light. These substitutions of abstract for concrete are not, taken in isolation, especially significant, but they point to a general tendency in the syntax of French literature from the 1850s on, which ultimately left a strong impress on poetic language and which bears some affinity with seventeenth-century high style in the manner of François de Malherbe. We begin to find the habit of using verbal nouns as concretes, as in Hugo's *arrachement*, the turning of the modifier into an abstract chief noun, as in Mallarmé's *nudité*, the pluralizing of abstract nouns, as if they could be quantified, and the parallelism of abstract and concrete nouns ("congelés dans leur rêve et leur lividité," Leconte de Lisle, "Paysage polaire"). These usages invade prose as well as poetry, and they might best be explained as a way of expanding the vocabulary of a language that has feeble capacities for word formation or assimilation. Of course, the principle of concreteness in language, which is generally implicit in Leconte de Lisle and the practice of many subsequent poets, is, in a sense, violated, since even when used as concrete nouns, abstracts retain something of their origin. Corbière's concrete use of *vie* and *amour* represents such ambiguity, and his habit of using the particular for the general derives from the same acute stylistic consciousness of the abstract, the solid, the figurative, and the real.

In Mallarmé's later poetry there are abstractions used as glosses in short allegories: the flower-ideas in "Prose pour des Esseintes" or the cape of time in "Au seul souci." Elsewhere, there is the statue-like personification of "Angoisse" in "Ses purs ongles" or the "Orgueil" which is sunset light in "Tout Orgueil." We commonly think of Mallarmé as a symbolist in distinction to the traditional allegorist, but actually he, like his contemporaries, tried both approaches to style. Perhaps the later poem in which allegorical abstraction is most strikingly and abundantly used is "Le vierge, le vivace":

> Le vierge, le vivace et le bel aujourd'hui
> Va-t-il nous déchirer avec un coup d'aile ivre
> Ce lac dur oublié que hante sous le givre
> Le transparent glacier des vols qui n'ont pas fui!

Will this fresh, hardy, and beautiful new day tear open for us, with a drunken flap of its wing, this hard, forgotten lake, haunted under the frost by the transparent glacier of unflown flights?

The lake is clearly a state of mind: this is the only way it could be haunted by memories of what was not. The image of being surrounded by one's mood is not at all incoherent or even unusual, but the mingling of a personification like "new day" with the curious glacier that is transparent, because it represents what never existed and therefore is a kind of nothingness, gives a strange effect of the semivisual.

One of the characteristic signs of allegory and poems using abstractions personified is that causality in them is somewhat cryptic:

> Un cygne d'autrefois se souvient que c'est lui
> Magnifique mais qui sans espoir se délivre
> Pour n'avoir pas chanté la région où vivre
> Quand du stérile hiver a resplendi l'ennui.

A one-time swan remembers that he is the one who, though magnificent, is struggling hopelessly to free himself, because he did not sing of the region of life when the ennui of sterile winter shone.

One of the reasons we think of causality (why did the swan not sing of the region of life? Pride? Stubbornness?) in reading this kind of poem is its general formulation: the swan is a traditional symbol for the poet and we tend, in the presence of abstractions or images with a long-consecrated significance, to expect didacticism.

> Tout son col secouera cette blanche agonie
> Par l'espace infligée à l'oiseau qui le nie
> Mais non l'horreur du sol où le plumage est pris.

> Fantôme qu'à ce lieu son pur éclat assigne,
> Il s'immobilise au songe froid de mépris
> Que vêt parmi l'exil inutule le Cygne.

His long neck will shake off the white agony inflicted by space on the bird which denies its existence, but he cannot shake off the horror of the ground where his feathers are caught. Like a ghost destined by his pure brilliance to this spot, he becomes motionless as he dreams the cold, scornful dream that envelops the Swan in the midst of his useless exile.

The bird's scorn, the uselessness or needlessness of his situation, his denial of the external world's existence suggest that he is an idealist in the solipsistic fashion expounded by minor symbolists, maintaining, in the face of his dying away into a ghost, that the world is his idea. The swan sonnet is unusual in Mallarmé's work for its somewhat commonplace-seeming moralistic implications (the swan should have sung of life, and so forth) and the abundance of psychological abstractions half-imaged, such as cold dream, white agony, shining ennui.

In the lesser poets of the 1880s and 1890s, we find much mingling of the concrete and abstract in poems suggestive of an allegorical quest. These lines are from Gustave Kahn's *Les Palais nomades:*

> Reine des lys, blonde oublieuse, enfant perdue,
> La cime des regrets dans les brumes se dore
>   Et s'adore
> En un réveil des fronts appâlis et fondus.
>
> Les midis jaunes et les soirs blancs,
> Tristesse morne des pensers lents,
> Chaloupe oscillante aux palans
> Appareille vers plus troublant.
>
> Se fondre! ô souvenir des lys, âcres délices!
> Plus de fanal au port, et plus d'espoir aux lices:
> Enterrez plus profond les vases des prémices!

Queen of the lilies, blond and forgetful, lost child, the top of regrets is gilded in the mist and worships itself in an awakening of pale, melted foreheads. The yellow noons and white evenings, the dreary sadness of slow thoughts, weaving launch with tackles, set off for more disturbing. To melt! O memory of the lilies, acrid delight! No more lamp in the port or hope in the lists: bury deeper the vessels of first-fruits.

Kahn's poetry is often difficult in that individual pieces seem like fragments from an allegory of quest or a journey into memory, but there is almost never enough context for one to say decisively or definitively what the guiding idea is. The kind of results one may obtain from intense scrutiny of a Mallarmé poem tends not to turn up very much in Kahn's verse. Adolphe Retté's poems are, on the other hand, much simpler than Mallarmé's beneath some initially rather cryptic imagery. One can isolate in them phrases that easily explain the whole. In the introductory poem to *Cloches dans la nuit* (1889), the "éternal mendiant" comes into the nocturnal, rainy city of autumn, knocks at the "palais du Savoir et les portiques du Dire" and asks, "Faites-vous pas l'aumône de l'idée?" The magicians send him to wander "A jamais à jamais par le Vide et le Noir." This kind of expansion of the concrete-of-abstract metaphoric formula is called allegory, but, of course, it is the opposite of *állo agoreúein*, to say something other than what appears to be meant: such metaphor says exactly what it means and is short on Mallarméan mystery.

The mingling of abstract and concrete ranges from something close to old-fashioned rhetoric, as in Retté, to curious new kinds of combinations in Mallarmé; taking them all together, we are justified in seeing this category of figurative language as one of the major ways in which poets sought to repoeticize verse after the prosaic practice of the Parnassians. The varied success of these stylistic effects should not prevent us from seeing how broad and important an idea in diction they represent. This is also one aspect of French Symbolist poetry which corresponds to no general movement outside France, although this is not to say that we do not encounter it: it occurs in a poet of very mixed diction like Hart Crane, as, for example, in "For the Marriage of Faustus and Helen." However, it is precisely the kind of figure the Imagists avoided; Pound's diction, especially, is generally free of such effects. A very unusual version of the mingling of abstract, concrete, and figurative also occurs in Rilke's *Duineser Elegien*.

While we examined Verlaine chiefly in terms of his reaction to the Parnassian conception of prosody, syntax, and image—a narrow if valuable way of seeing him—our investigation into Mallarmé led from sentence structure to the grammar of metaphor and peculiar characteristics of it in French Symbolist poetry and elsewhere. What we must now do is envisage the lexicon of late nineteenth-century poetry in a broad fashion, in practice as well as in theory. For the theory we have the idea of decadent style. Decadence in this technical sense has nothing to do with the romantic agony; it does not even necessarily betoken a belief in social decay, much less the expression of it, and above all it implies that decadence is a high form of originality, not etiolated imitation.

3. Decadent Style

The theory of decadent style holds, in essence, that the word is more important than the sentence, the sentence more than the paragraph, and so forth.[2] Put in this schematic way, it may not seem very remarkable, but it must be understood in the context of the dominant bourgeois taste of the nineteenth century, academicism, with its French connotation of official art. Academicism was compounded of some surviving elements of seventeenth-century literary theory and the numerous strains of sentiment discovered in the eighteenth century. It held to the general ideas of unity and decorum of style, although not applied with the exactness of high neoclassicism. Decadent was a term first used of Hugo, and it contained three slightly different notions: the use of morbid subjects with a vocabulary that rendered them vividly (as in some of *Les Orientales*), startling innovations in metaphor and other stylistic techniques, and hence, an uneven texture caused by the strangeness and brilliance of its individual elements, which tended to be connected by less ostentatious writing (Hugo's poetry of the 1830s exemplifies this). Although we cannot feel it as sharply today, the reader imbued with academic taste found the multiplicity of visual particulars, whether figurative or descriptive, impaired unity of style and fragmented the attention. The task that both Flaubert and Leconte de Lisle set themselves, consequently, was to weld together all the innovations of high romantic style, which meant for them essentially Hugo's work, into a polished seamless unity of effect, and that is the way we see their achievement today. Later Mallarmé and Valéry attempted a new kind of homogeneity of complex, periphrastic style, which has not infrequently been compared with neoclassicism; while this ideal did not greatly interest Eliot, Pound, and the English-language modernists, there is something of it in George's work and a very remarkable form of it in Ungaretti's last and most ambitious work *La Terra Promessa*.

The new unity of effect we see in Flaubert or Leconte de Lisle, while actually in one sense a rejuvenation of neoclassical concerns, often was built around a central point of view or images that were repugnant to academic taste. For unlike high French neoclassicism, academic taste espoused a view of the world that was self-satisfied and identified with the bourgeoisie. Yeats once remarked that when he was young, everyone talked of progress, and that annoyed him to the point of making him write his allegorical *Wanderings of Oisin*, which implies a denial of progress. Metaphysical questionings of a radical sort are an obvious form of the antiacademic style.

However, antiacademicism has a more specifically linguistic form, and that is decadent style. The low, the rare, and the surprisingly metaphorical are the categories of it which come immediately to mind, and they represent, in the late nineteenth century and in a more exaggerated form, the same tendencies that readers of the 1830s found in Hugo's work. But the linguistic innovations of Corbière or Rimbaud, are, at the same time, the expressions of social attitudes, bohemian and hostile, of a kind we do not find in Hugo, who preached but did not scorn. It is also obvious that the refined, rare, or precious term in style has an analogy to an aristocratic point of view, even if the aristocracy is only the one of art for art's sake writers; it is, of course, an objective fact that the institution of aristocracy was in decay and that any sympathy for it was decadent in that sense. The role of the argotic and proletarian in decadent taste is less obvious, however, but can be nonetheless analyzed. To begin with, the use of slang corresponds to nothing in the traditional canons of style, and its rudimentary syntax and focus on what is material are exactly contrary to the academic conception of development of style and distinguished sentiments. In Corbière, at times, the language is as antiprosaic as it is antipoetic; all notions of written style are dispensed with. Here is a poem on an unregistered prostitute, who works outside the city boundaries (hence the title):

A LA MEMOIRE DE ZULMA
VIERGE-FOLLE HORS BARRIERE
ET
D'UN LOUIS

Bougival, 8 mai.

Elle était riche de vingt ans,
Moi j'étais jeune de vingt francs,
Et nous fîmes bourse commune,
Placée, à fonds-perdu, dans une
Infidèle nuit de printemps . . .

La lune a fait un trou dedans,
Rond comme un écu de cinq francs,
Par où passa notre fortune:
Vingt ans! vingt francs! . . . et puis la *lune!*

En monnaie—hélas—les vingt francs!
En monnaie aussi les vingt ans!
Toujours de trous en *trous de lune,*
Et de bourse en bourse commune . . .
—C'est à peu près même fortune!
. . . .
—Je la trouvai—bien des printemps,
Bien des vingt ans, bien des vingt francs,
Bien des trous et *bien de la lune*
Après—Toujours vierge et vingt ans,
Et . . . colonelle à la Commune!
. . . .
—Puis après: la chasse aux passants,
Aux vingt sols, et plus aux vingt francs . . .
Puis après: la fosse commune,
Nuit gratuite sans trou de lune.

Translation is impossible in this case; the whole consists of playful allusions to the old expression *faire un trou à la lune,* "to go bankrupt, not pay one's debts," and the argotic *voir la lune,* "have sexual intercourse." The disappearance, at a certain point, of all feeling of a verse form is a brilliant technical achievement, mediocre poets being always the ones in French in whom prosodic forms are oppressive.

The popular and argotic is decadent not only from the narrowly grammatical point of view, however. While the twentieth century has favored myths of proletarian vitality, certain nineteenth-century

French writers saw in the working classes a decaying and abject part of the population—the breeding ground of the golden fly in *Nana*. In Zola, who recognized himself as an exponent of decadent taste, we see a particularly remarkable example of the union of the two sides of the antiacademic and antibourgeois imagination: the fascination with cultivated depravity and proletarian debasement.

Related to the interest in the popular and argotic is the important intuition that what traditionally might have been considered primitivistic is not at all unrelated to decadent complexity of feelings, as in the monologue of Mallarmé's faun. Again, it is the antiacademic that provides the link between previously discrete phenomena. Here is a poem by René Ghil in which the subject is a laundress; the style is at once esoteric and crude:

> Hors là, dans les prés grands sans eaux et sans ramée,
> Très dieu, le lourd soleil aux dièzes de violon
> Aime et viole la Terre: et, languide, assommée,
> D'un lourd viol, songe-t-on, large violée, et long,
> Tout à Terre elle s'ouvre: et des Taons vont, qui vont...
>
> Mais, les heures, et dur, sous ses poings aux os maigres
> A moussé le gros linge: et, pâle en les rameaux,
> Tandis qu'il pleure—ploq, pliq, ploq—et qu'eux, les aigres
> Ou les sourds, vont les Taons, sur le ru, glauques eaux,
> A l'air de nénuphars la mousse en des roseaux! ("Le Linge lavé")

Outside there, in the great fields without water or branches, very much a god, the heavy sun with violin sharps loves and rapes the earth: and languid, stunned, by a heavy rape, it seems, widely raped, and long, on the ground she opens, and horse-flies go, go. But, hours, and hard, under her thin-boned fists frothed the heavy linen, and pale, in the branches, while it weeps—splash—and they, bitter or deaf, go the horseflies, on the stream, green water, looks like waterlilies the froth in the reeds. ("The Washed Linen")

The laundress is raped by the sun as the poem proceeds. This amazing combination of onomatopoeias and unusual words is combined with a very subtle kind of syntax: one alternately perceives and loses the grammatical thread, although a little analysis proves the sentences to be whole, if rather exceptional in word order. Of course, no primitive ever expressed his vision of the forces of nature with this sort of primitivist style, any more than someone raised in an argot-speaking milieu would employ slang in the manner of Corbière: Ghil's style, like Corbière's, involves a highly calculated, even savant use of material outside the normal scope of literary language.

One further aspect of decadent diction in French derives from historical stylistics: whereas the Latinate, rare, or archaic word is associated in English with the high styles of Edmund Spenser and Shakespeare, it is more characteristic in French, along with the pun, of François Rabelais than of the better-known renaissance poets, and such devices call attention to the grotesque surface in Rabelais' work rather than to the concealed and substantific marrow. Rabelais created a disparity between inner meaning and outer expression; the decadent stylist, often choosing similar verbal materials, sought to create a language that would appear uniquely beautiful to the few and absurd to the many. Sometimes this difficult task is accomplished; at other times the result seems merely bizarre and in the vein of the *écolier du Limousin* ("Nous transfretons la Sequane au dilucule"). There are a number of minor poets, like Rimbaud's brother-in-law, Paterne Berrichon, who published decadent verse in little periodicals in the mid-1880s and whose intention as stylists is by no means clear; this *décadentisme cocasse* would seem to have elements of self-parody. Real satire, of course, may use the odd word brilliantly: "Mr. Eliot's Sunday Morning Service" ("Polyphiloprogenitive") and its ancestors in Rimbaud like "Les Assis" ("Le sinciput plaqué de hargnosités vagues") stand to one side in this question of intentions. But when we assume no satiric or parodic aim, we must recognize that there is a like principle, in the purely mechanical sense, at work in some of the successful poems of Laforgue or Mallarmé ("Je n'y hululerai pas de vide nénie") and in the merely mannered pieces of, say, the humorless Jean Moréas, when he brings forth what he called "d'impollués vocables." A marked irony, however, characterizes linguistic oddities at their best: the poem manages to be an ostentatiously aesthetic object, remote from the normal channels of speech and communication, and which defends itself against criticism by suggesting that its meaning is too fine to be conveyed other than indirectly. The peculiar device, such as Latinism or pun or inner rhyme, comes to have an absolute value, independent of variations in the poetic subject. Verlaine, for example, revived in diverse contexts strange echo effects sparsely used since the late Middle Ages and the poets known as *rhétoriqueurs:* "coeur qui s'écoeure." Here Apollinaire follows his lead:

> Les humains savent tant de jeux l'amour la mourre
> L'amour jeu des nombrils ou jeu de la grande oie
> La mourre jeu du nombre illusoire des doigts
> Seigneur faites Seigneur qu'un jour je m'enamoure

Humans know many games, love, la mora: love, the game of the navels, or of the greatest favors; la mora, playing at making an illusory number of fingers; Lord, make me one day fall in love.

The irony of "L'Ermite," from which these lines come, is pervasive, and it has as much to do with the fact that this is a poem and deals generally with the elusive value of holiness than with any particular point about specific longings of the hermit. Ultimately, the use of irony as an absolute mode of perception indicates not only unwillingness openly to celebrate transcendental ideas of beauty and elite destinies but also a certain hesitancy about the possibility of such affirmations in a world of prose and *bon sens.*

Although the principle of decadent style may be seen quite broadly in late nineteenth-century French poetry, the term is especially applicable to poets in whom we perceive divergent levels and sources of vocabulary. Laforgue exemplifies mixed style of one sort in French, Apollinaire another. In English we find a strong tendency toward the mixed, decadent style in Hart Crane, and there is one poem of Stevens in which we see with particular clarity the general relation of some of his poetry to the theory of decadent style. "The Comedian as the Letter C" is not perhaps Stevens' best poem, but it shows with great density stylistic traits to be found widely in *Harmonium.* The heavily nominal syntax and the variety of lexical provenance are evident at the beginning:

> Nota: man is the intelligence of his soil,
> The sovereign ghost. As such, the Socrates
> Of snails, musician of pears, principium
> And lex. Sed quaeritur: is this same wig

Of things, this nincompated pedagogue,
Preceptor to the sea?

"The Comedian" is an ironic portrait of the artist such as is found in Pound, Thomas Mann, André Gide, and Laforgue; the strange texture of the poem represents the fastidiousness of one whose art estranges him from the quotidian. In this ornate style we find elaborate contrasts between polysyllabic Latinate words and monosyllabic Germanic ones, a resource not available to Laforgue but one which he would surely have admired; proper nouns, rare words ("silentious," "lutanist," "thane"), removal of a word from normal context ("brunt," without "of" following, meaning the churning sea), foreign phrases ("ding an sich"), and much sound play (the "C" of the title in "Crispin concocted doctrine," "His cabin counted as phylactery," and elsewhere) characterize the poem as one where the detail tends to draw attention away from larger structures. The Crispinisms elsewhere in Stevens are less thickly employed, but their nature remains similar.

Baudelaire theorized that the dandy was the aristocrat of decadent periods, but the language of Stevens or Laforgue is, far more than anything Baudelaire conceived of, the dandy's poetic style, with its rare and valuable ornaments. There is, seemingly, an historical-cultural implication in their language, but such correlations must be approached with circumspection, since the opposite case arises with, say, Leconte de Lisle, who had a thorough-going conception of history as decline, but nothing of the decadent as a stylist. Again, the virulence of Rimbaud's satire, with its extraordinary mixed vocabulary, might seem to imply a belief in society's increasing degeneracy, but nothing we know about Rimbaud really permits such an affirmation. Sometimes a pattern like Eliot's frequent juxtaposition, in *Poems 1920*, of aesthetic objects and ugly realism can be taken as the outcome of a theory of history as decay, whereas in reality, like similar juxtapositions here and there in French poetry, it may only be the expression of decadent taste in the stylistic sense, the fondness for surprising detail over unity of effect. Present-day critics, for example, no longer take *The Wasteland* as primarily a lament for European civilization or the direct result of the First World War. We now see that the poem is about personal relations and only incidentally a *Blick ins Chaos*.

Underlying a good part of French literature in the late nineteenth century is an ambivalent feeling about the modern world as being at once agreeably stimulating and deleterious for the nerves. One's age may inspire misgivings, but it is difficult to reject completely the exacerbating fascination of, say, technology, which can be either diverting or dehumanizing or both at once. Poets like Apollinaire or Hart Crane, who are sometimes thought to be simplistic modernists because of the role of the Eiffel Tower or Brooklyn Bridge in their work, show the complicated way in which decadent themes and modernism join; in "Zone" and *The Bridge,* degraded eroticism and the deadly city contrast with images of the past, but the poet's redemption partakes of both older values renewed and modernist taste. Even poets who take an exclusively pessimistic view of the direction of history may relish new stylistic patterns, such as nominal syntax, rare words, low realism, metaphoric invention, and so forth. The whole novelty of the *symboliste* idea of decadence is that the poet is an innovator not an *épigone*, and that he delights in the artistic forms stemming from the decadence he may seem sometimes to deplore. One is almost tempted to consider pessimism about history to be a poetic strategy, a literary neurosis that permits the fullest deployment of stylistic means. Something of this can be felt, I believe, in Gottfried Benn's putatively scientific myth of history.

German is, in structure, a language involving much elaborate show of order (case relations, adjectival agreement, and varied, but codified word orders), and poets and prose writers of the beginning of the twentieth century like George, Rilke, and Mann quite carefully exploited the beautiful grammatical cohesion and even ostentation of German. In this literary context Benn's syntax is striking. In "Das späte Ich," terse but regular sentences—filled, however, with neologism—give way to fragments, as meditation turns to vision:

I
O du, sieh an: Levkoienwelle,
der schon das Auge übergeht,
Abgänger, Eigen-Immortelle,
es ist schon spät.

Bei Rosenletztem, da die Fabel
des Sommers längst die Flur verliess—
moi haïssable,
noch so mänadisch analys.

II

Im Anfang war die Flut. Ein Floss Lemuren
schiebt Elch, das Vieh, ihn schwängerte ein Stein.
Aus Totenreich, Erinnern, Tiertorturen
steigt Gott hinein.

Alle die grossen Tiere: Adler der Kohorten,
Tauben aus Golgathal—
alle die grossen Städte: Palm- und Purpurborden—
Blumen der Wüste, Traum des Baal.

Ost-Gerölle, Marmara-Fähre,
Rom, gib die Pferde des Lysippus her—
letztes Blut des weissen Stiers über die schweigenden Altäre
und der Amphitrite letztes Meer—

O you, look, wave of stocks, with which the eye fills, departing ones, self-everlasting flower, it's already late. With the last of the roses, when the fable of summer has long since abandoned the field, hateful I, still such maenadic analysis. In the beginning was the flood. A flow of ghosts pushes elk, herd, a stone impregnates it. From death-realm, memory, animal tortures rises God. All the great animals: eagle of the cohorts, doves from Golgotha valley; all the great cities: palm and purple borders, flowers of the desert, dream of Baal. East rolling rubble, Marmara ferry; Rome, give back Lysippus' horses. Last blood of the white steer over the silent altars, Amphitrite's last sea. ("The Late I")

The mixed, decadent kind of diction shows up in oddities like "Eigen-Immortelle," "Rosenletztes," the fragment of Pascal, and fitful syntax. This is the consciousness of the visionary such as we find it in a number of modern poems: as in *Une Saison en enfer*, Hart Crane's *The Bridge*, or the *Cantos*, the speaker participates in a mythic dimension of history while remaining a member of the world of men. He is both individual and exemplary.

Half-expressed recollections like the movement of decaying classical culture eastward, a confusion by which Golgotha becomes a valley (*Tal*), and, seemingly, the end of mythology have been evoked. Finally, the jungle alone is left and the I suffering from a degenerate late stage of evolution:

> Der Gummibaum, der Bambusquoll,
> der See verwäscht die Inkaplatten,
> das Mondchâteau: Geröll und Schatten
> uralte blaue Mauern voll.
>
> Welch Bruderglück um Kain und Abel,
> für die Gott durch die Wolken strich—
> kausalgenetisch, haïssable:
> das späte Ich.

The rubber tree, the bamboo-shot, the sea washes away the Inca terraces, the moon castle: rubble and shadows full of primeval blue walls. What brothers' happiness about Cain and Abel, for whom God struck through the clouds; causal-genetic, hateful: the late I.

Ellipsis, abundance of nouns without syntax, and parataxis of short sentences express an inability to grasp logically; only images and feelings are left. At first, the whole poem seems to describe the human adventure, the origins of religions, cities, and migrations. But we realize that this is not a cycle with a highpoint of culture and that the subject is the anguish of history seen as a mingling of excess and exhaustion, with no center of stability. Rudimentary grammar combined with a complicated vocabulary depicts the decay of a complex mind. Finally, the pseudoscientific account of early "de-brained" man (the term is Benn's) and late causal-genetic phases is as mythic as any scheme from theology or philosophical theories of history. The whole fantasy shows the decadent indifference to balanced cyclic notions of history, where decline would contrast with maturity and not with rude origins. Decadent taste likes juxtapositions on the order of barbarism and decay, crude vocabulary and precious expressions, primitive religiosity and scientific notions of decline, an aristocratic ethos and revolution, proletarians and nobles, asceticism and debauchery, Parsifal and Salome, objects of aesthetic refinement and realistic details of life, fertility cults and the quest for the Grail. This fondness for extremes, when perfectly good middles exist, is one of the reasons why a satisfactory historical scheme is difficult to derive from *The Wasteland*, to say nothing of the work of less distinguished poets. The whole tendency we have been calling decadent is very much of one piece with the notion of a modern man, *homo nervosus*, demand-

ing special qualities of extreme stimulus to his imagination and de-
lighting in irregular or complicated forms. These inventive decadents
take such pleasure in their own modernism that they appear totally
indifferent to classicism in any sense. In the lesser decadents there is
much that is shallow and silly, but some of the same imaginative tendencies are to be found in the greater figures like Benn or George,
and, a far more important point, these tendencies can lend themselves
to the most varied kinds of actual elaboration.

A last and supremely interesting exponent of a decadent aesthetic
is Constantine Cavafy, the great Alexandrian poet in Modern Greek.
Cavafy employs a quite unique scheme of reference with a stylistic
basis that cannot be duplicated in other languages. Cavafy's earliest
work (such as "Artificial Flowers") shows traces of some of the
routine imagery of modern decadence in French and English, languages he was as at home in as in Greek. Indeed, it is surprising that
he did not become an English-language decadent poet, with the wider
public that would possibly have brought and since from his literary
origins one could not exactly predict that peculiar stylistic vision he
was to evolve in Greek. Like other Modern Greek poets Cavafy chose
to write in the demotic language rather than the puristic dialect which
had been developed in the aim of giving dignity to the written form of
what had become an obscure, uncultivated tongue under the Turkish
domination. But there was a great difference between Cavafy and the
other writers who took part in what was actually a violent linguistic
controversy in Greece, involving all manner of questions of national
pride, poetic creativity, and ultimately the nature of modern Greek
culture.[3] Whereas they, like the writers of other emerging national
literatures in the nineteenth century, had a folkloric bent, a belief that
the true Greek language and character were to be found in the villages
and countryside rather than Athens, Cavafy was not even a resident
of Greece; he was an Alexandrian and a city-dweller, whose cultural
points of reference did not include the folklore of the Hellenic main-
land or islands. The Hellenized Near East and Egypt were his subject,
whether a mythical past in which the pursuit of beauty was accepted
as the highest goal in life or erotic encounters in drab modern Alexandria, little epiphanies of the surviving Hellenistic spirit.

In Cavafy's visions of the Hellenistic age we have again one of those unbalanced antitheses of the decadent imagination, like Benn's view of history, which includes only primitivism and decline with nothing in between. It has often been remarked that Cavafy shows little interest in the phases of Greek culture—like Athens at the time of the great tragic poets—which seem to us not only important but essentially Greek; the half-oriental world he writes of belongs to the obscure by-ways of the history of art and literature and with its self-conscious *hellenismos* reflects the traditional conception of the word decadence, which is imitative effeteness. Turning this world into a vision of refined sensuality and life lived as an art, in the image of the hard gem-like flame, represents an imaginative feat, and the linking of this world with modern Alexandria through the imagery of mythic bodies in ugly modern dress, a kind of hidden world under the surface of the Arabo-European commercial center, creates one of those unusual contrasts the modern decadent imagination cultivated. This is not the banal opposition between high Greek culture and the modern world put forth in *Mademoiselle de Maupin* and other romantic works; rather, both moments in Alexandria's history are ones of provincial, *métissé,* and marginal existence. But Cavafy's effort of historical imagination is only possible through the mediation of a remarkable linguistic situation.

The numerous poems written by George and others on late antiquity, and of which Verlaine's "Langueur" is the best in French, good as some are, lack a certain linguistic authenticity that Cavafy can achieve, even though his Greek is demotic, by delicate adjustments with the classicizing formal prose language. A mere noun-ending, a dative case, the paraphernalia of earlier Greek grammar can color his style with the feeling of the mythic past. The analogy between Greek, eroded and poor in its modern form compared with the treasures of ancient style, and the dreary provincial world of the modern city, in which Greek fortunes are declining, is always present. What Cavafy achieves with his extraordinary grammatical imagination corresponds, in an abstract way, to the wave of archaism in Western poetry of the turn of the century—mild in George, pronounced and entirely new in French, as in Moréas' work, or continuing earlier tendencies as in Pound's English or D'Annunzio's Italian. However, the comparison is faulty: the relation of demotic Greek to classical is the opposite of what we find in the West, where the modern forms of language are the vehicles of the more complex systems of ideas. The ultimate paradox, however, is that the Hellenistic age to which Cavafy's myth of the past largely refers, left few monuments of high lyric expression and least of all monologues summing up a view of life and civilization; Cavafy's version of the mixed, decadent style, with its discreet use of classicizing forms, invests the past with a meaning and value it could hardly have understood.

In Cavafy, Benn, Stevens, Corbière, and Apollinaire we can see how the most diverse linguistic techniques are employed by the decadent ironist. Not all decadent stylists are ironic, however, as our example from René Ghil showed, any more than they all associate linguistic primitivism and decadence or see a vast historical myth in operation. These variables account for the enormous variety of poetry based on the decadent linguistic aesthetic, which, however, has as its unifying principle an acutely historical sense of style, precisely what was lacking in late antiquity, the prototype of decadent eras, when pastiche of Virgil was more frequent than innovation. In this sense the decadent aesthetic is the heir of that intense idea of modernism which characterized French romantic thinking about literature. Whereas English and German romantic styles are closely identified with the idea of returning to the national heritage after a period of estrangement, French romanticism, as it unfolded, was as much concerned with absolute innovation as renewal.

Decadent style is curious in the relationship between its beginnings and ultimate development. It started narrowly enough as a reaction against the extremely puristic notion of unity of style and limits of vocabulary in French literary language, which were considerably greater than any constraints obtaining in other Western literary languages, whose major literature might appear decadent—as *Hamlet* did—judged by French academic standards; it would not be an exaggeration to say that Hugo and Baudelaire are part of the movement. As it reached a peak, however, decadent style in French went much beyond the grammatical and lexical freedom of English, Italian, or German: first of all, perhaps, in Corbière and Rimbaud, then in the 1880s as a widely shared idea, the new experimentation brought writers quite close to exploding the structures of language, as evidenced by

Rimbaud's "Mes Petites Amoureuses," Apollinaire's "Palais," Albert Mockel's *Chantefable un peu naïve* (1891), some lyrics by Gustave Kahn, and much of René Ghil's production, all works whose syntactic dissolution or semantic obscurity defy commentary.

Contemporaneous with the exploration of syntax and vocabulary of the late nineteenth century is a closely related effort to rethink the relationship between prose and verse. Obviously, when grammar is called into question, prose is also, and if the organization of prose can be modified, so can that of verse: this is roughly the chronology of the experiments running from Rimbaud through Laforgue and to the early twentieth century.

4. Prose Poems and Free Verse

Like Laforgue's *complainte*, the prose poem is an "empirical genre" and a very ambiguous one as soon as any attempt is made to theorize about it. Its early history is related to but not identical with that of poetic prose, a sixteenth- and eighteenth-century phenomenon; the two coincide notably in "Ossian's" work, which was acclimated in French somewhat after it was in English. However, the development of the genre in the nineteenth century can be considered distinct and properly begins with Aloysius Bertrand's *Gaspard de la nuit* (1842) and Baudelaire's prose poems. In these poets we see a major bifurcation: with Bertrand we find a type of rather regular stanza-paragraph arrangement, sometimes accompanied by refrain, and a lyrical-descriptive content, while Baudelaire's most striking pieces are short scenes or narrations in an elegant, disciplined, dry, and ironic prose which differs from the language of other prose genres only insofar as its art surpasses that of most stylists. The work of Bertrand and Baudelaire has so little in common, despite the latter's professed admiration for the former's book, that we seem obliged to conclude that the prose poem is merely a short piece of finished writing related to one or another of more established literary genres. Another theoretical ambiguity arises if we consider the nature of the prose in which the prose poem is to be written. A few years before Baudelaire described, in his preface to *Le Spleen de Paris* (1869), the ideal of a perfect rhythmic language without rhyme or regular meter, Flaubert was postulating the same kind of language for the novel. Certainly there are passages in *Madame Bovary*, and even more so in *Salammbô*, which rise to the level of fine lyric poetry in every way except traditional metric form; very few prose poems can match the beauty of Flaubert's style at its most finished. So the ambitions of novelists in the wake of Flaubert usurp somewhat the domain the prose poet reserved for himself, as is particularly noticeable in *A rebours*, where Joris-Karl Huysmans, whose first book had been a collection of prose poems, tried to make of each chapter a coherent, richly textured, and to some extent independent whole. Des Esseintes' abortive trip to England is a fine example of narrative prose poetry, while the chapters on his collections are in the meditative, descriptive manner.

The lyrical-descriptive kind of prose poem is found side by side with narrative ones in Mallarmé's work in the genre, as in Verlaine's, Huysmans', and others' later on. I tend to see the descriptive mode as they practiced it as a minor aesthetic aberration of the period: the prose is less memorable than Flaubert's, and the structure of the poem is determined by rather mechanical repetitions when there is any particular effort toward cohesion. The first person narrative poems, on the other hand, have, at their best, a powerful unifying element in the point of view maintained, in the degree to which a character is created. Baudelaire was the master of this and, after him, Mallarmé. The latter concerns us here, not only because his narratives are distinguished as such but also because he was the only one in the nineteenth century besides Rimbaud to successfully cast his prose poems in an experimental style. In "La Déclaration foraine" the narrator and his mistress, who have been riding in the country, stop at a little carnival. Seeing the unlit tent of an old *forain* who has given up all hope of putting on a show and drawing a crowd, the poet's mistress orders him, the poet, to beat the drum to bring an audience and displays herself as the attraction. The poet is concerned that she might be considered an inadequate spectacle:

Net ainsi qu'un jet égaré d'autre part la dardait électriquement, éclate pour moi ce calcul qu'à défaut de tout, elle, selon que la mode, une fantaisie ou l'humeur du ciel circonstanciaient sa beauté, sans supplément de danse ou de chant, pour la cohue amplement payait l'aumône exigée en faveur d'un quelconque; et du même trait je comprends mon devoir en le péril de la subtile exhibition, ou qu'il n'y avait au monde pour conjurer la défection dans les curiosités que de recourir à quelque puissance absolue, comme d'une Métaphore. Vite, dégoiser jusqu'à éclaircissement, sur maintes physionomies, de leur sécurité qui, ne saisissant tout du coup, se rend à l'évidence, même ardue, impliquée en la parole et consent à échanger son billon contre des présomptions exactes et supérieures, bref, la certitude pour chacun de n'être pas refait.

Clearly, just as an electric jet from elsewhere darted on her, on me there burst the calculation that, in the absence of anything else, she, as fashion, fantasy, or heaven's mood modified her beauty, repaid, without adding any song or dance, for the crowd, the alms demanded in favor of some one of no importance; and at the same moment I realized my duty in the danger of the clever exhibition, that is to say, that the only way in the world to dissipate any lack in the spectacle was to have recourse to some absolute power, like a Metaphor. Quickly I decided to spiel until there would appear on many faces the clear look of secure certainty of those who, not understanding immediately, give in to the proof, however difficult, contained in the word and consent to pay their tuppence in exchange for the precise and superior pretentions of her performance, convinced, to put it briefly, that they are not being conned.

The metaphor he has recourse to is the sonnet "La chevelure vol," which he recites to the astonished crowd as an accompaniment to the display of his mistress' hair. They murmur and are satisfied.

This prose has a certain amount of hyperbaton, but otherwise its peculiarities are not those of Mallarmé's verse. The speaker's voice is nuanced in his decadent mixture of the recherché and the familiar (*dégoiser, refait*), but the effect of persona is conveyed above all in the elaborate abstractions and circumlocutions with which he approaches the concrete. These are not the evocative periphrases of Mallarmé's poetry but the expression of a mind acutely conscious of vulgarity. The intricacy of his thought and his tendency toward verbal nouns and other abstracts is heightened by the superabundance of prepositional phrases, whose density is far beyond that of normal prose. (Somewhat earlier in the poem there is a sentence with *twelve* prepositional phrases one after the other.) We find both a contrast with the extremely concrete language of the sonnet and at the same time a common ground in the complexity of relations among the words.

The elements of style in "La Déclaration foraine," taken individually, have a place in traditional prose; their hypertrophy is what separates it from the main stream of French style, along with an attendant disregard for rhythm in the Flaubertian manner. One cannot, in any case, call it a poeticized form of language in the sense of adopting the peculiarities of poetry. The major long prose poem of the nineteenth century, Rimbaud's *Une Saison en enfer,* is likewise free of obvious poeticisms of grammar, if not entirely of imagery, yet at the same time remote from the usual criteria of prose sentence structure. However, Rimbaud's poem does probably derive from an intensification of the broken, antirhythmic, jerky movement Jules Michelet's narrative has at times in later parts of the *Histoire de France.* Rimbaud creates a stream-of-consciousness effect, with a syntax opposite to that of "La Déclaration foraine": infinitive phrases, few adjectives, lack of logical sentence connectives, ellipses of thought and grammar, parataxis, infrequent subordination, repetition of *et* and *je,* nominal phrases for sentences, a punctuation of suspension points and colons, asyndeton, and imperatives make up a prose movement which seems at times actually to border on the dissolution of recognizable forms of literary language. It certainly is bolder as monologue than the stream-of-consciousness language in *Les Lauriers sont coupés.*

With both "La Déclaration foraine" and *Une Saison en enfer* we draw near language which is not prose or verse. There is a considerable body of expression that stands outside the norms of literary language and even customary language systems. We saw an earlier example of it in the colloquialisms of Corbière and Laforgue, which fit no criteria of written language, any more than does the pseudoprose of Louis-Ferdinand Céline. In addition, one can make combinations of words that are understandable but not possible in the grammatical system of a language: the Latinisms of Góngora, Giosuè Carducci, John Milton, and sixteenth-century French prose are attempts to introduce into the structure of a language combinations that violate it. Yet the potential of their being comprehended, by at least the highly literate, is not to be denied and constitutes the fascination of this going beyond the limits of a grammatical system. Some modern writers have worked in this domain; in English, for example, there is a notable case of nonprose being introduced into a prose context in some of the stream-of-consciousness passages in *Ulysses.* But Joyce goes even further. In the sirens episode English syntax is abandoned in favor of expressive word orders:

Bloowho went by by Moulang's pipes, bearing in his breast the sweets of sin, by Wine's antiques in memory bearing sweet sinful words, by Carroll's dusky battered plate, for Raoul.

Yes, bronze from anear, by gold from afar, heard steel from anear, hoofs ring from afar, and heard steelhoofs ringhoof ringsteel.

With grace of alacrity towards the mirror gilt Cantrell and Cochrane's she turned herself.

Two sheets cream vellum paper one reserve two envelopes when I was in Wisdom Hely's wise Bloom in Daly's Henry Flower bought.

In cry of lionel loneliness that she should know, must Martha feel.

Sound combinations are Joyce's greatest concern in this chapter and create from beginning to end extraordinary word patterns from the point of view of syntax. The meaning is not undecipherable in the context of *Ulysses;* the grammar can be analyzed, but the language remains outside the structured system of English and therefore outside the boundaries of English prose, which is not, of course, simply anything written down in linear sequence, but a rhythmic construct derived from sentence forms.

It is important to keep in mind the fact that there is a nonprose, nonverse possibility of expression when studying the *Illuminations,* for there Rimbaud goes much farther in exploring this domain than any other French writer, except for Mallarmé in his last poem, making at times of the "prose" poem an entirely new form of language with its own structures. A case is "Métropolitain."

Du détroit d'indigo aux mers d'Ossian, sur le sable rose et orange qu'a lavé le ciel vineux, viennent de monter et de se croiser des boulevards de cristal habités incontinent par de jeunes familles pauvres qui s'alimentent chez les fruitiers. Rien de riche.—La ville!

Du désert de bitume fuient droit en déroute avec les nappes de brumes échelonnées en bandes affreuses au ciel qui se recourbe, se recule et descend, formé de la plus sinistre fumée noire que puisse faire l'Océan en deuil, les casques, les roues, les barques, les croupes.—La bataille!

From the indigo straits to the Ossianic seas, on the pink and orange sand washed by the winy sky, have just risen and crisscrossed crystal boulevards immediately inhabited by poor young families who buy their food at the fruit store. Nothing rich.—

The city! From the asphalt desert there fly straight in defeat with the layers of fogs rising in horrid bands in the sky which curves back, retreats, and comes down, the sky formed by the most sinister black smoke the mourning Ocean can emit—there fly helmets, wheels, boats, croups.—The battle! ("Subway")

Sentences whose pattern strains the possibility of inversion beyond what is tolerable in normal prose standards are punctuated with a summarizing noun. Then the sentence patterns break under the weight of nouns and their modifiers; while in some abstract way a sentence remains, the grammatical equipment no longer supports a structured meaning:

> Des routes bordées de grilles et de murs, contenant à peine leurs bosquets, et les atroces fleurs qu'on appellerait coeurs et soeurs, Damas damnant de longueur,—possessions de féeriques aristocraties ultra-Rhénanes, Japonaises, Guaranies, propres encore à recevoir la musique des anciens—et il y a des auberges qui pour toujours n'ouvrent déjà plus—il y a des princesses, et, si tu n'es pas trop accablé, l'étude des astres—le ciel.

> Roads bordered with gates and walls, barely containing their groves, and the horrible flowers you could call hearts and sisters, Damascus damning with length—the possessions of fairy tale-like aristocracies from beyond the Rhine, or Japanese, or Guarani, still suitable for receiving the music of the ancients—and there are inns which already are closed forever—there are princesses, and, if you are not too overcome, the study of the stars—the sky.

The punctuating noun continues as an organizing link between paragraphs as we reach the end:

> Le matin où avec Elle, vous vous débattîtes parmi les éclats de neige, ces lèvres vertes, les glaces, les drapeaux noirs et les rayons bleus, et les parfums pourpres du soleil des pôles,—ta force.

> The morning when, with Her, you struggled among the brilliance of snow, the green lips, the ice, the black flags and the blue beams, and the purple perfumes of the polar sun—your strength.

Here all is simplicity finally; the pattern of the poem is disintegration of the sentence, till we are left with only a noun phrase, and ultimately, greater clarity of images: the personification of strength and the poet struggling in the snow. And, of course, as we look back, there is a progression from sea to country to sky to pole (which must be imagined in the cosmology of the *Illuminations* as very elevated); height and morning conclude what appears to be an implied quest. Elsewhere there are patterns of increasing and decreasing sentence formation ("Parade" and "Enfance" I). In "Being Beauteous" a paragraph in which sentences are constructed with the very literary pattern of syntactic elements arranged by two's and three's is followed by abrupt noun exclamations to bring the poem to a close: Rimbaud frequently finds a special syntactic contrast for the end of the poem. In "Après le déluge," which is structured by temporal indicators, the final reversal is introduced by imperatives. In "Villes" I the sentences are elaborately varied in position of verb and length of material preceding and following it, but they are connected by a common system of prepositional phrases, along with auditory and light images; this prose is rounded off by two alexandrines, a rhythmic structure completely unlike anything that has come before. "Nocturne vulgaire" shows a sense and syntax correspondence: as the drunken narrator falls down, the elegant sentence structure and punctuation grow incoherent. "Dévotion" borrows the nonprose form of a prayer, "Solde" that of an advertisement.[4]

There is one relatively old pattern of literary language which is not prose or verse, and that is the verset or biblical verse, as it appears in modern languages. It is characterized by a generally complete sentence isolated typographically and thus rhythmically. The ambiguity of it comes from its origins: what was a distinctly structured form in ancient Hebrew becomes approximate in translation; the parallelisms of syntax and image lose the wording of the original, and, in any case, they appear less firmly patterned in languages where meter and even rhyme are the criteria of verse. In French the verset was used in one famous romantic work, Félicité de Lamennais' *Paroles d'un croyant* (1834), but its most remarkable exploitation is to be found in the *Illuminations*, which owe their handling of it directly to Rimbaud's close study of the Bible. Rimbaud's versets are extraordinarily varied. In "Après le déluge" the pattern is one of parallel images in complete clauses: the visual is uppermost. On the other hand, "A une raison" employs repetition of t-sounds from beginning to end in a more abstract context. "Génie" is structured by an elaborate system of repeated words and syntactical patterns. One of the most beautiful examples of design is "Barbare," where the versets lose their normal grammatical structure:

Bien après les jours et les saisons, et les êtres et les pays,
    Le pavillon en viande saignante sur la soie des mers et des fleurs arctiques;
(elles n'existent pas.)
    Remis des vieilles fanfares d'héroïsme—qui nous attaquent encore le coeur et la
tête—loin des anciens assassins—
    Oh! le pavillon en viande saignante sur la soie des mers et des fleurs arctiques;
(elles n'existent pas.)
    Douceurs!
    Les brasiers, pleuvant aux rafales de givre,—Douceurs!—les feux à la pluie du
vent de diamants jetée par le coeur terrestre éternellement carbonisé pour nous.
—O monde!—
    (Loin des vieilles retraites et des vieilles flammes, qu'on entend, qu'on sent,)
    Les brasiers et les écumes. La musique, virement des gouffres et choc des gla-
çons aux astres.
    O Douceurs, ô monde, ô musique! Et là, les formes, les sueurs, les chevelures
et les yeux, flottant. Et les larmes blanches, bouillantes,—ô douceurs!—et la voix
féminine arrivée au fond des volcans et des grottes arctiques.
    Le pavillon . . .

Long after the days and seasons, and the creatures and countries, the pavilion of
bloody meat on the silk of seas and arctic flowers. (They don't exist.) Recovered
from the old fanfares of heroism—which still attack our heart and head—far from
the old assassins—Oh! the pavilion of bloody meat on the silk of seas and arctic
flowers. (They don't exist.) Sweetness! Embers raining in blasts of frost—
Sweetness!—Flames in the rain of diamond-wind, cast by the terrestrial heart, eternally charred for us.—Oh world!—(Far from old retreats and old flames, which
we hear and feel.) The embers and foam. Music, the revolution of abysses and the
impact of ice-drifts on stars. Oh Sweetness, oh world, oh music! And there: forms,
exudations, hair, and eyes, floating. And white tears, boiling—oh sweetness—and
the feminine voice in the depths of volcanoes and arctic caves. The pavilion . . .

This is constructed without finite verbs save in relative clauses and
parentheses. The pivot of the structure is the two participles *pleuvant*
and *jetée*, both with a strong frequentative sense, which take the place
of a main clause, the preceding prepositional phrase (*après*), nouns,
past participles (*remis* modifying an implicit *moi*) serve as introduc-

tion, the function clauses would have in normal syntax. The analogy holds in that these constructions are of a different order (*remis* is not frequentative like *jetée; participles vary in mood and aspect in French, even though the form is the same). The versets following "Les brasiers, pleuvant" contain repetitions, a formal rounding off of the central statement. Then a summary, "O Douceurs," draws together imagery before introducing one last surprising perfect active participle (*arrivée*) which contrasts with and complements *pleuvant* and *jetée* by its punctual character. The ingenious grammar of "Barbare" creates a more gentle, static effect than would the use of main finite verbs.

The nonprose *Illuminations* derive much of their effect by contrast of structure among them and by juxtaposition with the true prose ones, which constitute one of the most extraordinary achievements in French style. Particularly notable among the latter are the narratives "Ouvriers," "Royauté," "Aube," "Conte" (written with a nuance of eighteenth-century style), and "Vagabonds." These respond to the same kind of analysis as is appropriate for Flaubert's work, although it is permissible to deem that Flaubert never quite reached such a height of narrative art. However, the prose poets who were more or less influenced by the *Illuminations,* such as Kahn (in parts of *Les Palais nomades*) or Retté (in *Thulé des brumes*) tend to echo phrases with no very marked feeling for prose, when their sentences are grammatically whole, or for nonprose, when they use fragments. Saint-Pol-Roux's *Les Reposoirs de la procession* shows greater brilliance of imagery than the work of early imitators such as Germain Nouveau or Charles Cros. In regard to prosaic structure, Breton worked out, on the basis of certain passages in Rimbaud, a quite ingenious stylistic pattern which consists of writing sentences that in their form and sequence adhere rigidly to the conventions of literary style, while employing combinations of words and images that completely violate the conventions of sense.

It is sometimes said that two *Illuminations,* "Marine" and "Mouvement," are the first modern free verse poems in French, but if they are, their free verse, which is unrhymed, has nothing to do with the first lengthy uses of that form, Laforgue's last poems and part of Kahn's *Les Palais nomades.* In Laforgue above all, the "freedom" of the form is primarily the liberty to be dense and even terse in expression, to avoid padding; rhyme is frequent, and lines are often short. Concision is the essence of Laforgue's *vers libre*. Such is, by design, not the spirit of some later free verse, and prolixity also creeps into some free verse writers merely through failure of talent. There was a good deal of confusion in the French reading public about the boundaries between prose poetry and free verse; it was not due entirely to obtuseness. The free verse that appears perhaps to have been influenced by Walt Whitman, Gide's *Nourritures terrestres*, Paul Claudel and Charles Péguy's work, and Marcel Schwob's *Livre de Monelle*, has never responded well to analysis, as does Laforgue's verse, while at the same time its qualities as prose—except for the Gide—are questionable. Much more satisfying is the kind of free verse Apollinaire used in "Zone" or, especially, Cendrars in "Prose du transsibérien," which, willfully prosaic in some ways, constitutes the second major wave of free verse in France. There the arrangement into verse on the page corresponds to grammatical units whose rhythmic function it underscores. Emotive distribution of emphasis becomes clear, and punctuation is often omitted as idle, because of the clear indications furnished by typography. (This can certainly not be said of Claudel's sprawling verse.) As a kind of *monologue intérieur*, employing parallelisms and recurrent imagery as its cohesive principle, "Prose du transsibérien" is a remarkably thought-out work. A similar principle of clarification is to be found in Breton's best free verse: the line is rhythmically and syntactically determined so as to isolate and display the image. Gourmont's *Litanies de la rose*, drawing on liturgical inspiration, are another variation on syntactically ordered free verse, though their rhythmic pattern is much closer to traditional prose, as is the typography. In the opposite direction, Robert de Souza, unfortunately a better theorist than poet, worked out, before Pound, a system of varied indentations and breaks to indicate shades of relation in free verse phrasing.

The second wave of free verse in early twentieth-century France not only involves a reintroduction of prosaic syntax in the work of Apollinaire, Cendrars, and, eventually, the surrealists, but it also corresponds to a polemic against romantic emotion and a general turning away from the more intricate late nineteenth-century ideas of vocabulary and imagery. In the 1890s French, which toward the end of the eighteenth century had had the most circumscribed literary language in Europe, briefly had the most experimental. The new classicizing theories of the day took the practical form of using echoes of seventeenth-century French and neoantique subjects: many poets who had written in the manner of the 1880s and 1890s now changed to the new "classicism": these include Moréas, Samain, Régnier, André Fontainas, Hérold, and Jean Royère. Perhaps the characteristic figure was Francis Vielé-Griffin, but the major one was Valéry, who, however, for all his classicizing pastiches, remained deeply antiprosaic and influenced by Mallarmé's grammar. The new classicism of all these poets differs from that of the seventeenth century in that it is influenced by Goethe's conception of classicism, with its emphasis on nature: nature, reality, truth, and health are the interlocking ideas governing it. In terms of style, the rhetorically articulated analogy from nature, as in a number of Valéry's *Charmes,* and the maxim or other well-defined thematic statements distinguish it.

While neoantique subjects are to be found in Pound and especially in H. D. (Hilda Doolittle), there is no true counterpart to the new French conception of classicism except the classicizing theories of Thomas E. Hulme, which correspond ill to any classicism ever known, and ultimately those of Eliot, which are equally polemic and divorced from the realities of English literature. The fact that the word classicism evokes no viable models or precise connotations in English (Ben Jonson? Milton? Alexander Pope?) as it does in French, diminishes its descriptive importance. The term Imagism, on the other hand, brings concrete examples to everyone's mind, and it is only when we look into the variety and detail of principles and poems, neoantique and modernist, plainly stated and metaphorical, which it included at one point or another in its short active life, that it becomes clear just how narrow its polemic value was and how weak its descriptive force. Much the most interesting idea about poetry at that time in London, beyond the more widespread notion in the English-speaking world that prosaicness and conversational language were to be cultivated, was Ford Madox Ford and Pound's theory of the specific relevance to verse of certain French prose writers like Flaubert, Guy de Maupassant, and Stendhal.[5] The objectivity they seemed to have achieved depends on a remarkably homogeneous effect in vocabulary, syntax, and rhythm, free of uneven flights of brilliance and plodding passages. In Flaubert this includes, beyond the avoidance of obvious authorial intervention, great attention to descriptive writing and restraint in metaphor. The illusion of objectivity is further enhanced in all three writers by an often faint but thoroughly pervasive ironic tone, so subtle at times it is difficult to point to the specific words that create it. "His true Penelope was Flaubert," Pound says of Hugh Selwyn Mauberly, pointing out, in a poem where the influence of Gautier is traceable, the most significant exemplar of objective style. For while Gautier in *Emaux et Camées*, Leconte de Lisle, and at times some more recent poets held criteria of diction similar to those of Flaubert, the novelist remains the principal exponent of the effects Pound sought to endow English verse with.

The bilingual and French-educated Filippo Marinetti and Ungaretti introduced prose values into Italian verse. While the former's gifts were slight and his "futurist" production uneven, to say the least, the latter's fine, brief, often epiphanic poems in *Allegria di naufragi* (1919) appeared to be a kind of notes or diary jottings to early readers, so different were they from the rhapsodic syntax and sound plays of D'Annunzio's short-line poems like "Il Novilunio," which had come out not many years before in *Alcyone* (1903). D'Annunzio had also taken advantage of the enormous body of poetic words and poetic forms of common words that was the heritage of centuries. A striking contrast in the severe discipline of Eugenio Montale's vocabulary, which is large and varied but hardly vaporous or self-consciously poetic, can be found as early as *Ossi di seppia* (1925). Montale exploited the harshest sound clusters that can be obtained in Italian and followed prose word order (which, however, admits of inversions, as with subject and verb, far more freely than French).

This general movement of the early twentieth century toward pruning poetic diction of either old embellishments, as in English or Italian, or of recently developed stylistic practices, as in French, served as a permanent discipline for some poets and as only a temporary ascesis for others. It would be difficult to say, for example, just at what moment Pound's poetry was ever totally free from poetic peculiarities of grammar. Yeats, who had in his early verse eliminated much of the poetic grammar of the nineteenth century and espoused speech values in the second decade of the twentieth, was already moving toward the intricate anastrophes, ellipses, subjunctives, multiple meanings of *but*, inversions of conditional clauses, asyndeton, suspense syntax, and asymmetrical parallelisms of his poetry of the 1920s.

It is one of the paradoxes of twentieth-century literature that many poets, while renouncing intricacies of nineteenth-century style like the poetic language of English or Italian and the denser peculiarities of French Symbolist verse, created new kinds of difficult expression. The new forms of expression, however, are hard to imagine without the obsessive concern with the idea of style in the late nineteenth century which extended to the very choice of prepositions. The theory of decadent style, the movement toward free verse, and the prose poem had created the notion of style as the absolute value in literature.

Words, rather than ideas conceived of as paraphrasable, dominate when style is regarded as unchanging and inevitable. It follows that a lengthy poem elaborated under this conception will have less of an argument in the traditional sense than patterns of specific words. It may be plotted even somewhat schematically—which is not the same thing as simply. We are going to look briefly at five ambitious poems in the attempt to isolate some elements of word patterns. *Un Coup de dés* represents Mallarmé's poetry at its latest and barest; the *Four Quartets* are Eliot's most thoroughly composed work; *La Jeune Parque* was the exercise Valéry set himself in order to relearn to write verse; *Anabase* has a concision and density not to be found elsewhere in Perse, and the *Cantos* illustrate the larger problem of stylistic configurations in Pound.

5. Verbal Patterns in Mallarmé, Eliot, Valéry, Perse, and Pound

At the end of his life Mallarmé made his only move away from regular verse and prose; with *Un Coup de dés* he created a kind of concrete poetry based on a distinctive grammatical pattern, which involved syntactic structures with double functions, groupings of modifiers and parenthetical elements inconceivable in an ordinary linear form, and a parabolic treatment of the analogy. This poem is not symbolic or allegorical in the sense of having one term of the analogy suppressed; the figurative and literal relation is overt. The action of thought is presented in terms of a shipmaster, then his son, who, as the sinking boat is buffeted by the waves, must decide whether to cast the dice, whose result, insofar as it is a definite number, will eliminate chance, imaged by the sea's movement, but in another sense cannot, because throwing dice is a concession to chance and depends on it. The ship will not be saved, but a constellation appears, so that indeed something comes about other than destruction. The text, which I have included in an appendix, is shaped into patterns suggestive of the ship, waves, and stars.

The informing sentence which begins on the title page, "UN COUP DE DES JAMAIS N'ABOLIRA LE HASARD," stretches over the first two-thirds of the poem, providing an initial element of tension. There are others. The opening of the work is one of syntactic prolongations, such as that of "QUAND BIEN MEME LANCÉ." The first two-page development we come to (one reads across the two pages as if they were one) is also an adverbial delaying element: "SOIT que l'Abîme . . . résume ["takes in"] l'ombre." Normally this clause would be balanced by another (*soit*) *que* ("whether . . . or"); here either the second (*soit*) *que* is omitted to give an effect of opening syntactic structures that are not yet to be closed, or, better perhaps, we must take *soit que* in a kind of literal sense: "let it be that," "if." The latter ties in with the generally hypothetical character of the events Mallarmé notes in his preface.

"LE MAITRE . . . inférant . . . que . . . hésite" begins the next section. On these pages we observe not only appositions like "Esprit" and "cadavre," which refer to the master of the ship, we also find some finite verbs ("il empoignait," "un envahit"), which are best taken as parentheses. As we turn the page, the "unique Nombre" in the master's hand is not cast ("hésite . . . à n'ouvrir"). "Quelqu'un ambigu," the son, is mentioned, and the "celui" apposition with modifiers tells of the son's birth from the master and the sea. ("Démon . . . ayant . . . induit" is a normal enough participial parenthesis.)

The syntax of the modifiers that fill out these pages is not untypical of the poem, and with a little patience can be worked out, once we know what the main grammatical direction is.

The water patterns the words make on the page represent a great crashing, crushing wave coming down, as we reach the "N'ABO-LIRA," which belongs to the spine sentence. The threatening quality of the word is emphasized by the typographical arrangement. Here we encounter one of the great imaginative effects of Mallarmé's syntax: "LE MAITRE" can have either "hésite" or "N'ABOLIRA" as its verb; "N'ABOLIRA" can have either "UN COUP DE DES" or "LE MAITRE" for its subject. Mallarmé is careful to have "LE MAITRE," "hésite," and "N'ABOLIRA" in three different typefaces, so that we do not automatically and necessarily conclude that "LE MAITRE" goes with one or the other verb. These are not idle ambiguities; they form a definite pattern of meaning, which emerges gradually, and, from an artistic point of view, creates a kind of syntactic drama of rare interest. This use of grammatical ambiguities can be seen in other details, such as the way the word "folie" seems to refer back to the immediately preceding passage about the master's mating with the sea but, at the same time, to be an *apposition antécédente* to the great "N'ABOLIRA" that follows.

The wave movement is more gentle in the next three sections, the typeface becomes italic, and the son is introduced. The incumbent throw of the dice passes from father to son, evidently to indicate that it is a racial, ancestral curse. The fading out of the father and appearance of the son, occurring in the middle of the poem, is accomplished through a very deft movement of imagery: *"Une insinuation* ["curving"] *simple"* has *"plume solitaire"* in the next section as a kind of apposition. Then we see that the feather is on a *toque* worn by someone. This prince with a feather in his cap resembles Mallarmé's depiction elsewhere of Hamlet, an allusion strengthening the father-son theme and that of a duty to be performed by the casting of the dice. *"Une insinuation simple . . . voltige"* is surrounded by the italic capitals *COMME SI*, which, like the earlier "SOIT que" emphasizes the exemplary, hypothetical character of the poem. The grammar is odd and typical of Mallarmé's subtle syntactic imagination: *comme si* normally indicates a contrary-to-fact condition and takes the imper-

fect, but Mallarmé uses a present tense because what he depicts is possible. (Here English might use the present subjunctive or conditional
after if, Latin the present subjunctive.)

In the next section the lower part of the pages contains a syntactic
parenthesis presenting the son's union with a siren. The rock she slaps
with her tail *"imposa une borne à l'infini."* The *passé simple,* the
only one used in the poem, has a dramatic effect through its punctual
aspect, it being the only tense in French that has so sharp a one. Since
"infini" can be taken as the infinite variety of numbers produced by
chance, the connection with the spine sentence is evident. However,
chance has not been limited; the words at the top of the section will
lead us into the major statement about it in relation to the *"*unique
Nombre" the master had been holding in his hand. These words at the
top consist of adjectives trailing over from *"prince amer"* in the preceding section, *"muet rire,"* which is a descriptive apposition of the
vingt ans, cheveux blonds kind possible in written French, and finally, *"que si."* The latter depends on *"rire"* and introduces the conditional sentences of the next section. At this point we may recall that
the grammatical structure of the center of the poem is whole:
*"COMME SI une insinuation . . . voltige . . . plume solitaire . . . pour
. . . marquer . . . quiconque . . . s'en coiffe . . . prince . . . soucieux . . .
muet rire que si."* Now we are ready for a great conclusion, which,
however, will be only provisional.

"[Rire que si] *C'ETAIT LE NOMBRE . . . CE SERAIT . . .* LE
HASARD," is the contrary-to-fact condition we finally arrive at. The
cluster at the top of the page of imperfect subjunctives with inversion
are an archaic form of if-clause, parallel to *"C'ETAIT."* Just as there
was bifurcation in the verbs dependent on *"LE MAITRE,"* thus opening up the syntax, here two clauses dovetail, with *"*LE HASARD" as
complement. Both *"UN COUP . . . N'ABOLIRA"* and *"CE SERAIT"*
close with it, thus narrowing the previously expanded syntax. The
"Choit la plume" clause at the bottom of the section, despite the odd-
seeming inversion, is a new sentence, which follows normally in the
narrative. It, in turn, is followed by two others, *"*RIEN" spreading
over two sections and *"*Toute Pensée" briefly closing the poem.

We may represent the more complex syntax of the work as follows:

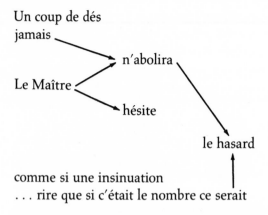

Un coup de dés
jamais
n'abolira
Le Maître
hésite
le hasard

comme si une insinuation
. . . rire que si c'était le nombre ce serait

The elegance of the scheme lies, of course, in the "rhythm of relations," to use Mallarmé's definition of poetic structure, as it is spread
out in time, spaces, pages, and the movement of the reader's mind.

We might now put together the chief sentences to see their relation:

1. Un coup de dés jamais n'abolira le hasard.
2. Le Maître n'abolira le hasard.
3. Si c'était le nombre, ce serait le hasard.
4. Rien n'aura eu lieu que le lieu excepté une constellation.
5. Toute pensée émet un coup de dés.

The elements of synonymity and analogy are worth noting: "Un coup
de dés" is the etymological meaning of "hasard." "Toute pensée" is
identified with it and thus leads back to the beginning of the poem.
The stars of a constellation have the form of marks on dice. "Le
Maître" and "toute pensée" are in a synecdochic relation, as are "Le
Maître" and the unique "nombre," which the master holds in his
hand. A constellation—and this one stops "à quelque point dernier
qui le sacre"—has a definite number of stars, and a die marks a
number when it ceases rolling. A subtle connection between the
contrary-to-fact condition and "excepté" can be seen in the fact that
the latter may be expressed as a condition: *ne fût-ce que, n'était.* By
playing with analogies we can restate elements of the poem:

1. Tout coup de dés émet un nombre.
2. Rien n'aura eu lieu que le nombre.
3. Le nombre n'abolira le coup de dés.

In other words, we can make relatively uninteresting material of Mallarmé's cosmic drama; the paradox of the dice still remains, but it seems considerably less gripping. The rhythm of relations is gone.

The relationship of syntactic tension in the first two-thirds of the poem have been discussed, but some consideration of their role in the end is important. "*Choit la plume*," the last sentence in italics dealing specifically with the son, breaks the taut grammatical movement, and the penultimate construction "RIEN . . . CONSTELLATION," if read carelessly, may seem to lack tension. Yet it is very ingeniously put together so as to contain three concessives, one within the other, arranged in a climax: "QUE LE LIEU," "EXCEPTÉ," and "pas tant qu'elle n'énumère." Thus the forward impetus of the poem, which had seemed dispelled with the feather's dropping, is renewed. The final statement, "Toute Pensée émet un Coup de Dés," is designed to contrast with the syntax of all the preceding sentences by its directness. It is not only direct, however; the maxim-like statement is full of pent-up energy and by its last words thrusts us back to the opening of the poem. This cyclic movement is an essential part of what Mallarmé is saying about thought.

The future of probability (*n'aura eu lieu*) and the contrary-to-fact conditional clauses in *Un Coup de dés* play an important role in the analogy between thought and the shipwreck illuminated by a constellation: Mallarmé chose to avoid the symbolic or allegorical method of representing figurative action as a real event taking place, and his choice of tenses, with their hypothetical element, is one of his particular means of creating a new effect, in which the concrete analogy is at once very vivid but always suggestive of the metaphysical drama. We are not asked to take a factually presented image and then to apply a conceptual framework to it.

We can hardly avoid thinking of verbal patterns in reading *Un Coup de dés*. Nor can we, if we approach *Four Quartets* from the perspective of Eliot's earlier work, with its normal sentence structure, which permits us to focus all our attention on images and personae. *Four Quartets* immediately impresses us with its syntactic peculiarities: parataxis plays a large role, joined with much connection through "and" and "or," which can actually be more complicated in implied relations than hypotaxis; words are repeated in what at times seems an almost spell-like fashion; we become aware of elaborate relations between abstract terms like "future" or "beginning" in their various combinations; the imagistic passages, instead of being juxtaposed in the manner of *The Wasteland*, have sometimes intricate connective material between them. The *Four Quartets* represent a new kind of building up of grammatical relations. Interestingly enough, the parallelisms that play such a large role in poets like Algernon Charles Swinburne ("Anactoria" is a good example) or Milton and his followers, are a characteristic aspect of this new style. While it is true that there are indeed parallelisms in *The Wasteland*, its style does not have the lulling, incantatory use of them that the *Four Quartets* do. There is an important way in which Eliot, in his last poem, revives literary effects he had once neglected and weaves them into a quite distinctive texture.

At the beginning of "Burnt Norton" there are tripartite formulas characteristic of this *Quartet*.

> Time present and time past
> Are both perhaps present in time future,
> And time future contained in time past.
> If all time is eternally present
> All time is unredeemable.
> What might have been is an abstraction
> Remaining a perpetual possibility
> Only in a world of speculation.
> What might have been and what has been
> Point to one end, which is always present.

With these last words a pattern becomes noticeable: an antithesis is established, only to have its two terms fall together and be related to a third. This verbal pattern, which for convenience might be called dialectic, is somewhat more elaborate than the antitheses or reconciliation of opposites so common in poetry. But this specific case needs some explanation. By verbal parallels Eliot identifies "what might have been" with "time future," "what has been" being, as we might expect, "time past." We may wonder what kind of future is "might have been." Eliot is using the term future to designate what is more precisely called the future-of-the-past, a time expressed in English by the conditional tense. "Emma thought she would be happy later." This tense, of course, is used in other constructions as well, which makes us hesitate somewhat, if we are in a present context: "I think Emma would be/would have been happy later." From there it is only a short step to "might have been." Furthermore, there is a point of bifurcation in the past between what was and what would/might have been. This point, which Eliot does not yet mention, will be very important in the thematics of the poem. As for the present, to which past and "future" point, it is not difficult to see how the alternatives of a situation past determine or influence the present. Finally, the opening words of the poem must be interpreted not with the normal meaning of "future" but in the future-of-the-past sense of what might have been: "Time present and time past/Are both perhaps present in time future"; that is, the present and the past are both contained in what might have been. Obviously Eliot's choice of the word "future" is stylistically more deft than the truly accurate grammatical term would be.

An illustration of Eliot's use of time references occurs immediately after the opening ten lines of "Burnt Norton": the door we never opened (what might have been) into the garden is evoked. Whereupon the tense changes to present and we move into the garden, thus illustrating how "time future" points to a present end. Of course, there is a great deal of ambiguity about the vision of the ghostly dancers in the garden. The point of bifurcation in the past has been moved to the present, but Eliot narrates the vision in the past. In part II we find references to still points or moments *out of time*, to which no tense is absolutely applicable and this is one of them, "where past and future are gathered." The general rhetorical formula of part II, both in the lyric and the longer lines, is reconciliation of the antithesis of past and "future" in the general category of time, which, through itself, is conquered, making place for the point of stillness. The antithesis of A and B is collapsed, and the resultant opposed to C.

In part III, the terms change slightly. Here, in the image of the limbo-like subway, "time before" and "time after" stretch out.

> Here is a place of disaffection
> Time before and time after
> In a dim light
> . . . .

> Men and bits of paper, whirled by the cold wind
> That blows before and after time,
> Wind in and out of unwholesome lungs
> Time before and time after.

What is between before and after is carefully left unstated: Eliot likes to vary his word designs. Obviously it is the possible point of bifurcation, where what might have been was excluded. Something we should note in the spatial representation of time in the subway is that it best suits the division between time before and after a point in the past. Thus we are dealing with the same past in which the garden door was not opened.

A variation on the same two terms occupies the beginning of part V: "the end and the beginning were always there/Before the beginning and after the end." Actually, of course, what is before and after time is the same thing, timelessness, so that this antithesis conflates into one: "And all is always now." Eliot returns to the tripartite formula ("Love itself is unmoving/Only the cause and end of movement") for a few lines and concludes with the garden image. The time implications at the end are an elegant example of useful ambiguity; "Quick, now, here, now, always" applies to a present context, the point of bifurcation in the past, now recreated in the present, while lines immediately following pick up a phrase from part III referring to the past: "Ridiculous the waste sad time/Stretching before and after." The latter preposition best fits the past, as we do not usually say "after now," but, of course, the whole theme of "Burnt Norton" is that the point between what might have been and what has been can be realized again in the present, to which it is always relevant.

The extreme overtness of verbal patterns in the *Four Quartets* makes for striking contrasts between them. The antitheses moving into A-and-B-versus-C formulas are abruptly dropped in "East Coker." There is a relationship, however, between the end before the beginning and the beginning after the end of "Burnt Norton" V and the opening paradox of "East Coker": "In my beginning is my end." This particular form of expression is a kind of antithesis with both literal and reversed meanings; it therefore generates movement to its opposite, which occurs in the last line of the *Quartet*, though not dialectic movement, which demands an element of reconciliation. Eliot immediately juxtaposes to his initial formula an enumeration with orderly gradation, which represents cyclic movement in time: "Old stone to new building, old timber to new fires,/Old fires to ashes, and ashes to the earth." The moment of vision in part I is of the life of past generations in their rural round of set activities. In the lyric section of part II we find a new kind of antithesis, that of irreconcilables in conflict:

> What is the late November doing
> With the disturbance of the spring
> And creatures of the summer heat,
> And snowdrops writhing under feet
> And hollyhocks that aim too high
> Red into grey and tumble down
> Late roses filled with early snow?

The imagery violates the preceding vision of cyclic natural order. Here, unlike the midwinter spring of "Little Gidding," the antithesis cannot be modified by any interpretation; it is absolute and betokens chaos. Another antithesis informs the rest of part II, between the "future," or what might have been, and what has been. Here there is no moment of bifurcation pointing toward present action, there is only the realization that:

> It was not (to start again) what one had expected.
> What was to be the value of the long looked forward to,
> Long hoped for calm, the autumnal serenity
> And the wisdom of age?

Part III escapes from this oppressive, doomed atmosphere of antithesis; it gradually builds toward dense statements of the classic Christian paradoxes: "In order to possess what you do not possess/You must go by the way of dispossession." Christian paradox is an antithesis in which meanings are reversed when they are taken in the spiritual rather than the bodily sense, or when something bad has a good result like the fortunate fall. Part IV contains three paradoxes: "ruined millionaire" (Adam), "frigid purgatorial fires," "call this Friday good," as well as other contrastive expressions.

Beginnings and ends, moments in between, and ends which are beginnings in a spiritual sense have occurred in "Burnt Norton" and the first line of "East Coker." Suddenly, in part V, Eliot creates a striking effect by opening up a middle: "So here I am, in the middle way, having had twenty years." This intermediate phase between true inception and conclusion is itself filled with worldly, aesthetic beginnings and ends: "every attempt is a wholly new start and a different kind of failure." The contrast with the spiritual sense of commencement and termination could not be more pronounced. It is as if Eliot had created a quite different dimension, a mundane one unknown to "Burnt Norton" and which will occupy a place in the last two *Quartets*. In the last verse paragraph of "East Coker" Eliot has still another variation on his patterns: a new kind of moment is evoked, a moment into which the cycle of life, the content of part I, is compressed: "But a lifetime burning in every moment,/And not the lifetime of one man only." Thus "East Coker" employs effects of both expansion and contraction: the period between my beginning and my end is revealed as the lengthy middle way of starts and finishes, while the great cycle of life of the individual and the generations becomes something one can perceive in an instant.

Setting out on the ocean, where "in my end is my beginning," concludes "East Coker" and leads to the sea imagery of "The Dry Salvages." Enumeration is the dominant rhetorical pattern of parts I, II, and V, and it signifies time as flux, which is distinguished from linear time, timelessness, and cyclic time, as we have encountered them up to now.

> The river is within us, the sea is all about us;
> The sea is the land's edge also, the granite
> Into which it reaches, the beaches where it tosses
> Its hints of earlier and other creation.

"There is no end, but addition," meaningless continuance. Part III represents flux as a Heraclitean paradox: you cannot step in the same river twice, and some antithesis accompanies this. The "calamitous annunciation" alluded to in part II is evidently the point of death, and "the moment in and out of time" from "Burnt Norton" is evoked in part V, as well as the tripartite pattern of reconciling past and "future" to move beyond them. Generally, "The Dry Salvages" adds little in word design to what we have seen in the preceding *Quartets,* save the representation of flux.

In the passage on midwinter spring that opens "Little Gidding" we see the union of things opposite in cyclic time, a vision "not in the scheme of generation."

> Midwinter spring is its own season . . .
> Suspended in time, between pole and tropic.
> When the short day is brightest, with frost and fire,
> The brief sun flames the ice, on pond and ditches,
> In windless cold that is the heart's heat . . .
> And glow more intense than blaze of branch, or brazier,
> Stirs the dumb spirit . . .

Here Eliot manages by his great art the difficult rhetorical task of reconciling antitheses whose members must still remain identifiable and distinct: "pentecostal fire in the dark time of the year," "transitory blossom of snow . . . neither budding nor fading." This unifying principle next takes a new kind of tripartite form: A-and/or-B-is-C. "It would be the same . . ./If you came at night . . ./If you came by day," "the timeless moment/Is England and nowhere." The synthesizing movement of "Little Gidding" produces new verbal patterns right from the start. After the meeting with Yeats' ghost during the air raid in part II, where the theme of the future-of-the-past, what might have been, recurs, as it does in the begnning of part III, a kind of reconciliatory enumeration comes to dominate part III: "These men, and those who opposed them/And those whom they opposed/Accept the constitution of silence/And are folded into a single party." With the lyric in IV, a new rhetorical device is introduced, the pivotal word with two meanings: the flaming dove of the beginning is both a pentecostal manifestation and a bomber; the double sense of fire in the redemption of fire by fire is the burden of the rest of the section. This is, of course, the opposite of the pattern we have seen earlier, where two words or things mean the same. The two verse paragraphs of part V employ all sorts of antitheses, paradoxes, and reconciliations relating to beginnings and ends; each reaches one of the tripartite formulas that distinguish "Little Gidding": "History is now and England," "And the fire and the rose are one." The last main verb

("And all manner of thing shall be well") is, interestingly enough, a future, a true future. We have finally reached the point, adumbrated in "Burnt Norton," where a new future can begin, a new choice of alternatives in the present renewing the seemingly irreparable point in the past where what has been and what might have been were divided.

We have seen the verbal tools Eliot uses in the *Four Quartets*: antithesis, identification, paradox, dialectic, and enumeration. With these comparatively few patterns applied to concepts of time, a great structure is erected, and one which employs no recondite conceptual material but rather notions generally familiar, sometimes specifically Christian, and occasionally mystic. While at times one must abstract thought from a passage, most often the thought is overt and is in the arrangement of the words themselves in basic patterns. In *La Jeune Parque*, on the other hand, we find less syntactic evidence of thought; the word problems are more semantic and derive from ambiguity. Valéry uses frequently elaborate grammar and imagery, so that the texture is less schematic than Eliot's; essentially, however, the problem in reading is again one of observing a limited number of words.

La Jeune Parque is a dramatic monologue of considerable length and sometimes intricate in the expression of simple things; it is written in what Valéry intended as a kind of purified *symboliste* style, free of most eccentricities of vocabulary, but not of periphrases and metonymies. Its slightly elusive quality does not obviate the possibility of close and successful explication, while providing a suitable medium for a mythological character of Valéry's own invention: a Parca is one of the aged Fates but this young one seems to owe her name to the fact that she herself is undergoing a fate in the course of the poem.

At the beginning of the first of the sixteen parts of *La Jeune Parque* the Parca has awakened to the dawn wind and the last stars: "Qui pleure là sinon le vent . . . avec diamants extrêmes?" She has not yet wept but feels someone is weeping who is evidently a part of herself:

> Cette main . . .
> Attend de ma faiblesse une larme qui fonde,

> Et que de mes destins lentement divisé
> Le plus pur en silence éclaire un coeur brisé.

This hand is waiting for my weakness to shed a melting tear which my broken heart, the purest, slowly separated from my destiny, will fill in silence with its light.

The Parca refers throughout this section and elsewhere to parts of her psyche or body in a kind of objective way; the *dédoublement* of herself she feels, which will be the major element in the poem's structure, is hinted at already. Alienation of herself is accompanied by a feeling that her familiar surroundings are strange; if she has become mortal, subject to the ill fate of death (*désastres*, "bad stars"), that would explain her lack of harmony with nature, but such an explanation is as yet merely a suggestion. As she observes her agitation, she recalls having seen, in the "depths of the forests" of her body, a serpent bite her.

In part two the imagery of wound, poison, and pain becomes no longer the manifestation of a serpent's attack, but the result of the Parca's soul betraying her:

> Va! je n'ai plus besoin de ta race naïve
> Cher Serpent . . . Je m'enlace, être vertigineux!
> Cesse de me prêter ce mélange de noeuds
> Ni ta fidélité qui me fuit et devine . . .
> Mon âme y peut suffire, ornement de ruine!

Enough. I have no need of your naïve kind, dear Snake. I twist around myself in my dizzy being! I no longer need you to lend me your imaginary knots and coils or your assiduity, slipping away or feeling me out. My soul suffices for the task, my soul, a destructive adornment!

The antithesis *âme-esprit* will be a structural element of the poem. She, possessed by herself alone and not by a serpent, is filled with a "sombre soif de la limpidité" and a new self, her "secret sister," arises. The snake will henceforth be seen variously as possible, hypothetical, symbolic, or imaginary; she no longer needs the serpent to explain what she understands her soul alone has done to her.

At this point the Parca's soul appears to be some sort of death-dealing, suicidal part of her, but in section three its opposite, her *esprit*, is described with similar suggestions of mortality:

Ma surprise s'abrège, et mes yeux sont ouverts.
Je n'attendais pas moins de mes riches déserts
Qu'un tel enfantement de fureur et de tresse:
Leurs fonds passionnés brillent de sécheresse
Si loin que je m'avance et m'altère pour voir
De mes enfers pensifs les confins sans espoir . . .
Je sais . . . Ma lassitude est parfois un théâtre.
L'esprit n'est pas si pur que jamais idolâtre
Sa fougue solitaire aux élans de flambeau
Ne fasse fuir les murs de son morne tombeau.
Tout peut naître ici-bas d'une attente infinie.

Now I am less surprised, and I see the situation clearly. I actually expected no less from the rich deserts of my mind than the creation of the snake's furious tress-like coils. The impassioned horizon of my inner deserts gleams with drought, however far I advance, ever thirstier, into these pensive hells in search of their hopeless borders. I know. Sometimes my weariness is like a theater. My mind is not so pure and self-sufficient that it never raises its torch-like eagerness to dispel the feeling of closed walls in its dreary tomb and to search for another's presence. Anything can appear if you wait long enough.

Now we are to understand that solitude and sterility of *esprit* created the serpent rather than *âme*. This kind of reversal, confusing at first, will lead to a rather elaborate system of antitheses. In the next section the serpent's bite will be real and beneficent and the Parca's previous existence empty of feelings, in keeping with the desert-tomb imagery we have just seen.

Dramatically the tense shifts to the imperfect in part four with perhaps the meaning of "just now":

Mais je tremblais de perdre une douleur divine!
Je baisais sur ma main cette morsure fine,
Et je ne savais plus de mon antique corps
Insensible, qu'un feu qui brûlait sur mes bords:
Adieu, pensai-je, MOI, mortelle soeur, mensonge . . .

But I was just afraid of losing a divine pain! I kissed on my hand the delicate bite, and I knew nothing any more of my former insensitive body than fire burning on my edges: farewell, I suddenly thought, MYSELF, mortal sister, lie.

The pleasure and pain felt by her new self are joined and opposed to insentience, an important detail, because, as the poem unfolds, the

Parca's "new" body will be subject to destruction as well as quickening. There are paradoxes here: the Parca's "former" body and existence have been described in images of a desert and tomb, but that insentient state is not the result of death, in a cycle of life and death, so much as an inorganic existence, free from all vital processes including death. However, words are ambiguous, and so the Parca calls her old, unfeeling self mortal, because it vanished with the coming of the serpent and life into her existence.

Modifications or even reversals of meaning are basic to the method of *La Jeune Parque*. In part five the Parca recalls her former existence in an entirely different way from previously: she was not imprisoned in a tomb lit only by her torch-like moods but was one with nature under the sun, this being not a *songe* or *mensonge* but a purely harmonious and palpable state. Here we see her worshipping and dancing:

> Quel éclat sur mes cils aveuglément dorés,
> O paupières qu'opprime une nuit de trésor,
> Je priais à tâtons dans vos ténèbres d'or!
> Poreuse à l'éternel qui me semblait m'enclore,
> Je m'offrais dans mon fruit de velours qu'il dévore;
> Rien ne me murmurait qu'un désir de mourir
> Dans cette blonde pulpe au soleil pût mûrir.
> . . . .
> Puis dans le dieu brillant, captive et vagabonde,
> Je m'ébranlais brûlante et foulais le sol plein,
> Liant et déliant mes ombres sous le lin.

What brilliance on my eyelashes, golden in the blinding light, O eyelids against which gleams a gilded night. I prayed, groping, in your shadows of gold! Penetrable by eternity, which seemed to enclose me, I offered myself like some velvety fruit it devours. Nothing whispered to me that a desire for death could, in the sunlight, ripen in my blond pulp . . . Then, in the god's brilliant light, wandering yet captive, burning, I set myself in movement, treading the firm ground, joining and moving apart the shadows of my limbs on the earth under my linen robe.

The desire for death is also, viewed differently, a desire for life as well, a refusal of the Parca's semideity. We see that a system of images and connotations is being constructed whereby, in the domain of immortality, there is both a positive solar aspect and a negative sepulchral one; balancing these are life and death, the two poles of an

organic world. The larger antithesis has, for each term, another bipolarity. The elaboration of this system is the basic thematic material of
La Jeune Parque.

Part six contrasts the Parca's dance in the sun and her former
wholeness, when she was "une avec le désir," with her present self of
inner darkness: her eye is foreign to the sun's light; she is a captive
"loin des purs environs." This is the imagery of present mortality and
the solar past, but, gradually, in the course of parts six and seven the
solar past turns into a sepulchral one:

> O dangereusement de son regard la proie!
> Car l'oeil spirituel sur ses plages de soie
> Avait déjà vu luire et pâlir trop de jours
> Dont je m'étais prédit les couleurs et le cours.
> L'ennui, le clair ennui de mirer leur nuance,
> Me donnait sur la vie une funeste avance:
> L'aube me dévoilait tout le jour ennemi.
> J'étais à demi morte; et peut-être, à demi
> Immortelle . . .

Oh the danger of fixing one's glance on oneself! For in their silken regions, my
mind's eye had already seen too many days gleam and grow pale, whose course and
color I had predicted. Weariness, the bright weariness of reflecting their hues gave
me a deadly anticipation of my lot. Dawn revealed to me the whole inimical light of
day. I was half dead, and perhaps half immortal.

We have returned to the thematics of part three, and each of her past
days was a "tomb." What is now clearer is that, before the night of
the serpent, the Parca was already undergoing a change: her semi-
immortality seems to mean that she had lost half of her original deity.
Thus the Parca has at times denied the reality of the nocturnal attack
and bite. There is still, however, an element of confusion in her
mind. She has attributed her new state, on the one hand, to her soul
and the nighttime experience, and, on the other, to the cumulative
ennui of her divine monotony of existence. She cannot yet be certain
what her feeling of mortality means, something she will know only
when mortality will come to signify life to her as well as death.

The remainder of part seven and part eight are taken up with the
Parca's reproaches to herself about the change already occurring in her

on the previous day. The next dramatic reversal takes place in part nine: the Parca demands first an altar in the sky, the death of an immortal, who simply goes through a change, so despairingly is she torn between revulsion from her former state and inability to accept the new one. Just as the other death, that of a mortal, begins to overcome her, however, she realizes that mortality brings not only death but life, and the invocation to the spring begins. The pattern of the poem is here at its most complex. As part ten begins, the Parca is resigned to eroticism and its burning, feels the tear from the soul come which is mentioned in part one but cannot flow until her mortality is achieved, and is tempted to leap over the cliff in suicide.

After intervening visions of dawn, the Parca, in part thirteen, recalls the "divins dégoûts" of her immortal self and the passage through the death of the soul which leads into the new life of the soul. The fourth possibility for her fate, the death of an immortal, the dispersal into nature, "plus transparente mort," comes to her mind in part fourteen. But she brushes aside this thought and inquires of herself how she escaped suicide and how the serpent vanished. With part fifteen the Parca falls asleep in the time preceding part one, thinking over her fourfold possibilities of destiny and her once deathly "purity." The reconciliation of her new body with the sun will be the essential last thematic touch in part fifteen.

The basic word pattern of *La Jeune Parque* comes from the *dédoublement* of self the Parca feels during much of the poem and which has as a fairly frequent manifestation the contrastive use of *âme* and *esprit* (or *spirituel*). Each of the Parca's identities which we may also call immortal and mortal, has the possibility of a kind of death, that of the immortal self consisting of dispersal in nature and insentience through length of lassitude. The mode of feeling of the immortal self is the perception of changelessness or nature as sun, that of the other one, the inner world of erotic disturbance. The word design of the poem is complicated through the double polarity of *nuit, soleil,* as well as *mort, corps,* and related terms: each enters into an antithesis within the realm of *âme* or *esprit* in addition to being part of the opposition between these two terms.

Valéry was inclined to consider poetry to be a matter of word patterns evoking emotion rather than as a mimesis in any objective sense. What he called myth is characteristic: "le nom de tout ce qui n'existe et ne subsiste qu'ayant la parole pour cause." With this in mind we should avoid temptations to allegorize *La Jeune Parque* too rigorously; at the same time, we cannot avoid perceiving that the Parca's former state is described in terms of the *symboliste* imagery of pure beauty: her golden dance in the sun, the velvet fruit of her body, even the clean dry lines of her inner desert, like a stylized stage setting ("Ma lassitude est parfois un théâtre"), suggest artifice. Her coming to awareness of eroticism and to life has been read as a general drama of consciousness or ego, but perhaps the Parca's overt awakening from narcissism into outwardly turning sexuality is a sufficient subject, especially if we see it as a comment on the limitations of certain *symboliste* ideas of art, in the name of truth, health, nature, and reality, the ideals of the new classicism. But Valéry clearly wanted the reader to be most of all aware of the verbal patterns, of the dialectical scheme of wholeness, division, and return to integrality, which is so widespread that its commonness to many subjects should make us hesitate before giving it a univocal interpretation. Furthermore, Valéry in his essays suggests that philosophy in poetry had little weight for him. Such an attitude is uncongenial to some readers, but it has the value of drawing attention to the verbal construction of the work of art. Finally, Valéry, by the very form of his poem, invites us to look at the relationships in it and their complexity. The division of the poem into fragments which do not follow a chronological sequence, the strong element of discontinuity, makes the reader focus on the presence of similar and divergent patterns.

Shortly after Saint-John Perse's *Anabase* was published, a French critic gave titles to its parts, and Eliot drew on them in the preface to his translation of the poem. They are of the following order: "Arrival of the Conqueror at the city," "Tracing the plan of the city," "Foundation of the city," "Decision to fare forth," and so on. Although modifications have been suggested, the best attempts at explication continue this tradition of tracing a plot in *Anabase*, albeit a loose one. It does not seem unlikely that, in Perse's first conception of the poem, there was some kind of plot line. The question is whether, in the poem's final form, enough plot exists to make it a useful or even necessary element in interpreting the poem. I feel Eliot's advice that one look above all for imaginative coherence of imagery provides a more valuable approach. There is certainly an artistic progression in the poem, but the usual search for plot seems to me to create certain problems, while leaving others unsolved. All the motifs of which the traditional plot descriptions are made can, indeed, be found in the poem, but the difficulty is whether they indicate, canto by canto, the relations of a leader to his tribe and the external actions of that tribe.

Leaving aside for the moment the introductory "Chanson" and taking the title in the two general senses of "horseback riding" and "movement of an army upland," we can see how the opening canto of the poem has traditionally led to difficulties in reading. A voice speaks in a majestic language whose idiosyncratic syntax resembles in no way the mannered art language of the 1890s; nor does the verset, with its strong divisions into six, eight, ten, and twelve-syllable groups resemble the loose free verse of the early twentieth century. No prose poetry or verset since Rimbaud's has such vigor and resonance:

> Sur trois grandes saisons m'établissant avec honneur,
> j'augure bien du sol où j'ai fondé ma loi.
> Les armes au matin sont belles et la mer. A nos
> chevaux livrée la terre sans amandes
> nous vaut ce ciel incorruptible. Et le soleil n'est point
> nommé, mais sa puissance est parmi nous
> et la mer au matin comme une présomption de l'esprit.
>
> Puissance, tu chantais sur nos routes nocturnes!... Aux
> ides pures du matin que savons-nous du songe, notre
> aînesse?

I have built myself, with honour and dignity have I built myself on three great seasons, and it promises well, the soil whereon I have established my Law. Beautiful are bright weapons in the morning and behind us the sea is fair. Given over to our horses this seedless earth delivers to us this incorruptible sky. The Sun is unmentioned but his power is amongst us and the sea at morning like a presumption of the mind. Power, you sang as we marched in darkness.... At the pure ideas of day what know we of our dream, older than ourselves?

The thing we are most sure of is that the voice is at once regal and hieratic. Details are seemingly contradictory or unrelated: the law is founded on an apparently infertile soil; the sun deity has not been named as in the normal establishment of a shrine, and the god's direction is felt rather at night than in the morning. The voice seems to be the god's at times: "Au seuil des tentes toute gloire! ma force parmi vous"; despite the founding of the law, no city will be founded, no alliances made with the peoples of the other shore. A mysterious time point is given: "Pour une année encore parmi vous." After the three asterisks the voice says "Or je hantais la ville de vos songes" and one might interpret it, as has been done, as belonging to another, countervoice, one which goes on to praise a future march through the desert and to make a catalogue of men, the first of a number of such passages in *Anabase*, whose rhythm and syntax make a striking contrast with the rest.

The question that the reader may well ask in regard to this canto is whether the speaking voice and his people are stopping or moving, how the founding of the law on the land and the exhortation to move on fit together. First we should note that the details pertaining to stasis are generally of a social and hierarchic order: they seem to characterize the speaker in regard to his men, and their new relation: "Pour une année encore parmi vous." The speaker, the priest-king, represents a god whose ritual is stable ("et l'idée pure comme un sel tient ses assises dans le jour") but whose power directs men to the west, just as the sun is at once a figure of immobility at noon and movement throughout the day. The speaker can be identified with the "Etranger" of the "Chanson" and other parts of *Anabase*, whose function is to lead men onward, but one should, here perhaps most of all, refrain from trying to interpret the detail of the poem as if there were a concealed plot, having motives and conflicts. The speaker's voice, whoever it is—and later it does not always sound necessarily like a priest-king's—speaks for all. The mode of the poem is mythic rather than realist-psychological, as the extraordinary new kind of rhythmic verset implies with its stately movement. Finally, it is part of the proportions and design of the longer cantos of *Anabase* that the imagery of movement and of stasis occur in conjunction in varying degrees; from a purely artistic point of view the exclusive representation at extreme length of either immobility or motion would be unsatisfactory and not suggest the rising and ebbing which is the rhythm of life and that of *Anabase*. Thus in canto three, the opening words "A la moisson des orges l'homme sort" have an ambiguous quality; they are followed by images of either movement or planning of movement (more likely the latter), yet the end of the canto suggests contemplation and stasis:

> A la moisson des orges l'homme sort. L'odeur puissante m'environne, et l'eau plus pure qu'en Jabal fait ce bruit d'un autre âge. . . . Au plus long jour de l'année chauve, louant la terre sous l'herbage, je ne sais qui de fort a marché sur mes pas. Et des morts sous le sable et l'urine et le sel de la terre, voici qu'il en est fait comme de la balle dont le grain fut donné aux oiseaux. Et mon âme, mon âme veille à grand bruit aux portes de la mort—Mais dis au Prince qu'il se taise: à bout de lance parmi nous
> ce crâne de cheval!

Man goes out at barley harvest. The strong smells encompass me, and the water more pure than that of Jabal makes sounds of another age. . . . On the longest day of the bald year, praising the earth under grass, I know not what being of strength has followed my pace. And the Dead under the sand and the urine and the salt of the earth, it is done with these as with the husks whereof the grain was given to the fowls. And my soul, my soul keeps loud vigil at the portals of death—but say to the Prince to be still: on the point of a lance, amongst us, this horse's skull!

There is a beautiful joining here of the static—suggested by the past, the dead, recollection—the still look of the present with what appears to be a ceremony going on, and the impelling anticipatory note of a mysterious power (which earlier "speaks over the roof"). It is characteristic that the third canto have this quality of balance and hesitation: variations on movement and stasis are the whole principle of the poem. Interestingly enough, the march through the desert before the quite unambiguous founding of the city in canto four is not described, whereas a later march before the founding of a new city is (canto eight). These combinations more than a plot line determine sequence in *Anabase*. Thus the end of canto four, in which a city is established, consists of the image, found earlier, of a man advancing to the edge of the desert in sign of departure. Five is the canto of night, dreams, dream-water, insubstantiality, solitude, and the desire for moving on; its imagery is suggested by a few lines of cantos one and three (this is a characteristic kind of interrelationship in the poem), and the reader might take this as signifying departure in some kind of story of the tribe. Yet this is not unambiguously the case; canto six is an evocation at once of alliances, movement to the west, violent conquest, and a still center of "nos pays de grand loisir et . . . nos filles," where "nous établîmes en haut lieu nos pièges au bonheur."

By sufficiently elaborating the idea of a plot, we could account for the relationship between canto four and what follows, saying that a substantial enough amount of time has elapsed since the founding of the city for dissatisfaction to arise and that in canto six the tribe divides into a stable central population and armed bands moving out from the "haut lieu." It seems to me, however, that, as we read this, we do not encounter or feel the same distinctions between individuals and collectivities of various sizes, the same firm sense of the identity of the actors, or the same analogy with time in our everyday circumstances as we do when we read a novel. There are logical categories we do not need to or always feel the need to apply to *Anabase*. Furthermore, the images of movement are, in a mythic poem like this one, as potent in the thematics of the work if they designate the impulse to fare forward as when they indicate its physical realization. Sometimes the insistence and detail of the imagery makes us incline to feel that genuine action is involved, as in canto four, describing the founding of a city. Elsewhere, as in canto five, we may find that it makes no difference, that we experience no need whatsoever to decide whether the urge toward further travels is embodied in action or not.

The great catalogues of men in their diverse activities as in canto ten or of movement and conquest in six must not obliterate the fact that the life force manifests itself as much in contemplation, in the search for inner depths, as in the élan forward in space. Canto eight, one of recollection before departure ("Nous n'habiterons pas toujours ces terres jaunes, notre délice") is the most developed illustration of this; the following passage is related to ones we have seen in cantos one and three:

Et à midi, quand l'arbre jujubier fait éclater l'assise des tombeaux, l'homme clôt ses paupières et rafraîchit sa nuque dans les âges. . . . Cavaleries du songe au lieu des poudres mortes, ô routes vaines qu'échevèle un souffle jusqu'à nous! où trouver, où trouver les guerriers qui garderont les fleuves dans leurs noces?

Au bruit des grandes eaux en marche sur la terre, tout le sel de la terre tressaille dans les songes. Et soudain, ah! soudain que nous veulent ces voix? Levez un peuple de miroirs sur l'ossuaire des fleuves, qu'ils interjettent appel dans la suite des siècles! Levez des pierres à ma gloire, levez des pierres au silence, et à la garde de ces lieux les cavaleries de bronze vert sur de vastes chaussées!

And at noon, when the jujuba tree breaks the tombstone, man closes his lids and cools his neck in the ages. . . . Horse-tramplings of dreams in the place of dead powders, O vain ways swept away by a breath, to our feet! where find, where find, the warriors who shall watch the streams in their nuptials? At the sound of great waters on march over the earth, all the salt of the earth shudders in dream. And sudden, ah sudden, what would these voices with us? Levy a wilderness of mirrors on the boneyard of streams, let them appeal in the course of ages! Erect stones to my fame, erect stones to silence; and to guard these places, cavalcades of green bronze on the great causeways!

The individual plunges into the past, future, and eternity. Here we see a particularly striking example of how natural movement, that of the sun in space and time, contains at the same time a natural manifestation of stasis and the atemporal in noon. The bipolarity of existence is the basic informing principle of *Anabase*.

The mythic mode of *Anabase* is characterized by an avoidance of coherence in detail: thus agricultural and nomadic customs are both mentioned, travel by horseback and by ship, superstitions of all orders, varying social structures, and so forth. In this we see an extreme example of a verbal pattern typical to a greater or lesser extent of much modern poetry: from large numbers of examples the reader must synthesize basic common elements or principles. In *Anabase* there is a notable absence of general statements or connection between images, while at the same time the most vast general principle, that of the bipolarity of human and natural existence, governs the poem. The process of reading it is a complex one in that one must delight in the variety of the imagery while avoiding becoming lost in tangential associations. The structural method of *Anabase* is to be found in many short lyrics where antithetical groupings of images are easy to perceive; it is unusual for a purely bipolar or cyclic pattern—since the gradations of Perse's poem produce a cyclic impression—to assume so protracted a shape.

The most remarkable example in twentieth-century poetry—for its ambition at least—of a very long poem eschewing argument in the traditional sense for word patterns is Pound's *Cantos*. The scale of the design is so large that related passages may be widely separated: in the *nekuia* of the first canto, Odysseus, momentarily distinguished from "ego scriptor cantilenae" although elsewhere identified with him, seeks knowledge from the dead; much later, in canto 47, he sails off for his meeting with Tiresias, and juxtaposed is a section on the natural fertility cycle joining man and nature; this we may take to be at least one kind of knowledge he attains. Finally, in *The Pisan Cantos, ego scriptor*-Odysseus has a vision of Aphrodite, the goddess associated, un-Homerically, with him in canto 1. We may take Aphrodite to represent sexuality in an idealized form, as Circe represents it on a more physical level. The wide separation of this material is countered by its stylistic coherence and distinction and by the fact that it is clearly discernible in the mass of other imagistic and thematic material in the *Cantos*.

Although making connections between more or less remote areas of the *Cantos* is one necessary task in reading them, the design of the poem is not simply one of scrambled pieces or even scrambled pieces arranged in a strikingly interesting order, although the latter is certainly one of the aesthetic principles involved. While lengthy sections of the poem seem conceived as a kind of impersonal meditation or recounting, the framework is very much one of personal vision, the sign of which, among other things in the early cantos, is recurrent variations on the phrase "And we sit here . . . There in the arena." Indeed, the sequence of the material in cantos 2 to 7 or 10 is less important for whatever themes we may choose to derive from the images and which do not all recur by any means, than as a dramatic prelude establishing mood and point of view. For example, the passages on Dionysus, Troy, Danaë, and Actaeon deal with the splendor, violence, and tragedy of men encountering the will of gods; through Troy in Auvergne and Itys-Cabestan a temporal transference is made to Provence. Conflict between men and gods ultimately has no special stable or repeated thematic value in the *Cantos*; the importance of this violent or tragic material is to contrast with the images of the "thin husks" of etiolated contemporary men in canto 7. We must see present torpor against past action in order to be receptive to more central thematic elements like antinatural economic disorder. Certainly the vision of the gods in cantos 2 or 4 hardly resembles that of later cantos; the mythic past will by no means seem a tragic past: that coloring is only used to establish a time scheme of robustness as opposed to deliquescence. The prolongation of the classical past in Provence is primarily a means of drawing toward medieval and renaissance Italy, which will occupy a number of cantos. All this corresponds not to an impersonal thematic design, such as we see in *Anabase*, but to the dramatic, visionary sequence in the mind of *ego scriptor*.

There is some overt discursive language providing thematic articulations in the *Cantos:* thus the mythological "vision" of cantos 2 to 6 is contrasted with the "clock ticks" and contemporary scenes "in 'time'" of canto 7, which is further commented on by "Time is the evil" (canto 30) and, in contrast, by the examples and language of cyclic natural time in cantos 47 and 52. The pity canto (30) and the usura ones (45 and 51) are likewise discursive statements. But equally important in the *Cantos* is the kind of juxtaposition or stylistic connection which, as we have seen, tells us indirectly what kind of knowledge Odysseus is to acquire. It is characteristic that a statement is not countered by another statement but rather by some thematic abstraction we must make from imagery or other details: thus the first Kung (Confucius) canto (13), speaks of order, and we must read "disorder" as the meaning of the material in cantos 12 and 14, even though nothing so specific is said. This method has its ambiguities: are we to take Chinese order as the opposite of Italian renaissance disorder in cantos 8 to 11, or does the latter merely contrast with modern effeteness? What possibly could be made of a contrast between mythological violence in cantos 2 or 4 and Confucian order? The joining of Kung and Eleusis in cantos 52 and 71 remains cryptic. In reading the *Cantos* it seems best to proceed by dialectic movement (mythological energy—modern weakness and confusion—Chinese discipline) rather than to seek one large bipolar pattern. If there is a general thematic organizing principle in the *Cantos*, it is the idea of nature, but that is a somewhat hollow abstraction, because nature divides up into the various notions of mythological wholeness (Aphrodite and the cycle of the seasons), moral discipline (Confucius), and sensuality. An unexpected comparison may occur, as when, in canto 52, Chinese moral order is revealed as analogous to the pattern of the seasons, but the vision of sensuality in the Odysseus cantos (39 and 47) hardly seems to square rationally or imagistically with the Confucian theme. Again, the opening visions of the *Cantos* do not seem to make a rational thematic connection with the rest since they deal often with violence in marriage (as opposed to the fertility unions of cantos 39 and 47), but, as we have seen, the technique of rapprochement demands some subtlety in application.

Rather than charging it with confusion, I think we should admire in Pound's technique the varied images and ideas that a general notion such as nature generates: hierophanies are natural, modern economics is not; the burden of history and historical time is unnatural, the Confucian "ch'êng," precise definition in language like a direct sun beam, is not; humility is natural (canto 81), pity is not (canto 30). Such complicated ramifications make a poem which, in spite of some of the obsessive harpings, has remarkable gradations; Pound is certainly not a simple dualist. The method of tacit rapprochement between statement and style, as when we understand that praise of *ch'êng* is concretely embodied in the *ch'êng* of the quotations from nineteenth-century presidents or in the fertility lyricism of canto 47, is certainly a highly imaginative use of stylistic patterns, its only drawback being that its limits and proportions are perhaps not so easily determined as those of a poem with a traditional argument structure. Certainly the open-ended form Pound left the *Cantos* in reflects this. On the other hand, the extremely schematic quality of some patterning is avoided.

The detailed working out of the verbal patterns in the *Cantos* involves many extraordinary effects. Since the *Cantos* move both forward and backward in time and thematic relation and since the episodes range from hierophany through narration to anecdote, the ordinary forms of English prosody and syntax with their connotation of direct, sequential movement, are rejected in favor of special ones. The typical verse line is one of three or four accents, the unaccented syllables varying in number and position, and end-stopped. The inspiration for this line is variously ascribed to Old English, the elegiac distich, and the *Cantar de mio Cid*, all of which could be suggestive of a

syllable and accent grouping that corresponds more to English phrasing than do the major traditional patterns. Certainly Pound's line is
flexible in the way it can vary from dynamic to static, its constant
virtue being the refusal of *remplissage*. Within this framework the
handling of the verb tends to determine the feeling of movement.
Many finite verbs provide a quite natural narrative rhythm; more interesting, however, is the yielding of finite verbs to participles:

> Beneath it, beneath it
> Not a ray, not a slivver, not a spare disc of sunlight
> Flaking the black, soft water;
> Bathing the body of nymphs, of nymphs, and Diana,
> Nymphs, white-gathered about her, and the air, air,
> Shaking, air alight with the goddess,
>   fanning their hair in the dark.
> Lifting, lifting and waffing:
> Ivory dipping in silver,
>   Shadow'd, o'ershadow'd
> Ivory dipping in silver,
> Not a splotch, not a lost shatter of sunlight. (Canto 4)

(This passage contains the occasional variants of five- and two-accent
lines.) English is exceptional in the Western European languages for
the wide variety of uses of its present participle, which has a notably
durative quality. Pound has carried further than usual this structural
characteristic of English, producing a kind of participial style which his
German and Italian translators cannot match, being obliged to supply
finite verbs frequently, since the participle of those languages simply
does not have the strength of the English one. The strong participle in
English, being imperfective, slows forward movement while retaining
some verbal qualities.

Pound's grammar has other interesting resources as well. In canto
17, which contains invented episodes in Odysseus' wanderings, like
his somewhat anachronistic visit to Venice, there are only nine finite
verbs, and some of them have implied pronoun subjects rather than
stated ones, a device that attenuates the preterite-propulsive movement by depriving the clause of one element of sentence structure:

> Koré through the bright meadow,
>   with green-gray dust in the grass:

'For this hour, brother of Circe.'
Arm laid over my shoulder,
Saw the sun for three days, the sun fulvid,
As a lion lift over sand-plain;
           and that day,
And for three days, and none after,
Splendour, as the splendour of Hermes,
And shipped thence
      to the stone place,
Pale white, over water,
      known water,
And the white forest of marble, bent bough over bough,
The pleached arbour of stone,
Thither Borso, when they shot the barbed arrow at him,
And Carmagnola, between the two columns,
Sigismundo, after that wreck in Dalmatia.
    Sunset like the grasshopper flying.

The delicacy of this kind of narrative, moving ever so gently, depends not only on the omission of pronouns, but on the ellipsis of verbs in several places, where a verbal element is implied by adverbial expressions: "Thither Borso." This movement by the reader's supplying an idea of verbal action, if no specific verb, is an amazingly imaginative use of syntax. One advantage offered by Pound's ways of avoiding finite verbs is that the transition between episodes, as in canto 17, is made so deftly, through the absence of the harshly sequential preterite, that it is almost imperceptible. It is an important part of Pound's technique in the *Cantos* that heterogeneous episodes should, when they are not abruptly and violently juxtaposed for effect, be able to melt into one another.

The verb element, or the noun in the absence of a verb, is the basic unit of syntax; the coordinating of these, in a highly stylized grammar like Pound's, demands particular attention. In keeping with his general simplicity of means, Pound makes great use of "and," which can have diverse functions. Here the "and" is cumulative, with an incantatory, ecstatic effect:

Gods float in the azure air,
Bright gods and Tuscan, back before dew was shed.
Light: and the first light, before ever dew was fallen.

> Panisks, and from the oak, dryas,
> And from the apple, maelid,
> Through all the wood, and the leaves are full of voices,
> A-whisper, and the clouds bow over the lake,
> And there are gods upon them,
> And in the water, the almond-white swimmers,
> The silvery water glazes the upturned nipple,
>   As Poggio has remarked. (Canto 3)

Elsewhere the same word is disjunctive, implying weariness, confusion, or the inexorable monotony of time:

> And, in Este's house, Parisina
> Paid
> For this tribe paid always, and the house
> Called also Atreides',
> And the wind is still for a little
> And the dusk rolled
>   to one side a little
> And he was twelve at the time, Sigismundo,
> And no dues had been paid for three years,
> And his elder brother gone pious;
> And that year they fought in the streets,
> And that year he got out to Cesena
>   And brought back the levies,
> And that year he crossed by night over Foglia, and ... (Canto 8)

There is a quite striking contrast in the Malatesta cantos between the elaborate diplomacy of the letters quoted and the brutal reality of events rendered by the "and's" which reduce causality and time to something at once oppressive and empty.

The distinctive features of Pound's syntax include the type of inversion of subject and verb current in Old English (or Italian), frequent omission of the article, and a general tendency toward parataxis; what is absent of traditional grammar is as important as what is preserved. When hypotaxis is used, it is often the sign of prose being quoted or imitated: it is important to Pound's design to be able to encompass a wide range of language, but the styles are meant to be separated and contrasting. A particularly remarkable effect in the quoting of prose is to use fragments, so that the sense is incomplete but the feeling of a type of prose and style persists:

> Your courts are shut down, justice VOID
> I have not drawn a writ since the 1st of November
> if this authority be once recognized
> > ruins America
> I must cut down my expenses.
> For my ruin as well as America's . . .
> To renounce under tree, may under the very branch
> where they hang'd him in effigy . . .
> > UNANIMOUS for Gridley, Jas Otis, J. Adams
> pray that the Courts may be opened
> > (original of this is preserved)
> If what I wrote last night
> > recall what Lord Bacon
> wrote about laws . . . invisible and correspondences
> > > . . . that parliament
> hath no authority
> > to impose internal taxes upon us. (Canto 64)

There are many places where the tone of prose and the cast of mind behind it seem to be more the point than the actual content, which is fragmentary. Likewise, the anecdotes told in colloquial language or dialect often seem to be brought in for a stylistic purpose: there is an important sense in which styles alone indicate the values embodied in the *Cantos*. Certainly the effect of the Chinese ideograms in the later cantos is as much stylistic as anything else: they transform the somewhat banal declarative Confucian style, as it appears in canto 13, into something lapidarily monosyllabic and memorable. Often foreign languages in the *Cantos* are used to reflect some small nuance of color rather than to indicate basic meaning. Finally, style is an analogue of Pound's economic theories: production of goods is the equivalent of *ch'êng*, or precision in language; usury corresponds to inflated style, words unnaturally divorced from things.

If nature can be taken as the subsuming idea of the *Cantos*, to which themes like time or economics are related by processes of derivation or contrast, these ramifications of the idea can most richly be expressed not in abstractions, but in their various embodiments in history and the poet's vision, which means, in Pound's case, discriminations of style. The fruitful modernist notion of juxtaposing styles receives greater elaboration by Pound than by any other poet; these styles, which are cultural symbols, are not simply worked out in oppositions. While Laforgue at times and Eliot in *The Wasteland* use contrasting styles in one work, their juxtaposition has a simpler function than the great range of verbal patterns included in the *Cantos;* there is much more to Pound's method than putting side by side the distinguished and the vulgar, the recondite and the colloquial. Just as we have observed the presence of many thematic gradations in the *Cantos,* so the voices of John Adams, the chronicler of Chinese rulers, the medieval lyricist (cantos 39 and 36), or Pound out of Divus out of Homer each bring a special authority and implication of values to the poem.

The five works we have just examined are all refractory to paraphrase. I have shown how *Un Coup de dés* can be reduced to some general statements, of which the principle one is the paradox that casting dice does not eliminate chance. Our other poems also yield very little: for example, the statement in the *Cantos* that time is evil scarcely subsumes the poem. With *Anabase* it is hardly possible to say more than that a tribe either migrates or stays where it is. *La Jeune Parque* describes an awakening to sensuality, but to epitomize it thus gives no idea of the exact content of many of its parts. Finally, we could extract many propositions about time from *Four Quartets,* but they do not add up to much out of context. Our poems all collapse, so to speak, when we seek in them an argument in the traditional fashion. That "rhythme de rapports" which Mallarmé saw as the essential characteristic of art is close to being the matter of these poems. It is illuminating to contrast these works with other modern poems in which a discursive armature is preserved: Valéry's "Le Cimetière marin" and Steven's "Sunday Morning" contain the thematic statements and even commonplaces that would permit a prose résumé to be easily and adequately made of them.

We are in a much better position to discuss our five poems when we observe not so much what words mean in them as how words behave. Then we see that *Un Coup de dés* is a kind of grammatical drama created by tensions between words which are syntactically related but separated on the page. The words on the page, furthermore, rise and fall with the sea and stars in the imagery. The role played by etymology is also characteristic of complex patterning: the meaning of casting dice lurks in "hazard," making curious paradoxes in the poem. In *Four Quartets*, the interplay of antithesis and tripartite formulations sustains the texture, and *Anabase* is entirely worked out in terms of the large antithesis of stasis and movement. With *La Jeune Parque*, we encounter another bipolar arrangement of words: the two categories are those of *esprit* and *âme*, but Valéry makes a very complicated pattern in his poem by a further subdivision. There is a life and death of the mind and a life and death of the soul: these are quite distinct, although, of course, Valéry uses the same words, *vie* and *mort*, for both. Pound's kind of verbal design relies on his virtuoso's ability to write in several styles; he goes far beyond mere antithesis.

One of the most interesting things about the poetry of verbal patterns is that mimesis, the reference to reality, is often uncertain. In *Anabase*, for example, we do not always know whether the poet is speaking of actions, intentions, or daydreams. The exact status of the serpent in *La Jeune Parque* is not altogether clear, either in the Parca's mind or ours. Mallarmé casts *Un Coup de dés* in a curious hypothetical mode so that the whole question of the literal and the figurative is obviated. In many places in *Four Quartets*, we find more references to temporal points than to the thoughts or actions that occur at such points: the design receives more attention than the content. Finally, Pound's narrating voice in the *Cantos* seems to shift from one role to another, moving between various planes of history or myth. If, when we approach the *Cantos*, *La Jeune Parque*, or our other poems, we look for objective representation of acts or facts, we will find interpretation more difficult than it need be. The formal pattern must be perceived first, and then details can be accounted for.

There is one large-scale element of design in all five of our poems: cyclic structure. This may be a narrative arrangement, as in *La Jeune Parque*, where later events are told first, with the poem eventually coming back to them. In *Anabase*, the natural cyclicity of day and night or the seasons reflects the tribe's periods of settlement and periods of migration. *Un Coup de dés* is constructed as a circle, the last words pointing to the first words. Eliot conveys the cyclic idea through natural imagery as well as recurrent material, and Pound relies chiefly on the periodic reappearance of Odysseus in the *Cantos*. The frequency with which cyclic patterns are found in modern literature seems to come, at least in part, from the disappearance of a poetic argument in the traditional manner.

While studying verbal patterns in our five works, I have avoided dwelling on the presence of symbols in them. None of them actually makes great demands on our sense of figurative language and its traditions. Now, however, we shall turn to poems in which the density or unusualness of the symbols suggest an allegorical dimension of meaning.

III
Symbolic
Structures

1. Introduction: Verlaine

The symbolism of romantic and earlier French poets belonged to
the usual categories of Western, Christian, literary analogy: while
they drew on correspondences between macrocosm and microcosm,
on selective elements of classical mythology, on early encyclopedic
science, and on folkloric elements such as animal symbolism, the imagery and types of the Bible were perhaps the greatest contributors. In
the broadest sense the divine and the demonic were the organizing
poles; order, disorder, virtues, vices, and moral-psychological qualities constituted the reference of most of this symbolism. Its pervasive moral coloring gave it a didactic value, which, even when only
implicit, nevertheless was always ready to be exploited.

Hugo and Baudelaire were the most specific, if fragmentary,
commentators on symbolism among the French romantic poets. The
former used expressions such as the book of nature, the latter, writing
significantly about Hugo, referred to the idea of universal analogy.
They relied not only on intuitively understood symbols or ones whose
use was so frequent as to make their meaning highly conventional;
they and other romantic poets were also given, in regard to stylistic
techniques, to quite explicit analogies. Similes and personifications
play a noteworthy role in Baudelaire's poetry, for example. The bipartite analogical poem like Mallarmé's Baudelairean "Les Fenêtres" is a
characteristic pattern. This is orderly symbolism with few con-
junctures that could impair its rhetorical force.

The traditional principles of symbolism through the romantic
period in France include certain clear-cut distinctions: levels of mean-

ing played some role in poetic practice as well as theory, at least in early poetry, and far more important are the notions that the outer symbolizes the inner and that the lower and terrestrial reflects the higher. Such categorizing becomes less relevant however, as one grows less sure that the poet recognizes sharp differences between the traditionally transcendental or objective and the content of mind. For Baudelaire and Hugo, the received principles seem to have held valid, but the new poetry of the late nineteenth century uses symbols that are above all psychological in nature. It is quite clear that for Verlaine before his conversion, for Mallarmé, for the Rimbaud of the *Illuminations*, there is no unambiguous transcendency, no cosmic scheme of analogy supported by the traditional kind of metaphysics. Our first example will be a fairly accessible psychodrama, Verlaine's *Fêtes galantes*, in which there occurs a new use of color symbolism free of earlier associations and a new form of a relatively new category of symbols: those of a historical period, a kind which eventually, in "decadent" poems on late antiquity or in Rilke's *Neue Gedichte*, was to achieve further elaboration. The title *Fêtes galantes* refers to the subjects of certain eighteenth-century painters and marks the replacement of biblical, mythological, and literary typology by symbolism at once *plastique* in origin and indebted to the new historical imagination of the nineteenth century.

In *Fêtes galantes* Verlaine drew together some elements of his earlier poetry: the unstated subject and the menacing time scheme of "Chanson d'automne," the neoclassical garden, whose symbolism is uncertain in "Nuit du Walpurgis classique," and the imagery of *fadeur* from "Melancholia." *Fêtes galantes* is not, however, a collection of poems of various periods and inspiration for which subsequently a meaningful pattern has been found, as is the case of *Les Fleurs du mal*; rather it is a carefully composed work, written over a short space of time. The difference lies essentially in the fact that, taken separately, many poems of *Fêtes galantes*, unlike those of *Les Fleurs du mal*, have little point; isolated, their function in setting tones and providing articulations within the whole is lost. Even those that are sufficiently self-contained to appear in anthologies acquire their full force only in context. *Fêtes galantes* consists of twenty-two poems, of which the first is distinctly introductory, the seventh an initial indication of a time pattern, the fourteenth marking a new thematic phase, and the last a conclusion. The care for symmetry is evident.

The opening "Clair de lune" stands out by its overtly symbolic character:

> Votre âme est un paysage choisi
> Que vont charmant masques et bergamasques,
> Jouant du luth, et dansant, et quasi
> Tristes sous leurs déguisements fantasques.
>
> Tout en chantant sur le mode mineur
> L'amour vainqueur et la vie opportune,
> Ils n'ont pas l'air de croire à leur bonheur
> Et leur chanson se mêle au clair de lune,
>
> Au calme clair de lune triste et beau,
> Qui fait rêver les oiseaux dans les arbres
> Et sangloter d'extase les jets d'eau,
> Les grands jets d'eau sveltes parmi les marbres.

Your soul is a choice landscape enchanted by masks and Bergamo clowns, playing the lute and dancing and almost sad beneath their fanciful disguises. While singing, in the minor mode, of conquering love and a lucky life, they do not seem to believe in their happiness, and their song mingles with the moonlight, the calm, sad, beautiful moonlight, which makes the birds dream in the trees and the fountains sob with ecstasy, the great slender fountains among the marbles.

The *votre* (there is no *vous*-reader in the volume) sets the tone of subdued intimacy; commedia dell'arte figures are suggested by *bergamasques* but merge imperceptibly in the second stanza with masked noble ladies and gentlemen; the modifiers in polysyndeton of the first stanza and the apposition (l. 8) drawing in a further apposition of the long sentence in the second and third stanzas represent Verlaine's meandering syntax at its most effective, and the final, casually introduced image of the fountains deftly symbolizes the fragile, lovely, and defeated aspirations described in the second stanza. As often in Verlaine, relaxed grammar should not make one lose sight of the intricately plotted character of the images.

Stylized figures from the commedia dell'arte are the subject of "Pantomine"; by their frank actions and desires they express what the noble actors of the other poems conceal or treat ironically: gluttony, sorrow, the urge to rape, and erotic longings seemingly arising out of the landscape. Moving, as often in *Fêtes galantes,* by contrast (in prosodic form always, as well as in content) "Sur l'herbe" next is a slightly drunken and lustful moonlit dialogue, unresolved like the snatch of melody (C, E, G, A, B). ",L'Allée" in *rimes mêlées* (a favorite neoclassical form) then presents a genre picture of a painted, dull-witted, and elegantly gowned lady taking the air. With "A la promenade" the decor of another bland *conversation galante* introduces us to the peculiar quality of light, air, and greenery which informs much of *Fêtes:* the sky is white, never blue, which is the color of shadows, and despite the evident opulence of the characters, the trees in their garden are *grêles,* the pool *humble.* Insipidity characterizes the landscape. "Dans la grotte," which follows, is a declaration written in a pastiche of eighteenth-century poetic style with its conventionalized mythological references. Finally, "Les Ingénus" takes leave of lechers to depict, ambiguously and by innuendo, an erotic initiation:

> Le soir tombait, un soir équivoque d'automne:
> Les belles, se pendant rêveuses à nos bras,
> Dirent alors des mots si spécieux, tout bas,
> Que notre âme depuis ce temps tremble et s'étonne.

Evening was falling, an ambiguous autumn evening: the belles, hanging dreamily on our arms, spoke then, in a low voice, such specious words that our souls since have been trembling and stunned.

Shock, wonder, faintness, and fear are implied in the old sense of *s'étonner:* a note of spontaneity is introduced into the weary round of *galanterie,* and a sudden feeling of temporal depth occurs as the first past tense verbs in the collection appear. We now, in the seventh poem, have an intuition of time passing, of the unsubstantiality of the *fêtes.* Another lady with her train, slave, and monkey; an erotic compliment in the form of a conceit; another commedia dell'arte poem, suggestive this time of crime, magic, and lust; and an amorous picnic are the short poems forming the middle section of *Fêtes.* Number ten, "En patinant," which is almost at the midpoint of the volume, is by far the longest poem and attempts to sketch the cycle of love and the seasons, with spring's befuddling the mind, summer's overly ripe emotions, and the sensible correction of gusty feelings brought on by autumn and winter.

The last part of *Fêtes galantes*, from number fourteen to the end, is much darker in certain parts, which stand out against the gracile and tenuous poems. Suddenly the neoclassical landscape becomes almost supernaturally threatening as intimations of a somber time to come obtrude:

> Un vieux faune de terre cuite
> Rit au centre des boulingrins,
> Présageant sans doute une suite
> Mauvaise à ces instants sereins
>
> Qui m'ont conduit et t'ont conduite,
> —Mélancoliques pèlerins,—
> Jusqu'à cette heure dont la fuite
> Tournoie au son des tambourins. ("Le Faune")

An old terracotta faun laughs in the middle of the bowling greens, presaging doubtless a bad end for these serene moments, which have led us, you and me, melancholy pilgrims, as far as this hour whose flight whirls to the sound of tambourines. ("The Faun")

The "pilgrims" are searching for their destiny, which the statue and the moment reveal. The sinister time point is marked ironically by the festive clinking of tambourines. The musical metaphor leads into the next poem, a contrasting one that demonstrates certain recurrent stylistic traits of *Fêtes*. Under singing boughs (a favorite image of Verlaine's) we find a *concert champêtre:*

> Les donneurs de sérénades
> Et les belles écouteuses
> Echangent des propos fades
> Sous les ramures chanteuses.
>
> C'est Tircis et c'est Aminte,
> Et c'est l'éternel Clitandre,
> Et c'est Damis qui pour mainte
> Cruelle fait maint vers tendre.

Leurs courtes vestes de soie,
Leurs longues robes à queues,
Leur élégance, leur joie
Et leurs molles ombres bleues

Tourbillonnent dans l'extase
D'une lune rose et grise,
Et la mandoline jase
Parmi les frissons de brise. ("Mandoline")

The serenade givers and beautiful listeners exchange insipid remarks under the singing boughs. There is Tircis, and Aminta and the eternal Clitander, and Damis who for many a cruel one makes many a tender verse. Their short silk jackets, their long dresses with trains, their elegance, their joy, and their soft blue shadows whirl in the ecstasy of a pink and gray moon, and the mandolin chatters amid the quivering breeze. ("Mandolin")

To create an effect of faded charm, Verlaine borrows names from neoclassical comedy; the second stanza contrasts sharply with the fourth where, moving into his own distinctive imagery, he has the lovers vanish in a complex of movement, emotion, attenuated light and color, and sound. One important stylistic invention of *Fêtes galantes* is the conveyance at once of lyric beauty and insipidity: the neoclassical figures must appear alternately or even simultaneously exquisite and colorless.

A serenade-like lyric, a *précieux* verse letter imitated from Théophile de Viau, and another *conversation galante* precede the final and most symbolic of the commedia dell'arte poems. In it, the male characters dance around Columbine, who lures and spurns them. She become a malevolent force, like the faun, leading them to *désastre*, in the original astrological sense of fated by an evil star. Another statue, more past tenses, and a significant time point bring us closer to the emptiness that lies at the end of *Fêtes:*

Le vent de l'autre nuit a jeté bas l'Amour
Qui, dans le coin le plus mystérieux du parc,
Souriait en bandant malignement son arc,
Et dont l'aspect nous fit tant songer tout un jour!

> Oh! c'est triste de voir debout le piédestal
> Tout seul! Et des pensers mélancoliques vont
> Et viennent dans mon rêve où le chagrin profond
> Evoque un avenir solitaire et fatal. ("L'Amour par terre")

The wind the other night threw down the Cupid, who, in the park's most mysterious corner, smiled while slyly stretching his bow, and whose look made us so pensive for a whole day. Oh, it's sad to see the pedestal upright all alone. And melancholy thoughts come and go in my reverie, in which deep sorrow summons up a lonely, destined future. ("The Fallen Cupid")

Just one more poem of languorous ecstasy in half-light remains before "Colloque sentimental," the winter's night walk of two ghosts, of which only one can remember shared pleasures.

Fêtes galantes symbolizes the conflict of libido, represented by commedia dell arte figures, and repression, through politeness or irony, embodied in the elaborately conventionalized neoclassical scenes. Desire is connected to the fear of fate and death, and the subtle time scheme of the work suggests ever more urgently that instincts will lead to *désastre*. In the actual conclusion, however, fate is contained by politeness and mitigated by insentience, a triumph of convention and repression. The latter are rendered most extraordinarily in the poem by the imagery of attenuation: even ecstasy appears with faint colors and insubstantial outlines. The insipidity of the garden setting, with its pale statues, absence of flowers, and stunted trees conveys safeness and protection from catastrophes of desire. This symbolism recurs elsewhere in Verlaine, as well as its opposite; here brilliant color is painful:

> Les roses étaient toutes rouges,
> Et les lierres étaient tout noirs.
>
> Chère, pour peu que tu te bouges,
> Renaissent tous mes désespoirs.
>
> Le ciel était trop bleu, trop tendre,
> La mer trop verte et l'air trop doux.
>
> Je crains toujours,—ce qu'est d'attendre!
> Quelque fuite atroce de vous. ("Spleen")

The roses were all red, the ivy all black. Dear, if you move even a little, all my despair is reborn. The sky was too blue, too tender, the sea too green and the air too mild. I still fear—it can be expected: a horrible escape on your part. ("Spleen")

All the imagery of *bercement, fadeur, langueur, pâleur,* and *monotonie* in Verlaine is an attempt to conjure away violent emotions with their unwanted consequences.

The symbolic technique of *Fêtes galantes* is not entirely unrelated to fragmentation, such as we encounter it, say, in Pound, although the texture is comparatively simple. Bits of scenes, mood poems, are combined with a very few lyrics which state a theme quite explicitly, like "Le Faune." The relation of tones, the juxtaposition of images, and the subtle, dynamic use of time points permit us to perceive an interplay of libido, fear, and containment seen against the background of aging. This psychological drama has none of the dimensions frequent in French Symbolism—the conception of solipsism or subjective idealism, the exaltation of beauty or the creative imagination—nor is the thematic material derived from the French romantics; rather it foreshadows later conceptions of the warring forces of the mind.

2. Minores

French romantic literature is filled with all kinds of nearly unbearable tensions, ranging from the divine and demonic opposition of *Les Fleurs du mal* to the antitheses in fiction between the individual and society or between reverie and reality or action. Late nineteenth-century poetry also contains dualisms, though often of a different order, and less frequently embodied in large antithetical designs within one poem. Exploring the literature of the period, we encounter the imagery of purity, as in Valéry's "Les Vaines Danseuses" or "Hélène," or allusions to legends involving asceticism and renunciation. The story of Parsifal in particular gives rise to numerous analogous plots; variations include, for example, Merrill's "Conte" or Hérold's "Floriane et Persigant." Hérold also wrote a playlet in verse with another typical plot structure: "La Dame parmi les lys" waits for a perfect knight; waiting or exile is a counterpart to the quest. We see in these examples the action of grace, visions of beauty, and a sexually idealized figure. There is a pronounced degree of correspondence between them: the general idea of purity embraces more than one kind of waiting, quest, or vision. A sacred virgin, the female equivalent of the chaste knight, sometimes appears, and the favorite images of the contemplation of pure beauty—moon, water, garden, unicorn, birds—often surround an idealized feminine waiting figure. The divine and the aesthetic are difficult to disentangle, and in a sense it is artificial to separate them. Multiple meanings are a characteristic of allegorical symbolism, which is also suggested by the frequent medieval or romantic setting; however, the religious interpretation of romance, which was uppermost in a medieval understanding of Parsifal and his legend, is qualified by the fact that the most intense religion for many late nineteenth-century poets was that of art. In these poems fragments of sacramental medieval legend occur, but the meaning of grace is more the attainment of beauty than anything properly religious; the general transference of religious vocabulary to art is widespread and accounts for much imagery. Purity is not always expressed in the setting of romance, however, and when the scene is modern, dying flowers and sickness may convey beautiful spirituality as in Rodenbach's poem on hands; medieval imagery, frequent as it is, is by no means the only way to suggest art, grace, and idealized sexuality.

Here is one of Samain's poems on beauty; like many, it manages, while not a piece in a framework of romance, to convey something otherworldly:

> J'adore l'indécis, les sons, les couleurs frêles,
> Tout ce qui tremble, ondule, et frissonne, et chatoie,
> Les cheveux et les yeux, l'eau, les feuilles, la soie,
> Et la spiritualité des formes grêles;
>
> Les rimes se frôlant comme des tourterelles,
> La fumée où le songe en spirales tournoie,
> La chambre au crépuscule, où Son profil se noie,
> Et la caresse de Ses mains surnaturelles;
>
> L'heure de ciel au long des lèvres câlinée,
> L'âme comme d'un poids de délice inclinée,
> L'âme qui meurt ainsi qu'une rose fanée,

Et tel coeur d'ombre chaste, embaumé de mystère,
Où veille, comme le rubis d'un lampadaire,
Nuit et jour, un amour mystique et solitaire. ("Dilection")

I love the indeterminate, frail sounds, and colors, everything that trembles, undulates, and shivers, and glistens, hair and eyes, water, leaves, silk, and the spirituality of slim forms; rhymes brushing against each other like doves, smoke in which dreams spiral, the bedroom in the twilight, where Her profile grows dim, and the caress of Her supernatural hands; the bright hour caressed along the lips, the soul bent as if beneath a burden of delight, the soul dying like a withered rose; and a heart of chaste shadow, fragrant with mystery, in which a mystic, lonely love keeps its vigil night and day, like the ruby of a holy lamp. ("Delight")

Here the aesthetic, erotic, and religious ideals mingle inextricably, although ultimately it seems to be the first category to which the others are analogous, above all if we look at the broad tendencies of late nineteenth-century poetry.

The opposite of the imagery of purity is that of life and its *tragique*. It has often been said that there is no tragedy in the nineteenth century, that its counterpart was Dickens' novel of pathos, or else that genuine tragic emotion is to be found rather in Herman Melville, Soren Kierkegaard, or Fyodor Dostoyevsky. While I do not disagree with the last proposition, I think that an important manifestation of tragedy occurs in certain poets. In Baudelaire, for example, the dualisms of romantic literature have the seriousness and elevation of tone we associate with tragedy, and the thematics of *Les Fleurs du mal* have the broad cultural significance we find in Shakespeare, Jean Racine, or Sophocles. In later French poets, we find that the disappearance of Christianity left a series of paradoxes about life, which can be called a *tragique*, a lyric and ironic epitome, in the absence of formal tragedy. These paradoxes are far from being the idiosyncratic vision of merely three or four poets; they underlie pieces of fiction as well, and can be illustrated in the work of that large body of distinguished painters and graphic artists of the turn of the century whose work has a thematic relationship with Symbolist poetry and who have only recently begun to attract the attention of art historians.

The tragic thematics of poetry in the 1880s and 1890s is conveyed most often in implied rather than openly stated paradoxes, which we must read in the context of waning religious belief. First of all, the figure of the prostitute, depraved woman, or sorceress suggests that eroticism, which should be fecund, leads to sterility and death. The desire for death generally is the great tragic paradox of life in this literature. Ephraïm Mikhaël's "Florimond" is a typical poem of a quest that fails and ends with entrapment in *mauvais amour*. Parsifal's encounter with Kundry and the flower maidens provides the model, and, while in the many variations like Edouard Pilon's "Les Tristes" (*Le Poème de mes soirs*, 1896), the knight does not always succumb, the peculiar beauty of the women is dwelt on at length. Vivian, as in Jean Lorrain's "Brocéliande" (*La Forêt bleue*, 1883) and Salome are favorite archetypes. The latter is found not only in well-known pieces but in such places as O. W. Milosz's "Salomé" (*Le Poème des décadences*, 1899) and in Samain:

> Des soirs fiévreux et forts comme une venaison,
> Mon âme traîne en soi l'ennui d'un vieil Hérode;
> Et prostrée aux coussins, où son mal la taraude,
> Trouve à toute pensée un goût de trahison.
>
> Pour fuir le désespoir qui souffle à l'horizon,
> Elle appelle la sombre danseuse qui rôde,
> Et Salomé vient dans la salle basse et chaude
> Secouer le péché touffu de sa toison.
>
> Elle danse!... Oh! pendant qu'avec l'éclat des pierres
> Au soleil, tes deux yeux brûlent dans leurs paupières,
> Mon âme, entends-tu pas bêler dans le verger?
>
> Tu le sais bien pourtant que l'enfer te l'amène
> Et qu'elle va, ce soir, réclamer pour sa peine
> L'Agneau blanc de ton pauvre coeur pour l'égorger. (*Au Jardin de l'Infante*)

On evenings feverish and strong as venison, my soul drags with it the ennui of an old Herod; and prostrate on pillows where its pain drills into it, finds a taste of treachery in every thought. To escape despair blowing on the horizon, it summons the roving dark dancer, and Salome comes into the low, hot room shaking the dense sin of her mane. She dances. Oh, while with the gleam of stones in the sun your two eyes burn in their lids, my soul, don't you hear the bleating in the orchard? You know all the same that hell brings her to you, and that she is going to demand this evening for her trouble the white lamb of your poor heart, to slaughter it.

Men, of course, are the willing accomplices of the depraved woman, as Samain's poem makes clear: it is their desire for death which creates the relationship, one in which sexuality must be understood as a facet of the larger *tragique*.

In the convention of romance the theme that glory is an illusion is an expression of the *tragique;* it can be combined as in Régnier's "Salut à l'étrangère" (*Poèmes anciens et romanesques*, 1892) with servitude to the sorceress. The medieval setting occurs also in the many poems about destruction and the triumph of barbarians over civilization, an expression of the tragic irony of history, with its oscillation between excess and effeteness (Mikhaël offers more than one example: "Hiérodoule," "Le Mage," "L'Etrangère"). The prostitute is an important figure in more or less realistic poems like Ghil's "De long en large" (*Légendes d'âmes et de sangs*, 1885); she enslaves like the sorceress of romance (and of course here we see another link with the contemporary novel). The modern city is her domain, and the many urban poems of the late nineteenth century tend to express, with or without the prostitute figure, the deathly quality of the setting man has made for himself: Verhaeren and Rodenbach are particularly powerful poets of the city. There is not only a human expression of life's *tragique*, the prostitute, and an artificial one, the city, but also a natural one: in both medieval and modern poems the sunset, the *agonie du soleil* and *sang du crépuscule*, symbolize the desire for death in life. Sometimes it has erotic overtones:

> Comme ce soir d'octobre, anxieux et puissant,
> Qu'empourpre de sa mort, splendeur désespérée,
> Le plus royal soleil de la saison dorée,
> Voluptueusement dans mon âme descend!
>
> O fureur des baisers! Jets de flamme et de sang!
> Rouges lèvres que mord une bouche égarée!
> Derniers cris de la chair misérable et sacrée!
> Votre ivresse est pareille au ciel éblouissant! (Albert Giraud, "Automne," *La Guirlande des dieux*, 1910)

How voluptuously into my soul descends this October evening, anxious, powerful, which the most royal sun of the gilded season reddens with its death, a desperate splendor. O fury of kisses, streams of flame and blood! Red lips bitten by a wild mouth! Last screams of the wretched, sacred flesh! Your intoxication is like the dazzling sky! ("Autumn")

The sunset is a major symbol of life's paradox in Laforgue and occurs in most other poets of the period; it is the principal cosmic metaphor of the late nineteenth century, appealing to poets for both the imagistic possibilities inherent in it and the contradictory associations of glory, death, beauty, and wounds. Here it is combined with unusual scientific imagery, and poison is distilled from it:

Les vitres tout à l'heure étaient pâles et nues,
Mais peu à peu le soir entra dans la maison;
On y sent à present le péril d'un poison.
C'est que les vitres, pour le soir, sont des cornues
Où se distille on ne sait quoi dans leur cristal;
Le couchant y répand un or qui les colore;
Et pour qu'enfin le crépuscule s'élabore,
L'ombre, comme pour un apprêt médicinal,
Semble y verser ses ténèbres, d'une fiole.
Dans les verres, teintés de ce qui souffre en eux,
Un nuage s'achève, un reflet s'étiole;
Il est en germe quelque chose de vénéneux,
Menaçant la maison déjà presque endormie;
Et c'est de plus en plus le nocturne élixir . . .
Ah! les vitres et leur délétère chimie
Qui chaque soir ainsi me font un peu mourir! (Georges Rodenbach, "Le Soir dans les vitres" XI, *Les Vies encloses*)

The windowpanes were just now pale and bare. But gradually the evening entered the house; you now feel in it the danger of a poison. That is because the panes in the evening are retorts, distilling something unknown in their crystal; the sunset spreads gold, coloring them, and finally, to create the twilight, shadow, as if preparing medicine, seems to pour into them its darkness from a vial. In the panes, tinted with what is suffering in them, a cloud dissipates, a reflection grows faint. There is in potential something poisonous threatening the already sleeping house. And it is turning more and more into the night elixir. Ah! the panes and their noxious chemistry, which thus each evening kill me a little! ("Evening in the Windows" XI)

The particular force of this sunset imagery is strengthened if we remember that day is commonly described as smoky and foggy, a quite realistic representation of a northern metropolis like Paris, London, or the Belgian cities in the coal-burning nineteenth century.

While the imagery of purity and life's *tragique* usually do not occur at the same time in lyrics, we find them so widespread that we can speak of them as together forming an imaginative configuration in late nineteenth-century poetry. The underlying idea is that life is death and that purity, renunciation, asceticism, spirituality, and barely incarnate beauty (Samain's "formes grêles") alone are not touched by death. They are ambiguous, of course, in that they suggest not so much life as the otherworldly and the unattainable. The analogy with the Christian paradox of losing life in order to gain it is important, and, in general, the fact that Christianity arose in an epoch of decadence and was originally oriented to the life beyond accounts for the tonality of the abundant religious imagery we find. Life as death and the true life as the beyond are most significantly symbolized by the depraved woman and the virgin. The antithesis is accompanied by a similarity: neither is fecund (prostitutes are commonly represented as sterile in the nineteenth century). The symbolic denial of fecundity in life might best be explained by a reference to Zola's realism, where the spawning proletariat is represented as degenerate and therefore blighted in its pullulation: reproduction is genetic decline. The notion of fertility is displaced onto the artist and his creation, which may be represented as the achievement of purity or merely a struggle toward beauty. The antinatural invention of the black flower, a recurring image with varying values, sometimes stands for the will to artifice, as does the theme of clown or circus. These attempts to transcend life in life do not succeed—the case of Des Esseintes—for beauty is tragically situated in a beyond. The tormented desire to rise above life is sometimes represented by the Chimaera, with its French connotations of a fantastic dream.

It is important that we do not assimilate these themes and images to the symbolism of good and evil (despite use of words like sin), such as we find it in Baudelaire and other romantics. This poetry is generally free of true theological conceptions. (Exceptions like Dujardin's *Antonia* trilogy, where the virgin-depraved woman ultimately gives birth to a redeemer, are quite explicit.) Traditionally nature is the source of images of the good; evil implies contrivance and the inorganic; multiple details derive from these broad categories. Here, however, antinature images belong in part to the positive values of beauty; the traditional symbolism of evil is split up and rearranged. Artifice, craft, sterility, and the rejection of nature's laws suggest the eternity of beauty. All this follows from the denial of fertility in both life and the realm of the beautiful. It would, of course, be possible in a larger view to conflate the antithesis of life and art and maintain that the total symbolism of the late nineteenth century is demonic with reference to earlier symbolic designs. This would perhaps provide a useful definition of the word decadent as applied not to style but to a world view.

In our symbolic patterns we find, not unexpectedly, variations according to taste and talent. Laforgue, for example, handles ironically the depraved woman and virgin in *Derniers Vers* in keeping with a realistic convention. Quillard's short play *L'Errante*, which takes place on life's winter- and sunset-suffused rock, envisages an anarchist revolt against the *tragique*. Quest poems may have, rather than an implicit meaning, a kind of discursive mode, often with personifications or sharply explicit analogies: Fontainas' *Les Vergers illusoires* is of this type. Sometimes the quest takes the form of memory, seeking for what has been lost: this we find in Kahn's work. Régnier, whose poems are among the most interesting of the *minores'*, introduces the symbols of a failure of union or marriage and of the wasteland. His best *Poèmes anciens et romanesques* (1892) are pure allegorical symbolism with no discursive glosses or personifications:

Nul luxe épanoui de roses par l'Eté
Ne pare l'Ile aride où vient un vent de cendre,
De l'aube au crépuscule, inexorable, épandre
Un destin de désastre et de stérilité.
. . . .
Un exil de jadis et de terres où rie
Autour des Villes d'ombre une fête de palmes
Pleure en leurs voix d'amour et veille dans leur songe;
Ah! quand viendront vers Elles le bruit lent des rames
Et la proue écumante et le rostre qui plonge
Et des yeux doux pour encor croire à leur mensonge!

Elles sont lasses de porter, les Vigilantes,
Les miroirs, les amphores vides et les lampes. ("La Vigile des grèves")

No luxuriant roses blossoming in summer adorn the arid isle where an ashen wind from dawn to twilight inexorably comes to spread a destiny of misfortune and sterility . . . An exile of long ago, from lands where festive palms laugh around the cities of shadow, weeps in their amorous voices and keeps vigil in their dreams. Ah, when will the slow sound of oars draw near them, and the foaming prow, and the plunging rostrum, and eyes gentle enough to still believe in their lie! They are weary, the watching women, of bearing mirrors, empty amphoras, and lamps. ("The Vigil on the Strand")

By no means were all of the minor poets of the 1880s and 1890s so confident in their handling of symbolism as to attempt to imitate the subtler tradition of allegory, which dispenses with the "land of sorrow" kind of metaphor or statue-like personifications of abstractions and adheres to the etymological sense of saying something other or in addition to the literal. The long poems are usually quite explicit in their general meaning. Generally the lesser poets' best work is in the lyric where a single symbol of destiny like the sunset or Salome conveys the burden of the poem without narrative or lengthy development. Régnier himself in one of his best long poems, "Motifs de légende et de mélancolie," merely accumulates varying forms of the symbol of the union that does not take place, the failure of the spiritual translated into physical terms.

It is remarkable how much of the poetry of the late nineteenth century turns around symbols of death in life and the aspiration to beauty, grace, and an idealized sexual figure. Of the mood poems we examined earlier, the ones by Verhaeren and Valéry, which have analogues in other poets' work, bear a definite affective relationship to this scheme, even if they cannot truly be said to contain in themselves the paradoxes, plurality of meanings, or contrasts that would make of them genuine symbolic structures. Certainly, however, it is legitimate to read them in the light of the larger picture of symbolism in the period. When we piece together a pattern of themes and images from many lyrics, some long poems, and a few short plays, we are generalizing from specific cases and making explicit what is clearly implied, so as to suggest a coherent way of reading much of the work of the period. The interest of doing this lies partly in the attempt to see how the notion of symbolism is applicable to it and partly in establishing a poetic order in relation to which we may place Mallarmé's verse.

3. Mallarmé

Some of Mallarmé's early *Parnasse contemporain* poems are very finished examples of romantic dualism and tragic emotion. They are organized around the opposite poles of art and life, in an adaptation of Baudelaire's great division of "Spleen et Idéal." The dominant symbol of art is *l'azur*, which is also associated in "Les Fleurs" with eternity ("vieil azur"), the moon, and otherworldly flowers, so often a symbol of poetry. Rebirth is an important theme: the world is reborn in the morning air in "Le Sonneur," but the tolling of the bells scarcely reaches the ringer, and he contemplates suicide because of his night-curse. It must be noted that, while the sky and air are symbols of art and the ideal in "Le Sonneur," Mallarmé uses them elsewhere, as in "Renouveau," to designate coarse, material life: this is the literal sky and springtime, which is opposed to the winter of artistic creation. These early poems seem at times very ambiguous because of the double sense of words like *l'azur* and winter carrying opposing connotations: in "L'Azur" bad weather is not the season of art but of carnal, gross comfort; the sky, glimpsed through holes in the smoky atmosphere, symbolizes the summons to artistic creation. In "L'Azur" art is a curse, not serene happiness: we see immediately that Mallarmé is complicating his themes. The winter sky, the blue sky, art, and life have conflicting associations of both pleasure and anguish. The danger of art is made most clear at the end of "Les Fenêtres," where, after leaping through the windowpane into art or *mysticité*, the poet may fall into eternal nothingness rather than attain beauty. The idea of possible rebirth in "Les Fenêtres" is continued in "Tristesse d'été," where the poet and his mistress will never be a single mummy, that is, a body prepared to live again, but the poet may alone aspire to the contemplation of *l'azur*. In "Angoisse" the sterile prostitute is the companion for a poet who is artistically barren. All these elaborate oppositions, the double meaning, literal and figurative, of *l'azur*, poetry as serenity or anguish, may seem like the work of a confused, immature artist overly influenced by Baudelaire (whose *poète maudit* figure, however, is ironically and even parodistically presented in "L'Azur"), were it not that Mallarmé draws these antitheses and similarities together in a perfectly articulated scheme in "Las de l'amer repos," an ars poetica, in which a number of the complexities of Mallarmé's mature syntax appear for the first time:

> Las de l'amer repos où ma paresse offense
> Une gloire pour qui jadis j'ai fui l'enfance
> Adorable des bois de roses sous l'azur
> Naturel, et plus las sept fois du pacte dur
> De creuser par veillée une fosse nouvelle
> Dans le terrain avare et froid de ma cervelle,
> Fossoyeur sans pitié pour la stérilité,
> —Que dire à cette Aurore, ô Rêves, visité
> Par les roses, quand, peur de ses roses livides,
> Le vaste cimetière unira les trous vides?—

Tired of the bitter repose by which my laziness offends a glory for which long ago I fled the adorable childhood of rose thickets under the natural blue sky, and seven times more tired of the harsh pact by which I dig, awake at night, a new grave in the miserly cold earth of my brain, a gravedigger without pity for my own sterility— what should I say to dawn, O Dreams, when its rosy light visits me, when, fearful of dawn's pale roses, the great cemetery closes up its empty holes?—

(These ten lines are merely the modifier of a *je* yet to come.) The graveyard imagery represents the paradox of the will to death in life, and the art it characterizes is poetry embodying that *tragique*. Mallarmé is careful to establish the antinatural quality of this art, which, however, will not be contrasted with poetry of life and nature of the ordinary European kind:

> Je veux délaisser l'Art vorace d'un pays
> Cruel, et, souriant aux reproches vieillis
> Que me font mes amis, le passé, le génie,
> Et ma lampe qui sait pourtant mon agonie,
> Imiter le Chinois au coeur limpide et fin
> De qui l'extase pure est de peindre la fin
> Sur ses tasses de neige à la lune ravie
> D'une bizarre fleur qui parfume sa vie
> Transparente, la fleur qu'il a sentie, enfant,
> Au filigrane bleu de l'âme se greffant.
> Et, la mort telle avec le seul rêve du sage,
> Serein, je vais choisir un jeune paysage
> Que je peindrais encor sur les tasses, distrait.

Une ligne d'azur mince et pâle serait
Un lac, parmi le ciel de porcelaine nue,
Un clair croissant perdu par une blanche nue
Trempe sa corne calme en la glace des eaux,
Non loin de trois grands cils d'émeraude, roseaux.

I want to abandon the devouring Art of a cruel country, and smiling at the old re-proaches of my friends, the past, genius, and my lamp, which certainly knows my agony, to imitate the limpid, delicate-hearted Chinese, whose pure ecstasy is to paint, on snow cups ravished from the moon, the death of a strange flower which scents his transparent life, the flower which as a child he felt grafted to the blue fili-gree of his soul. And, since my death would be accompanied only by the wise man's dream, serenely, I will choose a young landscape to paint absentmindedly on cups. A line of slim, pale blue would be a lake; in the sky of naked porcelain, a bright crescent moon lost in a white cloud dips its calm tip in the frigid waters, not far from the three great emerald eyelashes: reeds.

This spiritualized oriental art is remote from a dynamic, organic vi-sion of nature: it is moonlit, cool as the material it is painted on and, in contrast with European representations of nature, curiously sterile seeming. Here we reach the pattern of antithesis and similarity we have already seen: both kinds of art are nocturnal and suggestive of death ("la mort telle") and sterility; their opposition lies in the fact that the first one, the tragic art, signifies death in life, while the sec-ond proposes a vision of beauty beyond life. This is the translation of the symbolism of the prostitute and the virgin into opposing methods and contents of artistic creation. Mallarmé realized this antithesis, only to move beyond it two decades before it became widespread, and while we might, in a somewhat theoretical fashion, be able to trace sources for the poem, we would find that they do not fully account for it.

The crisis that Mallarmé underwent in 1866–1867 and that opened the way to his later art was one of felt thought, involving both philos-ophy and health. It began with anguish over a kind of antithetical thinking which he could have learned from his friend Henri Cazalis or some other writer interested in Hindu and Buddhist thought:

Yes, I know, we are but empty forms of matter, yet quite sublime for having in-vented God and our soul. So sublime, my friend, that I want to treat myself to the spectacle of matter—conscious of being and yet leaping wildly into Dream, which it knows doesn't exist—singing the soul and all the similar divine impressions which have accumulated in us since primitive times, these glorious lies, in the face of Nothingness, which is truth.[1]

The terms of Being and Nothingness will clarify this antithesis later on. The intellectual difficulty of the opposition is that it involves paradox, since Nothingness tends to swallow up Being, and the former cannot be conceived of save from the standpoint of the latter; it is a more radical kind of dualism than that which inspired the romantics. The solution to this dilemma, which put in question Mallarmé's existence as well as that of poetry, was in a tripartite, dialectical movement, which is expressed in more than one way. Mallarmé considered at one point that he was dead and reborn as an impersonal mind coextensive with the universe. Being, Nothingness, and the Absolute or Beauty as synthesis is another triadic formulation which emphasizes the work of art rather than the poet. The Absolute or transcendent Idea, as it is sometimes put, implies purity and the elimination of chance, *hasard*, from the work of art. Some contact with Hegelian thought, through intermediaries, had suggested the need of dialectic, the conception of an absolute, and the relationship between mind and being, although the result is a peculiarly Mallarméan adaptation. The escape from dualism by a three-stage movement remains the essential conquest of this crisis.

Mallarmé's letters during those years were filled with the announcement of poetic projects, despite a certain fear of sterility. When the crisis was over and its powerful intellectual impetus dissipated, Mallarmé may have produced very little—the dating of many poems is an insoluble problem—but he had written at least one poem demonstrating that the tripartite dialectic movement was a valuable acquisition for poetic technique:

> Ses purs ongles très haut dédiant leur onyx,
> L'Angoisse, ce minuit, soutient, lampadophore,
> Maint rêve vespéral brûlé par le Phénix
> Que ne recueille pas de cinéraire amphore
>
> Sur les crédences, au salon vide: nul ptyx,
> Aboli bibelot d'inanité sonore,
> (Car le Maître est allé puiser des pleurs au Styx
> Avec ce seul objet dont le Néant s'honore).

> Mais proche la croisée au nord vacante, un or
> Agonise selon peut-être le décor
> Des licornes ruant du feu contre une nixe,
>
> Elle, défunte nue en le miroir, encor
> Que, dans l'oubli fermé par le cadre, se fixe
> De scintillations sitôt le septuor.

With its pure nails lifting high their onyx, Anguish, a lampbearer, holds up, this midnight, many an evening dream burnt up by the sunset and not gathered in any amphora of ashes. On the credenzas in the empty parlor: no ptyx, the destroyed knick-knack of sonorous emptiness, (for the Master has gone to fetch tears from the Styx, with this, the only object honored by Nothingness). But by the window open to the north, a golden gleam is dying perhaps along the ornament of unicorns rushing fire against a water-sprite—her dead and naked in the mirror, although, in the oblivion surrounded by the frame, immediately there is fixed the sparkling septet of the Big Dipper.

Put quite succinctly, the starlight at the end of the poem represents a synthesis of light (day) and darkness (night). This severe patterning of images could be read metaphysically as Being, Nothingness, and Absolute, or morally, stars standing for hope. Its beauty derives at once from wonderful stylistic detail and from the austere tripartite structure. The objects, like the statue of anguish serving as a lamp base, the peculiarly concrete-nonconcrete burnt up dreams, the inexplicable ptyx, chosen for its mystery, and the mirror frame, with its carving of unicorns appearing to attack the sprite, have both a richly suggestive quality and a strict subordination to the dialectic design: this balance is one of the most difficult things to obtain in a purely symbolic poem, where detail often does not seem to fit in or else overwhelms the whole.

While day has vanished when "Ses purs ongles" commences, there is sufficient reference to sunset to establish that light as the initial stage of the dialectic of images. The specific character of the terms used is worth noting: evening dreams are burned up by the Phoenix's fiery death. Sunset implies quite clearly life's *tragique:* Mallarmé has taken a symbol which was to be widespread in the late nineteenth century and put it into a pattern with other symbols, the ptyx and the stars. This is, of course, a much more complex kind of symbolism than we find in most poets, where one symbol or a mere opposition suffices. Interestingly enough, Mallarmé can make a related image pattern with a different value: "La chevelure vol" deals with sunset, the hypothetical total darkness of night, and the new light that comes about, emanating from the lady. Here there is little symbolism, merely a conceit. The light-dark-light pattern in "Victorieusement fui" again is in the nature of a fanciful compliment. At most we could say that the lady's light is an escape from the natural cycle with its fatalistic implications. In "Quand l'ombre menaça de la fatale loi" it is the poet-*génie*, "dazzled by his faith," whose light shines through the cosmos of stars he has lit.

The correlation of the poet's mind and the universe Mallarmé spoke of in his letters of 1866–1867 is suggested by the cosmic imagery of "Ses purs ongles" and "Quand l'ombre." Much later, in Mallarmé's critical writings, we find another series of expressions that convey the need for images of some scope: the structure of poems can be ideally called "l'ensemble des rapports existant dans tout," "pur ensemble . . . des relations entre tout," "fils de ces rapports qui forment les vers," "Ligne espacée de tout point à tout autre pour instituer l'idée," "saisir les rapports . . . rares ou multipliés."[2] If the poems we have just mentioned seem to fit the idea of *rapports de tout* in the sense of imagery linking man with the universe, we must remember that they are only "teintés d'absolu," in Mallarmé's phrase. At the same time, we can see how the imagery of "Ses purs ongles" derives from the "page of sky" of the ideal theater and how its thematic content can be set beside the passion of man or the drama of the seasons, subjects suitable for the artwork of the future. Mallarmé felt that despite the disappearance of the Mass—as living theater rather than dead ritual—the time was not yet come for a new theatrical form whose music would be abstract relations instead of real sounds and the words of which would encompass the universe. (Mallarmé found Wagner's work to represent a crude compromise with the material side of music and the banal plot exigencies of nineteenth-century theater.) In the meantime, there was dance, the most poetic theatrical form, and a kind of poetry in which myths, especially that of the solar cycle, could perhaps suggest to us some notion of the ideal *rapports de tout:*

M'introduire dans ton histoire
C'est en héros effarouché
S'il a du talon nu touché
Quelque gazon de territoire

A des glaciers attentatoire
Je ne sais le naïf péché
Que tu n'auras pas empêché
De rire très haut sa victoire

Dis si je ne suis pas joyeux
Tonnerre et rubis au moyeu
De voir en l'air que ce feu troue

Avec des royaumes épars
Comme mourir pourpre la roue
Du seul vespéral de mes chars.

If I intrude into your history, it is like a hero startled, if with his naked heel he has touched some territorial turf. I ingenuously do not realize it a sin to assault your glaciers, a victory which you will not have prevented me from laughing loudly at. Listen, how happy I am to see pierce the air, looking down on scattered realms, the fiery wheel, its hubs of thunder and rubies, dying as it were into the purple light, the wheel of my only evening chariot.

The sun's chariot leads the triumphal procession in this the middle-aged poet's only victory, a sexual conquest. The mythic and imperial imagery of "Victorieusement fui" recurs, as the poet's mistress becomes a subdued land invaded by him, who is now assured of a place in her chronicles.

The *char vespéral* in "M'introduire" has given more than one commentator some difficulty, and it suggests the problems that arise with the *rapports de tout*. Mallarmé had a series of terms he used more than once to try to convey something about the detail of the *rapports:* evocation, allusion, *état d'âme*, symbol, suggestion, near creation, mystery. These words are attempts to situate poetry somewhere between pure mimesis or the descriptiveness Mallarmé deplored in poetry and an incantatory self-contained pattern of words, in which, however, there would be "some reminiscence of the object." In practice, Mallarmé's peculiar mode of diction tends to involve mingling several kinds of figurative language, as here in the Verlaine *tombeau*, where we see that cosmic imagery is often relevant to poems of praise:

> Le roc noir courroucé que la bise le roule
> Ne s'arrêtera ni sous de pieuses mains
> Tâtant sa ressemblance avec les maux humains
> Comme pour en bénir quelque funeste moule.
>
> Ici presque toujours si le ramier roucoule
> Cet immatériel deuil opprime de maints
> Nubiles plis l'astre mûri des lendemains
> Dont un scintillement argentera la foule.

The black rock angered that the north wind rolls it will not even stop for pious hands feeling for its resemblance to human ills, as if to bless some fatal mold. Here, almost always, if the dove coos, this immaterial mourning presses in, with cloudy folds, on the ripe star of morrows, whose sparkling will silver the crowd.

Whether the rock is a tombstone or a black cloud is an initial difficulty; if it is the latter, then the immaterial mourning refers to it. Should tombstone be the reading, it becomes clearer how hands can touch the rock. The disembodied hands, which do not seem to be those of the crowd, measuring *maux*, the gratuitously appearing cloud (if, indeed, we take it as a cloud), the unexpected doves, which appear to represent Verlaine's poetry, the occurrences in the sky create that characteristic mingling of symbol, metonymy, visual periphrasis, and some vaguely real background that is so characteristic of Mallarmé: words belong to different categories of figurative language in so daring, so theoretically incoherent a way that the success of the poems is always astonishing.

The relationships of imagery in a poem like the Verlaine *tombeau* are intended to make one aware of the peculiar mode of existence of poetic language. As a synthesis of Being and Nothingness, we might expect it to convey something other than the representational content of ordinary literary language and take inchoate or decaying things into account. In the late poems commonly called the triptych, we meet such nuances:

> Tout Orgueil fume-t-il du soir,
> Torche dans un branle étouffée

Sans que l'immortelle bouffée
Ne puisse à l'abandon surseoir!

La chambre ancienne de l'hoir
De maint riche mais chu trophée
Ne serait pas même chauffée
S'il survenait par le couloir.

Does every pride of sunset go up in smoke, a torch put out with a swing of the arm, without the immortal puff being able to survive neglect! The former bedroom of the heir of many a rich but fallen trophy would not even be heated if he suddenly came through the corridor.

The passage into nothingness of the room corresponds to the death of the sun in its haughty, immortal, ever recurrent, display of dying light. The decline of a once great house, as in *Igitur*, *Axël*, or *A rebours*, is suggested, along with the illusory character of glory and the *tragique* of sunset. The contrary-to-fact condition is a characteristic example of negative elaboration, the first in a series that gives the triptych a very special place in the poems where Mallarmé is concerned with rendering the dissolution of Being.

Affres du passé nécessaires
Agrippant comme avec des serres
Le sépulcre de désaveu,

Sous un marbre lourd qu'elle isole
Ne s'allume pas d'autre feu
Que la fulgurante console.

No other fire is lit than, beneath the heavy marble top isolated by it, the blazing console, the necessary agony of the past gripping, as with claws, the tomb of disavowal.

The agony of the past—with the special sense of approaching death contained by the word *affres*—is the weight of family tradition, which is opposed to the disavowal of it suggested by the tombstone-table top. The console's empire legs are represented as clutching with lion's claws at the marble surface that would deny them. The light of the gilt legs is dying with sunset; as often in Mallarmé, a glow or glitter implies the persistence, albeit weakened, of life. The burden of all this imagery is the situation made explicit in a work like *Axël:* the ancestral summons to carry on the family is being neglected.

The opening quatrain of the night sonnet of the triptych exemplifies negative imagery, with a suggestion of incomplete Being:

> Surgi de la croupe et du bond
> D'une verrerie éphémère
> Sans fleurir la veillée amère
> Le col ignoré s'interrompt.

Risen from the rump and the leap of an ephemeral vase, the unknown neck of it breaks off, without adorning with a flower the bitter evening.

Whereas the vase is incomplete, the sylph of the ceiling (comparable to the unicorns and sprite in "Ses purs ongles") represents the virtual:

> Je crois bien que deux bouches n'ont
> Bu, ni son amant ni ma mère,
> Jamais à la même Chimère,
> Moi, sylphe de ce froid plafond!

I certainly believe that two mouths, neither my mother nor her lover's, ever drank from the same fantasy, I the sylph of this cold ceiling.

The many mysterious birds and other vaguely supernatural creatures in Mallarmé's poetry belong to a realm between Being and Nothingness, and in that sense they are highly poetic. Some, like the sylph, are unborn, others are ghosts. They serve to remind one of the essentially otherworldly nature of beauty.

The drink-kiss-union, which the sylph's mother and her lover did not join in, is connected with the vase of the first quatrain:

> Le pur vase d'aucun breuvage
> Que l'inexhaustible veuvage
> Agonise mais ne consent,
>
> Naïf baiser des plus funèbres!
> A rien expirer annonçant
> Une rose dans les ténèbres.

The vase empty of any potion save inexhaustible widowhood agonizes in death but does not consent to exhale anything announcing a rose in the shadows, a naïve funereal kiss.

The pure notion of poetry is always imaginative and therefore abstract in Mallarmé's conception. This rose, which is poetic creation itself, exists only in Mallarmé's idealism, which is not a Platonic system, but rather the ensemble of images engendered by words. This second sonnet fits into the series by envisioning an alternative to the procreation or ancestral summons of the first: a thing of beauty could redeem the night. However, there is no starlight as in "Ses purs ongles" and the curse weighs on the house.

With morning comes imagery especially rich in connotations:

> Une dentelle s'abolit
> Dans le doute du Jeu suprême
> A n'entr'ouvrir comme un blasphème
> Qu'absence éternelle de lit.

Lace vanishes in the uncertain light of the supreme Game and opens upon the blasphemy of an eternally absent bed.

The "Jeu suprême" is basically the seeming conflict of night and day, which the latter wins, but, of course, "Jeu" also suggests the heir's staking his life on some act of creation, a game with fate. The lace seems to be either the window curtains or bed curtains, growing pale and transparent in the morning light. The bed is more a place of birth than of sexual activity, and the blasphemy is against the noble heritage, which will die without children being born in bed.

Mallarmé has many delicate structural elements in the triptych: the relationships among the three sonnets, connected but not tightly so, include notably the birth theme, unstated as such in "Surgi de la croupe" and suddenly quite literal-seeming and prominent in the third sonnet. But within the third sonnet itself there are subtle articulations. The last line of the second quatrain corrects the violent impression of blasphemy in the first:

> Cet unanime blanc conflit
> D'une guirlande avec la même,

Enfui contre la vitre blême
Flotte plus qu'il n'ensevelit.

This unanimous white conflict of a garland with the same, waving against the pale windowpane, floats more than it buries.

The curtains ("guirlandes"), blowing together ("avec la même") in the breeze do not, as a matter of fact, reveal some "buried" or never born heir, or any intent to evade the ancestral charge to procreate. This neutralizing observation forms a transition to the thought of spiritual rebirth or artistic fecundity, the only true kind for the last heir of a great house, equipped, as his forebears had never been, with the superior intellect to understand that true procreation is artistic. This is the decadent myth of the last scion, as *Igitur* and *A rebours* embody it.

Mais, chez qui du rêve se dore
Tristement dort une mandore
Au creux néant musicien

Telle que vers quelque fenêtre
Selon nul ventre que le sien,
Filial on aurait pu naître.

But in whoever gilds himself with dream, there sadly sleeps a mandolin with hollow musical nothingness, a mandolin such that toward some window, by no belly but its own, filially one could have been born.

The concluding contrary-to-fact condition, comparable to certain passages in *Un Coup de dés*, shows Mallarmé's increasing fondness for only indirect affirmations; it is a fitting complement to the elaborate negations of the preceding sonnet. Insofar as the conditional designates rebirth into a world of art and musical order—a metaphysical notion implied already in "Les Fenêtres"—we can see why its extreme daring makes the tense of the impossible appropriate.

In the imagery of the triptych and other poems we can see, to some extent at least, what Mallarmé meant by such oft-quoted phrases as "tout existe pour aboutir à un livre" and the characterization of the ultimate poem as "l'explication orphique de la Terre." Mallarmé's old idea of the correlation of the poet's mind with the universe still holds. Nevertheless, Mallarmé came, in his lecture on *La Musique et les Lettres* (1895), to doubt apparently that idea, structure, and music in the Greek sense, by which he meant the principle of a poem's design, was more than an artist's illusion: "le leurre," "cet au-delà," "rien," "supercherie," "le manque chez nous," "ce qui éclate là-haut." These expressions characterize the deceptive meaningfulness of the cosmos, which seems to make up for the lack of any order on earth by a show, *là-haut* among the stars and beyond, of pattern. A certain ambiguity in *Un Coup de dés* betrays this concern, but it is most explicitly conveyed in the sonnet "A la nue":

> A la nue accablante tu
> Basse de basalte et de laves
> A même les échos esclaves
> Par une trompe sans vertu
>
> Quel sépulcral naufrage (tu
> le sais, écume, mais y baves)
> Suprême une entre les épaves
> Abolit le mât dévêtu
>
> Ou cela que furibond faute
> De quelque perdition haute
> Tout l'abîme vain éployé
>
> Dans le si blanc cheveu qui traîne
> Avarement aura noyé
> Le flanc enfant d'une sirène.

Beneath the overwhelming storm cloud, along the enslaved echoes of waves, a shoal of basalt and lava, what sepulchral shipwreck, unannounced by a worthless horn, destroyed the stripped mast, the topmost piece of the wreckage (you know, foam, but you just drool there)? Or is it that, furious through lack of some high perdition, the whole empty abyss of water outspread can have hungrily drowned, in the white line of foam trailing, the childish flank of a siren?

The question is essentially whether there is some "perdition haute," a malevolent scheme in the universe, *perdition* having both the sense of a sinking ship, *bateau en perdition*, and metaphysical destruction. Either man was destroyed, in some great design, or there was merely foam in the wake of a plunging siren. We have returned to the spectacle of the fitful, meaningless alternation of Being and Nothingness, which was Mallarmé's point of departure in his quest for metaphysical and artistic design.

In a simple reductive fashion it can be said that stars stand for hope in "Ses purs ongles" and *Un Coup de dés*, that "A la nue" is about fate, and that the triptych concludes with the notion that something positive still exists in potential. Many explications arrive at just such conclusions, and there is hardly any difficult modern poetry that cannot be made to yield similarly ordinary ideas. Mallarmé, however, offers an initial example of how such reductivism must be qualified. The suppositive mode of poems like "A la nue" or *Un Coup de dés*, the ambiguity of symbols (while a star may schematically stand for hope, it is also unearthly, inorganic, and remote from life, being even, at times, a *dys-aster*), and the synthesizing, embracing character of dialectic in Mallarmé's triadic poems suggest that besides looking for common shapes, we should make some distinctions about the content of various poems. So the constellation of *Un Coup de dés*, the Big Dipper of "Ses purs ongles," the sexual fulfillment of Hérodiade, and the contemplation of the birth of music at the end of the triptych are more similar movements than identical syntheses. For their art, in distinguishing it from the more ordinary antithetical patterns of contemporary poets, the triadic design, which it is possible to trace in *Un Coup de dés* or find the beginning of implicit in "A la nue," is of capital importance. For their meaning, the multiplicity of levels of reading must be stressed: rough distinctions could be made, for example, among the metaphysical, aesthetic, moral, and psychological or affective planes. This is not to say that symbols can mean anything one wants or that all interpretations seem equally pertinent: one reason we do not use the medieval fourfold levels of interpretation today is that one or two of the levels (especially the moral-imperative) seem irrelevant. But we could say, for example, that the triptych's light and birth imagery represents the drama of Being and Nothingness, that aesthetically the primacy of art over procreation is affirmed, and that the psychological content is the heir's tragic inability to rise to the summons of art. With "Ses purs ongles" one could affirm that the stars, if they signify hope on the moral plane, could also be interpreted as the existence of impersonal beauty as a contrast to man's cycle of hope and despair.

The relationship of Mallarmé's religion of art—from his earliest essays on he used religious analogies for art—to Christianity likewise needs to be approached somewhat tentatively. The triad of ordinary life-death-rebirth into impersonality, which he saw in his own life, bears an interesting resemblance to Christian patterns, but obviously has another emotive content. Whatever salvationist designs we perceive in Mallarmé, we must remember that orthodox redemption is based on a personal relationship with God that has no counterpart in religions of art; the intense fondness for comparisons with Catholicism that we find in late nineteenth-century writers is an attempt to capture certain aspects of religious thought and experience while vigorously rejecting the rest. It is essential to Mallarmé's conjoined ideas of philosophy and poetry that his art not be dominated by the merely antithetical; the resulting dialectic has a third stage, but to what extent we wish to assimilate this to salvation, rebirth, regeneration, or resurrection will depend on our definition of the affective value of the poetry and our willingness to move toward ever broader analogies. We must realize, in any case, that from the historical point of view Mallarmé was the first modern poet of somewhat hermetic tendencies to create a body of work whose symbolic structure makes at all possible a redemptive interpretation. Many such poets were to follow.

4. Illuminations

From almost the earliest of his preserved poetry on, Rimbaud's work shows strong thematic design bordering on the symbolic. In the poems of 1870–1871 there is a broad opposition between church, the bourgeoisie and its occupations, political institutions, war, and sexuality as regulated by society, on the one hand, and nature, including the idea of freedom, on the other. Nature is not just the countryside but organic processes as well, as in "Les Poètes de sept ans." Rimbaud also contrasted real crops and useful vegetation in "Ce qu'on dit au poète à propos de fleurs" with the artificial, monotonous constraint of literary descriptions of nature and their vocabulary. This vast but coherent conception of nature is more far-reaching than any previous one in nineteenth-century French poetry, and its stylistic ramifications are considerable. Most of Rimbaud's poetry through 1871 reflects this symbolic division between the natural and the antinatural.

With the poems of 1872 a great change takes place: the antithetical character of much of the earlier poetry vanishes, and the imagery of nature alone remains, but coupled in the most interesting poems with the new themes of thirst, hunger, forgetfulness of self, suffering or patience, secret knowledge (*science*), the consuming flame, the ocean of love, the castle, the desert of life, and the dark night. These symbols of spiritual life derive from the mystic tradition, although their peculiar combination with the pastoral is something Rimbaud devised himself:[3] the superimposition of the ways of nature, the mystic, and even the magician on each other creates a memorable complex of images. But almost as remarkable as the poems of 1872 are in themselves is the fashion in which Rimbaud used them the following year as part of the texture of *Une Saison en enfer*. Here Rimbaud's fondness for strong thematic design shows up in a complex dialectic of the divine and the demonic, the Christian and the anti-Christian. Poems of 1872 are quoted as part of the illustration of damnation through pursuit of the divine: the two poles are represented as so conjoined that each implies the other and may paradoxically become its opposite. *Une Saison en enfer* is based on one of the great antitheses of French romanticism, but its conclusion moves beyond the ineluctable union of the divine and the demonic by rejecting both categories. The "new hour" and "splendid cities" at the end of the poem have been purged of all traditional theological implications.[4]

The *Illuminations*, which are now accepted as having been written after *Une Saison en enfer*, have no order established by the poet, but their imaginative relations dictate patterns for arranging and interpreting them. As a point of departure we can take the rejection of Christianity, the divine *and* the demonic. "Dévotion" marks this with a temporal reference. The prayer-like movement depends on the understood expression *faire dévotion à*; first comes the list of persons (including "l'adolescent que je fus" and "Lulu—démon") to whom an act of devotion is made in farewell, then the indication of the present circumstances:

Ce soir à Circeto . . . pour ma seule prière muette comme ces régions de nuit et précédant des bravoures plus violentes que ce chaos polaire.

This evening in Circeto . . . for my only prayer silent as these night regions and preceding exploits more violent than this polar chaos.

The time of Christian—and anti-Christian—adoration ("notre vice sérieux") is over, and that of violence and renewal is at hand. The last words, after summing up the speaker's tempered regard for his past and now looking forward, are "Mais plus *alors*," the sense being "But no more after this point."

"Voici le temps des *Assassins*": the famous conclusion of "Matinée d'ivresse" relates this poem to the violence promised in "Dévotion." It likewise has a strong temporal indication right from the beginning, "Cela commença." Body and soul, which are disunited in Christianity, according to *Une Saison en enfer*, are joined, as at the end of that poem:

Rassemblons fervemment cette promesse surhumaine faite à notre corps et à notre âme créés: cette promesse, cette démence! L'élégance, la science, la violence! On nous a promis d'enterrer dans l'ombre l'arbre du bien et du mal

Let us fervently summon up this superhuman promise made to our body and soul at their creation: this promise, this madness! Elegance, knowledge, violence! We were promised the tree of good and evil would be buried in darkness

The triad of elegance, knowledge, and violence or the aesthetic, philosophical, and moral aspects of renewal is one of those occasional uses of abstractions that help us find our way in the imagery of the *Illuminations* and situate the poems with regard to Rimbaud's previous work. The "promise" of "Matinée d'ivresse" indicates that we are dealing not only with an ecstatic moment but with prophetic poetry.

The shifts of mode of discourse and style between thematically related *Illuminations* is one of the most fascinating qualities of Rimbaud's art. "Ouvriers," a poem about knowledge, is largely written in a realist narrative style dealing with the speaker and his wife in a large northern industrial city. At the end, however, as the wind blows from the south, the language grows allusive: "Le Sud me rappelait les misérables incidents de mon enfance, mes désespoirs d'été, l'horrible quantité de force et de science que le sort a toujours éloignée de moi." Fate has a strong sense here, designating almost a spell. The reference to physical strength (caught up in the last line where the speaker rejects his present life: "Je veux que ce bras durci ne traîne plus *une chère image*") connects this with the imagery of subjecting the body to the tests of cold and torture in "Dévotion" and "Matinée d'ivresse"; a strengthening physical trial ushers in spiritual renewal, as in the warfare imagery at the end of *Une Saison en enfer*.

The unilluminated industrial city of "Ouvriers" is the subject of "Ville," where the prose appropriately grows heavy:

Je suis un éphémère et point trop mécontent citoyen d'une métropole crue moderne parce que tout goût connu a été éludé dans les ameublements et l'extérieur des maisons aussi bien que dans le plan de la ville. Ici vous ne signaleriez les traces d'aucun monument de superstition. La morale et la langue sont réduites à leur plus simple expression, enfin! Ces millions de gens qui n'ont pas besoin de se connaître amènent si pareillement l'éducation, le métier et la vieillesse, que ce cours de vie doit être plusieurs fois moins long que ce qu'une statistique folle trouve pour les peuples du continent. Aussi comme, de ma fenêtre, je vois des spectres nouveaux roulant à travers l'épaisse et éternelle fumée de charbon—notre ombre des bois, notre nuit d'été!—des Erinnyes nouvelles, devant mon cottage qui est ma patrie et tout mon coeur puisque tout ici ressemble à ceci,—la Mort sans pleurs, notre active fille et servante, un Amour désespéré et un joli Crime piaulant dans la boue de la rue.

I am a transitory and not too dissatisfied citizen of a metropolis deemed modern because all recognized taste has been avoided in the furnishings and the exterior of the houses, as well as in the plan of the city. Here you could not point out the remains of a single monument to superstition. Morality and language are reduced to their simplest expression—at last! These millions of people, who have no need to know one another, conduct their education, occupation, and old age so similarly that their life span must be several times shorter than what crazy statistics establish for the peoples of the continent. Also from my window I see new specters rolling through the thick and everlasting coal smoke—our forest shade, our summer night!—new Furies, in front of my cottage which is my homeland and all my heart since everything here looks like this—Death without tears, our busy daughter and handmaiden, a despairing Love, and a pretty Crime whining in the filth of the street.

Abstraction dominates in this language, as is suitable for a people reduced to uniformity; through the ironic tone we perceive, however, at the end, that some human qualities persist, although in their least desirable form. The same imagery of despair in the modern city is the content of "Dimanches," part I of "Jeunesse," where it contrasts with memories of aspirations and present attempts at *étude* and the creation of the *oeuvre*. The latter word occurs in "Matinée d'ivresse" ("Hourra pour l'oeuvre inouïe") somewhat cryptically, and now its vast connotations become clearer. The *oeuvre* is the work of transforming mankind, here put in physical and aesthetic terms:

Mais tu te mettras à ce travail: toutes les possibilités harmoniques et architecturales s'émouvront autour de ton siège. Des êtres parfaits, imprévus, s'offriront à tes expériences. . . . Ta mémoire et tes sens ne seront que la nourriture de ton impulsion créatrice. Quant au monde, quand tu sortiras, que sera-t-il devenu? En tout cas, rien des apparences actuelles.

But you'll devote yourself to this work: all harmonic and architectural possibilities will rise about your seat. Perfect beings, unforeseen, will offer themselves for your experiments. . . . Your memory and your senses will be but the nourishment of your creative impulse. As for the world when you go outside, what will have become of it? At any rate, nothing like present appearances.

Knowledge, *science*, finds its application. Youth and its aspirations are also the subject of "Angoisse," where the *oeuvre* is described as a "féerie scientifique" and "mouvements de fraternité sociale"; here fear of failure balances ambition, love, and strength. "Guerre" is another brief poem of youth and vast projects. In "A une raison" the new mankind with its new love appears, and the burden of time recedes. New love is connected with the rejection of traditional unions: the "chère image" of the wife in "Ouvriers," the "ménages" of "Génie." The illuminated world is finally described, in the somewhat ambiguously titled "Soir historique," as visions of all times and places mingling, while the untransformed present is characterized interestingly as "personal," that is, as the condition of mankind divided and pervaded by malaise:

Le plus élémentaire physicien sent qu'il n'est plus possible de se soumettre à cette atmosphère personnelle, brume de remords physiques, dont la constatation est déjà une affliction.

The most elementary physicist feels that it is no longer possible to submit to this personal atmosphere, a fog of physical remorse, whose ascertainment is already an affliction.

The climate is that of "Ville." In "Mouvement" humanity sets forth on a voyage of discovery enlightened by *science*.

Themes of these various *Illuminations* come together in "Génie": the future, strength, and love reinvented. The old form of the physical world and the old religion ("Adoration" or devotion) are rejected:

Et si l'Adoration s'en va, sonne, sa promese sonne: "Arrière ces superstitions, ces anciens corps, ces ménages et ces âges. C'est cette époque-ci qui a sombré!"
Il ne s'en ira pas, il ne redescendra pas d'un ciel, il n'accomplira pas la rédemption des colères de femmes et des gaietés des hommes et de tout ce péché: car c'est fait, lui étant, et étant aimé.

And if Worship goes, ring, his promise rings: "Away with these superstitions, these old bodies, these couples, and these ages. It is this epoch which has foundered." He will not go away, he will not come back down from a heaven, he will not accomplish the redemption of women's rages and of men's gaieties and of all this sin: for it is done, because of his being, and being loved.

Redemption is now; the *génie*, unlike Christ, has no otherworldly refuge in heaven, no Second Coming. *Science* is balanced by *élégance* and *violence* as in "Matinée d'ivresse": "Son corps, le dégagement rêvé, le brisement de la grâce croisée de violence nouvelle!" The promise of the earlier poem is realized.

The *Illuminations* we have been considering are based on romantic theories of history, ranging from the relatively sober dialectic of Michelet to the prophetic discourse of the Saint-Simonians and Ballanche, and to the poetic visions of Hugo in *Châtiments* and *La Légende des siècles*. These thinkers foresaw a new religion to replace Christianity with its dualism and other contradictions, as well as social, moral, political, and psychological transformations of man. Physical, even biological changes were anticipated by the more visionary. The artist occupies a place of predilection in bringing about the illumination of the world in some schemes. These theories are not in themselves the content of the whole *Illuminations* but part of Rimbaud's great poetic design. They were, in any case, only relatively esoteric in the early and mid-nineteenth century; joined or not with occultist neoplatonism, modified according to the taste of the writer, they were expounded in many works and constitute a characteristic pattern of thought of the romantics.

"Soir historique" with its panorama of ages and places is related to a group of vast visionary poems, timeless, full of detail, and representing not so much humanity transformed as the joy and mystery of illumination. The themes of strength ("Métropolitain") and mankind's new task ("Villes") occur, but mostly these poems, including "Scènes," "Fête d'hiver," "Promontoire," "Les Ponts," "Mystique," and both "Villes," deal with a heightened form of perception. Perception is the original sense of aesthetics, and pure art, uncomplicated by moral or philosophical ideas, is the method and content of these poems. The "impulsion créatrice" of "Jeunesse" toward the making of fabulous architecture and beings is now given free rein. It is notable that the imagery of beauty in these poems often involves cold light or surfaces, intricate movement, the accumulation of visual notations to the point of spatial incoherence, sound, and even a certain suggestion of violence at times. The movement toward union with the "Being Beauteous" of the poem of that title takes place on a battlefield; this is not the still, contemplative poetry of beauty, so characteristic of other writers of the late nineteenth century; its *trop-plein* seems always to imply the possibility of further detail rather than achieving one definitive image of beauty. This dynamic quality is important because it leads us to the final stage of the quest for a new order.

In "Being Beauteous" there is an attempt at union between the speaker and the figure he sees. "Royauté," "Aube," and "Barbare" represent the attainment of serene illumination by the symbols of marriage, sexual congress, and the presence of a goddess. "Royauté" and "Aube" are written in the most pellucid style:

Un beau matin, chez un peuple fort doux, un homme et une femme superbes criaient sur la place publique: "Mes amis, je veux qu'elle soit reine!" "Je veux être reine!" Elle riait et tremblait. Il parlait aux amis de révélation, d'épreuve terminée. Ils se pâmaient l'un contre l'autre.

En effet ils furent rois toute une matinée, où les tentures carminées se relevèrent sur les maisons, et tout l'après-midi, où ils s'avancèrent du côté des jardins de palmes.

("Royauté")

One fine morning, in the country of a very gentle people, a superb man and woman were crying out in the public square: "My friends, I want her to be queen!" "I want to be queen!" She laughed and trembled. He spoke to friends of revelation, of a trial terminated. They swooned against each other. In fact, they were monarchs for an entire morning, during which the crimson hangings were raised on the houses, and for the entire afternoon, during which they moved toward the gardens of palm trees. ("Royalty")

The spell alluded to in "Ouvriers," where the couple will be disunited, is broken, the world transformed. In contrast to the intense seething of images in the visionary poems like the two "Villes," here the technique is to isolate details for stillness and salience. "Barbare" specifically indicates that its world is after time, after the invention of new beings and the visiting of new places, after the epoch of struggle and the "anciens assassins" of "Matinée d'ivresse." We reach here the end of the process which begins in "Dévotion" and proceeds through "Matinée d'ivresse" and other poems toward the achievement of a new beauty and feeling of wholeness. In the course of the *oeuvre*, in Rimbaud's special sense, the world is transformed; finally, however, there remains only the poet hearing the voice of the goddess in "Barbare." We have moved from isolation in "Dévotion" to visions of crowds in "Soir historique," "Villes," and other poems and back to a new solitude shared only with the goddess in "Aube" and "Barbare."

The cycle of the *Illuminations* has an ironic downward phase after the peak of "Aube," "Royauté," and "Barbare." This is very perceptible in the various temporal indicators of "Après le déluge," where, after illumination reaches its high point in the vision of spring, the poet calls for its destruction:

—Sourds, étang,—Ecume, roule sur le pont et par-dessus les bois. . . . Eaux et tristesses, montez et relevez les Déluges.
    Car depuis qu'ils se sont dissipés . . . c'est un ennui! et la Reine, la Sorcière qui allume sa braise dans le pot de terre, ne voudra jamais nous raconter ce qu'elle sait, et que nous ignorons.

Gush forth, pond; foam, roll above the bridge and over the woods. . . . Waters and sorrows, rise up and release the Floods again. For since they have vanished . . . it's tedious! And the Queen, the Soceress, who kindles her coals in the earthen pot will never be willing to tell us what she knows, and what we do not know.

The goddess has become a witch refusing full illumination and *science*. More reference back occurs in "Parade," which is the ironic counterpart to "Soir historique." In the latter the poet promises "la même magie bourgeoise à tous les points où la malle nous déposera," an everyday magic and vision accessible to all. In "Parade," on the contrary, magic belongs to a menacing group—the opposite of the new men of "A une raison"—who threaten the onlookers by their very being:

Il y a quelques jeunes,—comment regarderaient-ils Chérubin?—pourvus de voix effrayantes et de quelques ressources dangereuses. On les envoie prendre du dos en ville, affublés d'un *luxe* dégoûtant.

There are some young ones—what would they think of Cherubino?—possessed of frightening voices and several dangerous talents. Rigged out in a disgusting luxury they are sent into town to bugger men.

Homosexuality contrasts with the heterosexual unions of the high point of illumination. Theater, the opposite of that of "Scènes," is now "le plus violent Paradis de la grimace enragée." Violence returns directed against the *you* to whom the poem is addressed; the *I* speaking is now exclusionary: "J'ai seul la clef de cette parade sauvage."

The same exclusionary *I* offers his visions for sale in "Solde"; the new world is being abandoned:

A vendre ce que les Juifs n'ont pas vendu, ce que noblesse ni crime n'ont goûté, ce qu'ignorent l'amour maudit et la probité infernale des masses; ce que le temps ni la science n'ont pas à reconnaître.

For sale what the Jews have not sold, what neither nobility nor crime has tasted, what accursed love and the infernal probity of the masses do not know; what neither time nor science can recognize as theirs.

The realm beyond Christian good and evil, beyond time and banal science, as we must here understand the word, summarizes a great deal of the *Illuminations*. Here are specifically the unforeseen, perfect beings of "Jeunesse":

A vendre les Corps sans prix, hors de toute race, de tout monde, de tout sexe, de toute descendance! Les richesses jaillissant à chaque démarche! Solde de diamants sans contrôle!

For sale priceless bodies, beyond any race, any world, any sex, any lineage! Riches springing up at every step! Unrestricted sale of diamonds!

Elsewhere in "Solde" there are allusions to the migrations of "Mouvement" and other images of collectivity.

Exile and a spell have fallen on the two companions of "Vagabonds"; the speaker cannot effect the transformation he has promised:

> J'avais en effet, en toute sincérité d'esprit, pris l'engagement de le rendre à son état primitif de fils du Soleil,—et nous errions, nourris du vin des cavernes et du biscuit de la route, moi pressé de trouver le lieu et la formule.

I had in all sincerity of mind undertaken to return him to his primitive state of child of the Sun,—and we were wandering, nourished on the wine of caverns and the dry bread of travelers, while I searched continually to find the place and the formula.

The vocabulary of magic is particularly strong in the *Illuminations* of failing power and retreat from vision. The antimyth "Conte" is about a promise of supernatural eroticism that fails; these aspirations through magic are private, individual, and not destined for mankind as a whole.

Recollection, isolation, exile, and rejection of the goddess are the themes of "Enfance" and "Vies," the latter stressing the speaker's great age, the fact that his *oeuvre* is done, his descent from "gaîté divine." In these poems of decline, however, there is some reference to reversal of the process. When the poet of "Enfance" IV sits in his tomb-like underground refuge, he thinks, "Pourquoi une apparence de soupirail blêmirait-elle au coin de la voûte?" There is just a possibility that his isolation might end. Such effects not only contribute to the self-irony of these poems, whose speaker finds all affirmation excessive, even that of decline, but also suggests a continuous potential for movement back to the beginning of the cycle: "Qu'est mon néant, auprès de la stupeur qui vous attend?" ("Vies").

I think it is now clear that for the most part the *Illuminations* consist at the same time of groups of poems similar in theme and technique and also of ones directly contrasting in movement. In other words, they are not in any way miscellaneous or heteroclite, but tightly and complexly related. To put it in the most schematic fashion, poems anticipating a new adventure of violence after the unsatisfactory one of Christianity are complemented by prophecies of constructive change. These yield, in turn, to visions of a full, rich, almost chaotically transformed world. Violence in a muted form is not absent: "Les boutiques doivent contenir des drames assez sombres" ("Villes" I). But the narrator largely participates as a curious onlooker; his great height of experience comes only with the poems dominated by one or two figures, including a female one. Finally, however, come the poems of withdrawal, of retreat from other men; present experience may give way to recollection. But concluding the poems of remembrance we find ambiguous references to another future; in short, the relationship between poems is not only sequential or antithetical but also cyclical. The *Illuminations* are fragments of a cycle, a pattern that emerges most clearly in those that mark a time point between two eras or phases such as with "Dévotion," "Matinée d'ivresse," "Jeunesse," "Soir historique," "Après le déluge," "Solde," "Enfance," or "Vies." Now we must consider the general sense of the cycle.

"In youth he had read of 'Illuminati' and 'Eleutherarchs,' and believed he possessed the power of operating an immediate change in the minds of men and the state of society." Mary Shelley's remarks (in her note on the poems of 1871) about her husband suggest the particular kind of romantic imagination which had been Rimbaud's in 1871, and which is conveyed through the child's vision of life transformed in "Les Poètes de sept ans," which dates from that year. The "moi qui me suis dit mage ou ange" of the poems of 1872 and *Une Saison en enfer* turned primarily to a theological inspiration, though one grounded most concretely in experience, as the corresponding poems of Verlaine's show.[5] At this time the dominant idea of Nature vanished. As the theological phase of his thought resolved itself with the rejection of dualist Christianity, Rimbaud was left with just one of his themes, that represented by the boy's novel in "Les Poètes de sept ans," by the exhortations to invent images in "Ce qu'on dit au poète à propos de fleurs," and by the voyage of the *bateau ivre:* the faculty of the *voyant.* The content of the seer's vision had been identified by Rimbaud in 1871 as the universal intelligence, which many have taken to mean a kind of collective unconscious. As the seer's vision appears in the *Illuminations*, it would seem to grow out of much reading of romantic social thinkers and Rimbaud's subsequent reaction against this body of thought. The poet's mind takes cognizance of the late nineteenth-century industrial world, nourishes itself with romantic apocalyptics, reaches its fullest expansion, and then, disappointed by the disparity between its conceptions and the still unchanged world about it, recedes into irony. The work is symbolic in that the references to London, to Verlaine (in "Vagabonds," for example), or to anything else historical and objective are not part of a systematic exterior account but facets of the vast and intricate tableau of Rimbaud's imagination. It would not be an exaggeration to see allegorical levels of meaning at various points in the *Illuminations*. Thus the "Génie" could be taken to mean man himself, in a romantic humanist interpretation, or the new God, if we prefer to read a transcendental sense into the poem. The poems of the goddess or union express the wholeness of the imagination, but they are also open to a sexual reading, by which they contrast with the homosexual content of "Parade." Specific symbols give a color to the work unlike that of Rimbaud's earlier poetry: height and coolness, ice, snow, the North Pole, and cold waters express spiritual exaltation and self-sufficiency. The fantastic buildings and landscape of the two poems entitled "Villes" or of "Promontoire" convey the delight of imaginative, aesthetic discovery. The whole work is characterized by unusual viewpoints such as seeing history spatially in "Mystique" or reaching the end of the world in "Enfance" III, or other schemes of marked horizontal or vertical progression. These are intermediate between the extremes of height in "Dévotion," "Barbare," and "Génie" and the subterranean refuge of "Enfance" IV or the room of the lone visionary in "Jeunesse" IV or "Vies" III. Elements of systematic imagery, however, are not so obtrusive as to make the *Illuminations* schematic; rather, the extreme variations in form, syntax, and local imagistic effects make contrasts so pronounced as to obscure, without the most careful reading, the structure of the cycle.

When we reflect on the ultimate interpretation of the *Illuminations*, we cannot go very far without encountering the problem of the transcendental. There is nothing in Rimbaud's vocabulary to indicate to us in any certain fashion whether or not, at the height of the cycle, the poet is in direct contact with the divine. Nor do we have any information external to the work which would permit us to say unequivocally that Rimbaud believed in higher forces than man and his imagination. It seems unlikely that Rimbaud believed in God in the traditional manner, which involved a whole metaphysics of body and spirit, matter and mind, as well as an eschatology or view of the final end of the cosmos. But it is possible, of course, to have a belief in God which dispenses with all the old philosophical intuitions. Such a belief, moreover, can find a perfect expression of itself in poetry: the ambiguities of poetic, symbolic language do not oblige the poet to decide theoretical questions which he may be reluctant to face or may find idle.

There is a very interesting parallel to Rimbaud's symbolic poetry in Hart Crane's work, and some comparison will perhaps sharpen our apprehension of the subtleties involved in reading both of them. At the end of "For the Marriage of Faustus and Helen," which constitutes in some respects Crane's preparatory task for the elaboration of *The Bridge*, the cyclical theme of creation and destruction, love and death, is transcended. The "volatile blamed bleeding hands" of the years, a symbol of the poet's quest and struggle will

> thresh the height
> The imagination spans beyond despair,
> Outpacing bargain, vocable, and prayer.

Crane uses the key word of the English romantics, imagination, to express his aspiration to a supernal world. The image in "span" suggests to us a bridge, an old and almost universal symbol for prayer or for the passage from the visible to the unseen. Since the third part of "Faustus and Helen" begins with urban images, we have here a preliminary sketch of the way in which, in the first part of *The Bridge*, the "curveship" of Brooklyn Bridge rises from the foot of Manhattan, as if leading into the timeless and the apparently transcendental. Crane's city is not unlike Rimbaud's deathly industrial metropolis, with its base metal contrasting with the silver of the bridge:

Under thy shadow by the piers I waited;
Only in darkness is thy shadow clear.
The City's fiery parcels all undone,
Already snow submerges an iron year . . .

It has been observed that the movement from "Proem" to "Atlantis,"
the final section of *The Bridge*, can be symbolically summarized as
one from the iron year of the unilluminated city to the white buildings hinted at in the final revelation and present elsewhere in Crane's
work. In the concluding, apocalyptic imagery of *The Bridge*, Crane
does not speak of the imagination, as he had in "Faustus and Helen,"
but uses terms like "Myth," or "Deity's glittering pledge" for the
bridge and sees how, through the metal span "Deity's young name"
ascends. We think of Rimbaud's "génie" in connection with this
young deity and find that he, like the *génie*, will grant "pardon for
this history," that is, the mournful past of humanity. The "canticle"
of the bridge "fresh chemistry assigns/To rapt inception and beat-
itude." "Chemistry" is Rimbaud's term in the *Illuminations* for a
kind of visionary science. In the "rapt inception" of a new world,
there are "migrations that must needs void memory," as in Rimbaud's "Mouvement." I do not think that we should speak of influence here but of a coincidence brought about by the needs of both
poets as they attempted to build a modern image of the divine. Imagination is too profane a word to describe the faculty at work here, despite the English romantics' exaltation of the term. Visionary works
like the *Illuminations* or *The Bridge* describe either the transcendental or some psychological experience which is a replacement
for it. This ambiguity can never be resolved, since it really depends on
our conception of the theological and the divine.

One thing remains certain and striking: both Rimbaud and Crane
had the experience of vision failing, of a retreat from the heights.
Near the end of his life, in "The Broken Tower," Crane wrote his
equivalent of the *Illuminations* dealing with the downward phase of
the cycle:

The bell-rope that gathers God at dawn
Dispatches me as though I dropped down the knell

> Of a spent day—to wander the cathedral lawn
> From pit to crucifix, feet chill on steps from hell.

The poet's day, he realizes, was actually night, with its "antiphonal" or blasphemous music, and with the true day comes remorse and damnation. In a great clangor, "the bells break down their tower/And swing I know not where": the orderly world of God's bells becomes chaotic. The poet's "broken intervals" are matched by sounds outside him:

> And so it was I entered the broken world
> To trace the visionary company of love

Now the adjective "broken" has been transferred from the tower and sounds to the world, which was not of the poet's making. In the end the tower is rebuilt within the poet; the interiorization of what was to be the changing of life corresponds to the private "scène où jouer les chefs-d'oeuvre" of "Vies," though Crane's poem has none of Rimbaud's acidity.

Poems like "Génie" or the concluding section of *The Bridge* occupy a middle ground between the poetry of the imagination and theological revelations of the old kind. Although imagination is an adequate word to describe the faculty of a poet who refuses all transcendency, like Stevens in *Harmonium*, or to indicate the content of poetry of aesthetic discovery like "Villes" or "Promontoire" in the *Illuminations*, I find the term imagination is historically too closely tied to profane psychology to be used with regard to intuitions of godhead. At the same time, we sense that Rimbaud's and Crane's deities have little existence outside their poetry, something that cannot be said of Milton's God, for example. This problem of poetic deities and the faculties of the poets revealing them is not an idle question, for the way we look at private theological visions and transcendency will color our attitude toward some of the most important works of modern poetry. The redemptive implications we have seen in Mallarmé's work are a part of this issue, which I shall return to in my last chapter.

5. Conclusion

Although we can do very little about changing or restricting the various uses of the word symbol, we can attempt to clarify it somewhat by looking back over the early conceptions of symbolism and those peculiar to the late nineteenth and early twentieth centuries.

Much traditional symbolism owed its long life in part at least to commentaries, Biblical exegesis, compilations of mythology, and iconological handbooks: while works of art and literature might spontaneously convey somewhat new symbolic details and associations, the allegorizing cast of mind tended to conventionalize meanings, even in the case of multiple values of a specific symbol. A classical-Christian synthesis of moral conceptions, in addition to the all-embracing points of reference in theology called correspondences, made symbols part of a coherent system. It is important to insist on the stable quality of the traditional symbolism of the good and the bad, the divine and the demonic and their sublunary correspondences, because the use of it in modern literature is sometimes considered to be obscure: what is obscure, however, is not so much the symbols themselves as the elliptic or allusive treatment of them. Symbols like the contrasting fires of purification and lust, which are discursively presented in Dante and other earlier writers, may be merely suggested or else perhaps disguised in a realistic background. Eliot's poetry is characteristic in its often covert handling of conventional symbols which are explicit in other poets.

The obviously different values of much modern symbolism can best be characterized as psychological, whether it refer to moods, to situations in novels, like the golden bowl in James or Emma Bovary's frequent gazing out of windows, to the aesthetic imagination in the *Illuminations*, or to the ancestral summons to procreation in Mallarmé's triptych. Works may be devoid of any possible theological interpretation like *Madame Bovary*, or else the primary meaning is psychological, as many now think *The Wasteland's* to be. In the case of someone like Mallarmé, we perceive an intermittent level of metaphysical reference, but it consists so exclusively of the poet's own private adventure in thought that none of the generalizing value we expect of philosophy is present. Many of the actual symbols of earlier literature do persist, though with altered value, like Rimbaud's cities, Mallarmé's stars, or the ships they both made use of. The thematic content may sound metaphysical when briefly summarized but is regularly presented as an episode in individual psychology: innocence and experience, fate and freedom, wholeness and fragmentation of self, creation and sterility, or imagination and reality.

There are, to be sure, some new or relatively new symbols like Mallarmé's furniture, Rimbaud's North Pole, or Verlaine's anemic colors and landscape. These often appear in an antithetical or some other kind of relationship. Even with a mere antithesis, however, which is perhaps the simplest form of an original symbol system, there occurs a problem for the reader in that a great range of interpretative analogies often suggests itself. Irrelevantly Christianizing ones are often proposed. Of course, the less obviously the symbol is based on some easily made association, the greater the ambiguity or the possibilities for ever expanding commentary. One of the best examples is Wallace Stevens' early work. In *Harmonium* there are some static mood poems and some poems where an explicit analogy accounts for the images, but a very large number are based on a relationship, often an antithesis, between two things or creatures, and this relationship must be interpreted by the reader. Sometimes this is simple as in "Disillusionment of Ten O'Clock," where the colorless real houses contrast with the inner world of the old sailor catching tigers in red weather. Elsewhere the relationship may involve a contrast but not a true antithesis, and it may consist of an action or process. This is nicely illustrated by "Earthy Anecdote," which Stevens obviously placed first in *Harmonium* to establish this technique at the outset as characteristic of his volume:

> Every time the bucks went clattering
> Over Oklahoma
> A firecat bristled in the way.

> Wherever they went,
> They went clattering,
> Until they swerved
> In a swift, circular line
> To the right,
> Because of the firecat.

Or until they swerved
In a swift, circular line
To the left,
Because of the firecat.

The bucks clattered,
The firecat went leaping,
To the right, to the left,
And
Bristled in the way.

Later, the firecat closed his bright eyes
And slept.

We know from Stevens' more explicit comparisons elsewhere that imagination working on reality is a favorite pattern, and we realize that the firecat is shaping reality into perfect, aesthetically pleasing circular forms. Such a notion will do as a beginning for commentary, although it is rather lacking in nuances. Pursuit of analogies could lead one ultimately into theology or domains Stevens is not known to have touched on.

The relationship of these symbolic configurations with allegory deserves comment: in late nineteenth-century France the distinction which had been made in Germany and England between mechanical allegory and organic symbolism was hardly known. Ambitious *symboliste* poems, when they are more than explicit analogies, sometimes use the abstractions of one kind of allegory (the personification of "A une raison" in the *Illuminations*, for example), which is another way of providing commentary rather than pure allegory, "saying something else." When, on the other hand, no gloss is given, we may find an example of high traditional allegory such as *Hérodiade*; there is a vast difference between an action performed by Hérodiade and one accomplished by a personification called Beauty. However, we find that modern symbolic poems may differ significantly from allegory in that a thing like the drunken boat, which is not at all times like a child or the imagination, to use two common interpretations, replaces the traditional human or highly personified narrative figures. Another difference may be the use of thematic coherence without plot or with a highly elliptical one: the *Illuminations* are an example and have less of an initial impression of wholeness than allegory, the relationship between elements being harder to analyze. Juxtaposition of images in a lyric, such as "Ses purs ongles" (which Mallarmé called "allegorical of itself"), is another way of using symbolism which seems to leave connections to chance. Sometimes the generalizing quality we expect in allegory cannot easily be found, as when the figures in Rimbaud's "Mémoire" are taken to have purely autobiographical value. What of course is lacking is the organizing power of the rhetorical tradition, which clarifies and expands relationships. In fact, a lengthy commentary on poems like these could turn into a kind of plotting of themes just as one would have in summarizing an allegory. The look of an allegorical fragment which some modern poems have comes precisely from common elements, unsupported by the sustaining element of coherent narrative. Even the fuller landscape of allegory helps the sense. Something of this can be felt in the *Illuminations*, where the polar imagery of snow, ice, and cold waters seems concomitant with the state described by the title; however, this imagery occurs in a less orderly seeming progression than in older allegory. Narrative, landscape, and other detail in earlier poetry often have traditional typological values as well, but equally important perhaps is that, in the structure of allegory, we tend to note clearly defined stages or gradations, based frequently on ethical categories. To use the example of the *Illuminations* again, we can definitely perceive several phases in the cycle, but they refer to no clear, preexisting body of theological or philosophical distinctions. Another interesting difference is that modern symbolic poems sometimes make extensive use of magic to create an abrupt, elliptic pattern of causality; since magic became a myth by the beginning of the nineteenth century, it serves as a purely poetic device, an effect not possible earlier when magic was believed in and had a theory all its own. Finally, it is the existence of an acceptable and whole literal level in allegory which divides it often from modern symbolism; the tendency to perturb literal values increases hesitation about the symbolism. It is equally important to understand the differences and the similarities between medieval and renaissance allegory and recent symbolic poems: there are many comparable local effects that provide the same kind of aesthetic pleasure, and not all modern symbolism would be incomprehensible by any means in the intellectual framework of several centuries ago. Like twentieth-century poems, some earlier allegories contain numerous enigmas. At the same time, however, the older allegorist evidently felt clarity, discrimination, and firmness in a greater number of abstract entities than is common today, which permitted the construction of more elaborate discrete detail and lengthier developments. The feeling for such clear distinctions is also connected with the disputed question of levels of meaning in allegory, which is primarily a matter of habits of thinking. Whereas levels, if not always as many as four of them, obviously influenced the conception of some older poems, it might be denied that anything of the sort exists in modern works, were it not for the fact that some poets at least are reported to have insisted that, in Rimbaud's putative words, "I mean it literally and in all senses." Certainly we can distinguish aesthetic and religious levels in the Samain text we quoted earlier, and in *The Wasteland* there is a literal sense, the level of personal relationships, with metaphorical parallels in the quest for grace in the Parsifal story and in the revival of the land in the vegetation myth imagery; *The Wasteland* even has an intermittent fourth level in the references to Western history. However these levels, for most readers, tend to fall together into psychological complexes: we do not have the habit of sorting out the anagogical, the moral, and so forth.

There are two cyclical patterns under which we may subsume the themes and symbols of much modern poetry: the cycle of spirit and that of death or matter. In the former, some earlier state of aspiration or perfection is recaptured after a trial or decline. This may be death: in *Hérodiade* Saint John's search for beauty is completed in the union or marriage with Hérodiade that follows his death. Valéry's Parca is for the first time truly whole and alive at the end of the poem, after passing through the divisive phases of death in life and life in death. The appearance of stars in "Ses purs ongles" and *Un Coup de dés* represents a triumph of spirit so symbolic that we cannot say whether literal death has preceded them. The *Illuminations* form a complex pattern in that romantic myths of history embody the redemptive cycle, but it is the other, complementary cycle, that of death of spirit and the return to matter, which marks the final phase of the work. The mental and physical are intimately connected in these cycles, as in Benn's pseudoscientific vision of history ending in genetic decay.

This is true of the divorce of the male and female union in Rimbaud's "Mémoire," the failure to achieve union in Régnier's poems, the atmosphere of mourning that comes over Apollinaire's world when, as we shall see, the god dies and the profane replaces the divine. These cycles of defeat are implied in much late nineteenth-century literature.

The cycles of spirit and of death, or whatever terms one may prefer, are one of the most significant aspects of modern poetry in that, while their form is usually clear, their exact reference is often not: they create overtones or analogous patterns beyond the one we may consider basic to the interpretation of a specific poem. This is why affirmations about modern poetry's having poetry as its subject are frequently neither entirely right nor entirely wrong; it is also why Christian myth is easily read into poems where it may not belong. Perhaps our safest recourse in studying such poems is to be aware of the entire range of analogous patterns and to consider comparatively the variety of nuances and detail they acquire in major poetic works.

IV
Death, Renewal, and Redemption in Apollinaire, Montale, Lorca, Yeats, and Rilke

We have seen Rimbaud in "Génie" contrast Christian salvation with a new deity redeeming the world and Mallarmé employ rebirth or incarnation among his themes; the possibility of redemption or regeneration or their impossibility is a major subject in twentieth-century poetry. Frequently it is affirmed that modern poetry is primarily about poetry; art, however, when it is a theme, is often subordinate to larger, soteriological implications, and we shall now look at a variety of these.

Among the early poems Apollinaire published in *Alcools* (1913) is "Merlin et la Vieille Femme," whose subject is a variant on the Merlin and Vivian legend so frequently treated in the late nineteenth century. In it Merlin, before being made a prisoner of Vivian's spell, has a son by Memory, which, on the analogy of the birth from Memory of the Muses, indicates that his bequest to the world is poetry. The wedding of Merlin and Memory ("L'entrelacs de leurs doigts fut leur seul laps d'amour," in the typical, intricate diction) is accompanied by transformation of the landscape from winter into spring; this spring of the birth of poetry contrasts with the enchanted one when love in the form of Vivian will hold Merlin captive. We could say that the poem is prophetic or that Apollinaire was to impose on his experience the pattern of art being born while the artist is the prisoner of an incapacitating spell cast by a dead love. Certainly this describes the circumstances surrounding the creation of "La Chanson du mal-aimé," the long poem commemorating Apollinaire's attachment to Annie Playden.

Apollinaire knew how to achieve new beauty from types of poems, styles, and symbols that somewhat older poets had made much use of in the 1880s and 1890s; thus the legendary settings and decadent style used by the minor *symbolistes* are completely absorbed and surpassed by the skill of the poet in "Merlin et la Vieille Femme," and the imagery of sunset and the depraved woman undergoes an extraordinary transformation at the beginning of "La Chanson du mal-aimé":

> *Un soir de demi-brume à Londres*
> *Un voyou qui ressemblait à*
> *Mon amour vint à ma rencontre*
> *Et le regard qu'il me jeta*
> *Me fit baisser les yeux de honte*
>
> *Je suivis ce mauvais garçon*
> *Qui sifflotait mains dans les poches*
> *Nous semblions entre les maisons*
> *Onde ouverte de la mer Rouge*
> *Lui les Hébreux moi Pharaon*
>
> . . . .
>
> *Au tournant d'une rue brûlant*
> *De tous les feux de ses façades*
> *Plaies du brouillard sanguinolent*
> *Où se lamentaient les façades*
> *Une femme lui ressemblant*
>
> *C'était son regard d'inhumaine*
> *La cicatrice à son cou nu*
> *Sortit saoule d'une taverne*
> *Au moment où je reconnus*
> *La fausseté de l'amour même*

One half-misty evening in London, a hoodlum who resembled my love came in my direction, and his glance made me lower my eyes from shame. I followed this thug, who was whistling, his hands in his pockets. Between the houses, the open wave of the Red Sea, I seemed like Pharaoh, he the Jews. . . . At the corner of a street burning with all the fire of its façades, wounds of the bleeding fog where the house fronts wept, a woman resembling my love—it was her inhuman gaze, the scar on her bare neck—lurched out of a bar, just at the moment when I realized the falseness of love itself.

The imagery of the bloody sunset on the brick red streets is accompanied by strange confusions of identity: the persecutor and perse-

cuted are reversed in the Red Sea image; the triple *mauvais garçon,*
mon amour, and drunken woman turn an odd resemblance into something hallucinatory. The poet attempts to shake off this memory with
a mythological song about spring, and, as it ends, we find an important thematic statement:

> *Beaucoup de ces dieux ont péri*
> *C'est sur eux que pleurent les saules*
> *Le grand Pan l'amour Jésus-Christ*
> *Sont bien morts et les chats miaulent*
> *Dans la cour je pleure à Paris*
>
> *Moi qui sais des lais pour les reines*
> *Les complaintes de mes années*
> *Des hymnes d'esclave aux murènes*
> *La romance du mal-aimé*
> *Et des chansons pour les sirènes*

Many of these gods have died; over them the willows weep: great Pan, love, Jesus
Christ are indeed dead, and the cats mew in the courtyard. I weep in Paris, I who
know lays for queens, the ballads of my years, hymns of slaves cast to the eels, the
romance of the ill-loved, and songs for sirens.

The death of love is more than the end of a specific attachment; it is
the end of an era of feeling and being. Nature, Christ, and love form
an indivisible whole, the category of sacred, numinous existence. The
occasional religious vocabulary, hell or damnation, is part of the identity of the death of love with that of Christ. Of course, we must note
that rather than a theological hell—a demonic as opposed to a divine
domain—this is a secularized, profane world, following the disappearance of the divine, a *monde désacralisé* in which the cats mew in the
city and the poet is out of place because he knows songs for legendary
figures. As often in modern poetry, the demonic vocabulary does not
imply the dualistic world of a poet like Baudelaire or the Rimbaud of
Une Saison en enfer, but an antithesis of presence and absence,
mythic life and empty existence. Thus Apollinaire uses, rather than
references to God or Satan, the opposition between the world with
Christ and without; it corresponds better to the non-Manichean con-

trast he is trying to render. Naturally the orthodox definition of evil as the absence of good fits this, as it often does not the depiction of evil in literature.

The end of royalty, in the form of Louis II of Bavaria's death, is depicted, unhistorically, as related to the mad king's not having a consort; Wagner's patron, the favorite figure in modern political history of the *symbolistes*, is evoked as part of the final contrast in "La Chanson du mal-aimé" between mythic, numinous times and the era of the modern city; Louis II is a link between legend and the present. Another kind of contrast occurs in the related "L'Emigrant de Landor Road"; there the emigrant seeks to escape from the mourning city he has passed his days in; by implication it is the city in which love died. Spring in the form of flowers covers the ocean as his ship sails from the autumnal port, and he undertakes to marry a "modern" siren. Memory overcomes him however; modern sirens are no replacement for the dead era of love, and he drowns himself at the end. The poet's "dieux morts en automne" are also the subject of a number of short poems.

The analogy between the religious and erotic is explored in the prose Merlin story *L'Enchanteur pourrissant*, where parody of the Bible is coupled with the degradation of love. An equally curious work is the strange "Un Soir," where a dreary city is the scene at once of a new love and Judas' suicide:

> La ville est métallique et c'est la seule étoile
> Noyée dans tes yeux bleus
> Quand les tramways roulaient jaillissaient des feux pâles
> Sur des oiseaux galeux
>
> Et tout ce qui tremblait dans tes yeux de mes songes
> Qu'un seul homme buvait
> Sous les feux de gaz roux comme la fausse oronge
> O vêtue ton bras se lovait
>
> Vois l'histrion tire la langue aux attentives
> Un fantôme s'est suicidé
> L'apôtre au figuier pend et lentement salive
> Jouons donc cet amour aux dés

Des cloches aux sons clairs annonçaient ta naissance
Vois
Les chemins sont fleuris et les palmes s'avancent
Vers toi

The city is metallic, and it is the only star drowned in your blue eyes; when the streetcars passed, pale fires spurted onto scabby birds, and all that was trembling in your eyes of my dreams, which a single man was drinking, under the gaslight red like poisonous mushrooms. O woman clothed, your arm was coiling. See, the actor is sticking out his tongue at the women watching. A ghost has committed suicide; the apostle is hanging from the fig tree and slowly salivating. So let us gamble at dice for this love. The bells were announcing with clear tones your birth. See, the roads are covered with flowers, and the palms are coming toward you.

There is ambiguity here and probably ambivalence as well. Harsh mingling of traditional poetic language about eyes with sinister urban imagery—including the prostitute's streetlamp—gives way to allusion to the crucifixion, by implication from the death of Judas. The latter has a female audience, an image that continues the sexual polarity of the poem. The triumphal imagery of the entry into Jerusalem at the end is qualified by the fact that this love is a risk, being compared to the gambling over Christ's robe. The symbolic question is whether this love is possible after the death of Christ, that is, paradoxically, the death of love.

Sometimes Apollinaire's handling of themes becomes quite elliptic, as in "Le Voyageur," where the imagery of a river and travel includes this brief allusion to the end of the numinous:

Un soir je descendis dans une auberge triste
Auprès du Luxembourg
Dans le fond de la salle il s'envolait un Christ
Quelqu'un avait un furet
Un autre un hérisson
L'on jouait aux cartes
Et toi tu m'avais oublié

I stopped one evening at a melancholy inn near Luxemburg. At the end of the room a Christ was flying up. Someone had a ferret, and another man a hedgehog. They were playing cards. And you had forgotten me.

The passion, with the gambling of tradition as in "Un Soir," is super-imposed on the ordinary scene in the inn. In the course of the journey in "Le Voyageur," however, a new symbol appears: a bright mountain shining in the night with figures trying to climb it; the connection with theological symbolism of purgatory and salvation is clear, although the context is hardly orthodox. The death of the god is not followed by his resurrection; the poet alone is transfigured. We encounter, in other words, a historical pattern in which the god and his era are surpassed. "Les Fiançailles" illustrates this more lengthily despite considerable obscurity. An unusual juxtaposition of images is found in the opening of the poem: the spring of perjurious betrothal also has dulcet Christian associations:

> Le printemps laisse errer les fiancés parjures
> Et laisse feuilloler longtemps les plumes bleues
> Que secoue le cyprès où niche l'oiseau bleu
>
> Une Madone à l'aube a pris les églantines
> Elle viendra demain cueillir les giroflées
> Pour mettre aux nids des colombes qu'elle destine
> Au pigeon qui ce soir semblait le Paraclet
>
> Au petit bois de citronniers s'enamourèrent
> D'amour que nous aimons les dernières venues

Springtime lets the perjured betrothed wander and lets the blue feathers leaf out lengthily, shaken by the cypress the bluebird nests in. A Madonna took the eglantines at dawn; tomorrow she will come to gather the stock to put in the nests of the doves she intends for the pigeon who was like the Paraclete tonight. In a little lemon grove the last doves to arrive fell in love with a love that we too love.

This strange mingling of faithless lovers or doves (the reference of *venues* is ambiguous), of the erotic and the Christian, is an extreme example of playing on the double connotations of images like the dove or the betrothal to Christ, the bridegroom, to produce an effect whose purpose is initially quite mysterious. After the poet falls asleep and, waking in depression, sees his past, we understand that the initial imagery is designed to suggest the *mensonge* or deception of love which the poet only later realizes: a reference to the crucifixion of the lover justifies the Christian associations and Apollinaire's general parallel of Christ's life and death with that of love:

Un ange a exterminé pendant que je dormais
Les agneaux les pasteurs des tristes bergeries
De faux centurions emportaient le vinaigre
. . . .
Etoiles de l'éveil je n'en connais aucune
Les becs de gaz pissaient leur flamme au clair de lune
Des croque-morts avec des bocks tintaient des glas
. . . .
Des femmes demandaient l'amour et la dulie
Et sombre sombre fleuve je me rappelle
Les ombres qui passaient n'étaient jamais jolies

An angel put to death, while I was sleeping, the lambs, the shepherds of the sad sheepfolds. False centurions carried off the vinegar. . . . Stars of awakening, I don't know a one of them. The gas jets pissed their flame into the moonlight. Undertakers were clinking death knells with their beers. . . . Women demanded love and dulia, and somber, somber river, I recall the passing shadows were never pretty.

He has awakened to a new sky; the vision of the earlier night, with its reference to death and women demanding holy worship slowly vanishes, and the long, reflective central section of the poem deals with new creative powers: "Pardonnez-moi de ne plus connaître l'ancien jeu des vers." Allusions to the earlier mentions of flowers, night, the crucifixion, and the Virgin occur as the imagery of daylight and the end of a journey mark the beginning of the poet's regeneration:

A la fin les mensonges ne me font plus peur
C'est la lune qui cuit comme un oeuf sur le plat
Ce collier de gouttes d'eau va parer la noyée
Voici mon bouquet de fleurs de la Passion
Qui offrent tendrement deux couronnes d'épines
Les rues sont mouillées de la pluie de naguère
Des anges diligents travaillent pour moi à la maison
La lune et la tristesse disparaîtront pendant
Toute la sainte journée
Toute la sainte journée j'ai marché en chantant
. . . .
Au tournant d'une rue je vis des matelots
Qui dansaient le cou nu au son d'un accordéon
J'ai tout donné au soleil
Tout sauf mon ombre

Les dragues les ballots les sirènes mi-mortes
A l'horizon brumeux s'enfonçaient les trois-mâts

> Les vents ont expiré couronnés d'anémones
> O Vierge signe pur du troisième mois

In the end, lies no longer scare me. It's the moon cooking like a fried egg. . . . Here is my bouquet of Passion flowers, tenderly proffering two crowns of thorns. The streets are wet with recent rain. Diligent angels are working for me at home. The moon and sadness will disappear for all the holy day. All the holy day I've been walking and singing. . . . At a corner I saw sailors dancing barenecked to the music of an accordion. I have given all to the sun, all, except my shadow. Dredges, bales, half-dead sirens! Three-masted ships were sinking on the foggy horizon. The winds have died, crowned with anemones, O Virgin, pure sign of the third month.

Summer has replaced the earlier spring (the Virgin is the third sign of summer), and in general the detail of the imagery is significant with reference to earlier sections. The poet's regeneration is not to be confused with salvation in an afterlife, however; he has kept his shadow, the sign of mortality, and in the final section, he envisages dispassionately his extinction:

> Templiers flamboyants je brûle parmi vous
> Prophétisons ensemble
> . . . .
> Liens déliés par une libre flamme Ardeur
> Que mon souffle éteindra O Morts à quarantaine
> Je mire de ma mort la gloire et le malheur

Flaming Templars I burn in your midst. Let us prophesy together. . . . Bands loosened by a free flame, ardor that my breath will extinguish, O dead, at Lent. I contemplate the glory and the misfortune of my death.

The epigraph to "La Chanson du mal-aimé" says the poet's love will die and rise like the Phoenix; whatever the biographical allusions are, it is clear that Apollinaire intended the imagery of renewal through fire in "Les Fiançailles" to have a broad spectrum of connotations. "Le Brasier" refers more specifically to love:

> J'ai jeté dans le noble feu
> Que je transporte et que j'adore
> De vives mains et même feu
> Ce Passé ces têtes de morts
> Flamme je fais ce que tu veux

. . . .
Où sont ces têtes que j'avais
Où est le Dieu de ma jeunesse
L'amour est devenu mauvais
Qu'au brasier les flammes renaissent
Mon âme au soleil se dévêt

I have cast into the noble fire, which I carry and worship, living hands, and the same fire, the past, the death's-heads. Flame! I do what you wish. . . . Where are those heads I once had? Where is the God of my youth? Love has turned evil. Let the flames in the brazier rise again. My soul strips down in the sun.

We now see that in these later poems the symbolic scheme of "La Chanson du mal-aimé" has shifted; the time of Christ and love ended in suffering and can seem either an age of numinosity, as in the earlier poem, or a doomed, mendacious one compared with the new transforming life of fire. This old era of fury-ridden loves is summed up in one striking image, where the poet's inspiration, Memory, has transcended the violence of passion, represented by Helen and Clytemnestra, and made the snakes of the Eumenides into the flame of regeneration: "O Mémoire, Combien de races qui forlignent/Des Tyndarides aux vipères ardentes de mon bonheur." The end of renewal is knowledge, knowledge to the point of destroying the knower, who accepts his end: "J'aimerais mieux nuit et jour dans les sphingeries/Vouloir savoir pour qu'enfin on m'y dévorât." The Templars of the end of "Les Fiançailles" were also, like the sphinxes, repositories of secret lore; poetry is conceived of as revelation and prophecy. One poem, "Vendémiaire," has a ceremony of revelation as its content; in it the poet, become a macrocosmal figure, drinks blood and wine to perform the sacrifice leading to regeneration.

Apollinaire's symbolism has stable elements like the reference to Christ's life, but it grew and modified with the years. In "Zone," the last poem of *Alcools* to be written, he originally had used the comparison between the death of love and Christ's end: the poet was crucified with a thief on either side. He discarded this passage, however, and reworked the poem into something quite different: it is related to his earlier symbolism but not identical with it. The references to modernity at the beginning of "Zone" have a few parallels in earlier imagery such as the "roses of electricity" in "Les Fiançailles." The renewal of poetry is, of course, involved in Apollinaire's broad theme of regeneration, but in "Zone" we must not take the beginning as an independent statement about art; the comparison of modernism with Christianity is essential to the unfolding of the themes of the poem, quite aside from any desire to account for the prosaic movement of the poem itself:

A la fin tu es las de ce monde ancien

Bergère ô tour Eiffel le troupeau des ponts bêle ce matin

Tu en as assez de vivre dans l'antiquité grecque et romaine

Ici même les automobiles ont l'air d'être anciennes
La religion seule est restée toute neuve la religion
Est restée simple comme les hangars de Port-Aviation

Seul en Europe tu n'es pas antique ô Christianisme
L'Européen le plus moderne c'est vous Pape Pie X
Et toi que les fenêtres observent la honte te retient
D'entrer dans une église et de t'y confesser ce matin
Tu lis les prospectus les catalogues les affiches qui chantent tout haut
Voilà la poésie ce matin et pour la prose il y a les journaux

In the end you are weary of this old world. Shepherdess, O Eiffel Tower, your flock of bridges is bleating this morning. You've had enough of living in Greek and Roman antiquity. Even the automobiles look old here. Only religion remains perfectly new; religion has stayed as simple as the hangars at the airport of Juvisy. Alone in Europe you are not antiquated, O Christianity. You are the most modern European, Pope Pius X. And you whom the windows watch, shame restrains you from going into a church and confessing there this morning. You read the handbills, catalogues, posters that sing aloud—that's the morning's poetry, and for prose there are the newspapers.

The allusions to Pius X's blessing an aviator who won a race and to the fact that some early automobiles were made to look like carriages show that Apollinaire's poetic method will not be just modernism, but as often the juxtaposition of old and new. The reference to Pius X leads in fact to a long comparison between the ascending Christ and an airplane, in which Elijah, Apollonius of Tyana, and mythological figures are invoked. And it is a magic aspect of Christ, his ascension, which is emphasized; Christ's modernity lies in his *merveilleux*, in the supernatural, not in his humanity. In "Zone" Christ's divine life, not his crucifixion, is the point of reference.

The movement of "Zone," which is a long inner monologue during a walk through Paris, covering about twenty-four hours, proceeds by juxtapositions, as well as narrative; both inner and outer events play a role. The long description of an austerely thaumaturgical Christ flying with miraculous Chinese pihi birds, the phoenix, sirens, and the roc from the *Arabian Nights* is dropped abruptly for the picture of the poet's fall:

> Aujourd'hui tu marches dans Paris les femmes sont ensanglantées
> C'était et je voudrais ne pas m'en souvenir c'était au déclin de la beauté
> Entourée de flammes ferventes Notre-Dame m'a regardé à Chartres
> Le sang de votre Sacré-Coeur m'a inondé à Montmartre
> Je suis malade d'ouïr les paroles bienheureuses
> L'amour dont je souffre est une maladie honteuse

Today you are walking in Paris. The women are covered with blood. It was—and I would prefer not to remember it—it was at the time of the fading of beauty. Wrapped in her fervent flames Our Lady looked at me in Chartres. The blood of your Sacred Heart deluged me at Montmartre. I'm sick from hearing blessed words. The love I suffer from is a venereal disease.

Earlier there had been images of the narrator's childhood devotions: the underlying theme of the day's wandering in "Zone" is separation from Christ, and the profanation of love is illustrated with particular intensity near the end of the poet's evening when he visits a prostitute. By a series of analogies and contrasts the poem has moved from the initial vision of modernity and redemption to increasingly dark episodes: the early images of the modern city are not simply a kind of aesthetic manifesto, as is often thought; on the contrary, they represent the purposefully misleading mood of morning, which the narrator's meditations modify in the course of his peregrinations in Paris and in memory. In the early hours of the day Christ and the world seem in harmony, and Christianity suits the present as well as it has ever suited the past; only as afternoon and evening draw on does the narrator see that the divine miracle and his own life have become less and less connected. When he sees the sun rising before he goes to bed, it suggests the emotional violence and despair of his life, not the

Christ symbol of tradition: "Adieu Adieu/Soleil cou coupé." But there is one note of reconciliation with Christ:

> Tu marches vers Auteuil tu veux aller chez toi à pied
> Dormir parmi tes fétiches d'Océanie et de Guinée
> Ils sont des Christ d'une autre forme et d'une autre croyance
> Ce sont les Christ inférieurs des obscures espérances

You are walking toward Auteuil, you want to go home on foot and sleep among your fetishes from the South Pacific and Guinea. They are Christs of another shape and creed; they are the lower Christs of dark hopes.

Through his modernist love of primitive art the narrator finds a Christ in proportion to his aspirations; the thematic conflict of the poem is dialectically resolved. Apollinaire has constructed in "Zone" and earlier poems a pattern whose analogy with Christian redemption is stressed but which is not identical with it, for Apollinaire envisages regeneration within the limits of life only. The coloring of his symbols—the sphinxeries of "Le Brasier," the order of the Templars with its secrets, the fetishes—is magical and esoteric; while there is apparently no transcendental divinity in any way comparable to that of Christianity, there are mysteries. Apollinaire rejects the humanitarian versions of Christianity and primarily retains from it, like the author of the second gospel, the miraculous.

The technique of symbolism in Apollinaire rests on one important principle: as the images multiply, sometimes almost beyond our ability to order them, intermittent terse statements give us some sense of direction: "L'amour est devenu mauvais," "Ce sont les Christ inférieurs," "A la fin les mensonges ne me font plus peur." This balancing of symbol and partial gloss is the attempt to compensate for our incapacity to refer all the disjunctive imagery to a typology or to understand the relationship of its parts. This is the typical modern symbolic texture replacing the allegory of earlier periods, and the prototype for it is the *Illuminations*. We are not by any means able in every case to work out the connection of statement and symbol; Dylan Thomas' verse, for example, is notoriously difficult in this respect. However, the guiding aesthetic conception is understood as a convention by the reader of modern poetry, just as the language of traditional allegory was once current.

While the spring of "Les Fiançailles," the brazier, and many of the settings and objects in Apollinaire's poetry have no literal meaning, Montale usually makes his poems out of scenes that do have literal coherence. Within this sometimes quite realistic framework, actions and things take on symbolic significance; the structure is closer to allegorical symbolism in this respect. In Montale's first volume, *Ossi di seppia* (1925), the handling of symbolism is still somewhat discursive: the wall, the sea envisaged as freedom or repetitive movement, the chain of existence, motionless motion ("immoto andare"), circles of all kinds, examples of life barely surviving on the rocky Ligurian shore, all present a fairly explicit picture of life, reinforced, at times, by commentary. The sensory vividness of the language is so great, however, that the poetry never seems abstract or pallid.

The breaking of the chain, the disturbance of circular movement is called salvation in one or two places in *Ossi di seppia*, but we must not take the word in the most direct Christian sense, it being by no means clear what salvation would consist of beyond freedom. Nor must we take the opposite theological terms of damnation or hell in the ordinary way:

> Lo sai: debbo riperderti e non posso.
> Come un tiro aggiustato mi sommuove
> ogni opera, ogni grido e anche lo spiro
> salino che straripa
> dai moli e fa l'oscura primavera
> di Sottoripa.
>
> Paese di ferrame e alberature
> a selva nella polvere del vespro.
> Un ronzio lungo viene dall'aperto,
> strazia come un'unghia ai vetri.
> Cerco il segno smarrito, il pegno
> solo ch'ebbi in grazia da te.
> E l'inferno è certo.

You know: I must lose you again and I cannot. Like an accurate shot every action startles me, every shout, and even the salty breeze which brims over the docks and makes the murky spring of the Genoa harbor. Landscape of iron structures and of shipmasts thick like a forest in the evening dust. A long whir comes in the air; it grates like a fingernail on window panes. I am looking for the lost sign, the only pledge I received as a grace from you. And hell is certain.

This poem is the first of the "Mottetti" in *Le Occasioni* (1939), a striking group of short poems devoted to a female figure who sometimes is literally present, sometimes present as an intimated force.[1] Intuitions, visions, and signs, as in the above poem, play a large role. "The lost sign" is typical of Montale's language in its allegory-like insistence on an enigmatic object. The hell her departure and the loss of her sign bring about is a psychological state and no more literally hell than Jean-Paul Sartre's *enfer.*

Salvation is by no means a clear theme in *Le Occasioni;* indeed the female figure, Clizia or sunflower, as she is eventually called in accordance with the mythological associations of the name, appears bound up with the darkest events; in "Il Ritorno" there is an infernal boatman, furies, an obfuscate sun, and the poet says to her, "ecco il tuo morso/Oscuro di tarantola: son pronto."

Communication with Clizia sometimes takes other forms than the vision or intimation. In "Notizie dall'Amiata" the poet writes her a letter; the mountain resort in autumn is described with the richer, occasionally almost fantastic imagery Montale evolved after *Ossi di seppia:*

> Il fuoco d'artifizio del maltempo
> sarà murmure d'arnie a tarda sera.
> La stanza ha travature
> tarlate ed un sentore di meloni
> penetra dall'assito. Le fumate
> morbide che risalgono una valle
> d'elfi e di funghi fino al cono diafano
> della cima m'intorbidano i vetri,
> e ti scrivo di qui, da questo tavolo
> remoto, dalla cellula di miele
> di una sfera lanciata nello spazio—
> e le gabbie coperte, il focolare
> dove i marroni esplodono, le vene
> di salnitro e di muffa sono il quadro
> dove tra poco romperai. La vita

che t'affàbula è ancora troppo breve
se ti contiene! Schiude la tua icona
il fondo luminoso. Fuori piove.

The fireworks of the storm will turn into rain, like the murmur of beehives late in
the evening. The room has worm-eaten beams, and the odor of melons rises through
the flooring. The soft lines of mist, which rise along a valley of elves and mushrooms to the transparent cone of the peak, darken my windows, and I am writing
to you from here, from the faraway table, from the honey-cell of a sphere hurled
into space—and the covered cages, the hearth where chestnuts are exploding, the
veins of saltpeter and mold are the setting where shortly you will emerge. Life
which gives you the quality of a myth is too short if it contains you! Your photograph suddenly has a background of gold. Outside it is raining.

We note immediately the importance of a pleasantly closed-in space;
the beehive analogy is the first of the representations of clear shapes in
the poem. The poet feels the presence of Clizia, whose photograph
turns into an icon, seeming almost to come to life, and he undertakes
to explain to her what he has discovered and what he wants her to see
of his revelation:

E tu seguissi le fragili architetture
annerite dal tempo e dal carbone,
i cortili quadrati che hanno nel mezzo
il pozzo profondissimo; tu seguissi
il volo infagottato degli uccelli
notturni e in fondo al borro l'allucciolío
della Galassia, la fascia d'ogni tormento.

And would that you might follow along these fragile buildings black from time and
coal smoke, the square courtyards that have a very deep well in their center. Would
that you might follow the shrouded flight of the night birds and in the depths of the
ditch the glittering of the Milky Way, the bandage of all pain.

The binding Milky Way is a variant of the symbol of the chain of existence, but here it not only shuts in, it lenifies and heals anguish. The
buildings and well are static images of well-defined shape; that they
suggest a prison is relevant to later lines. The storm, we gradually
realize, means the disturbance of the chain or of the poet's perception
of it, the questioning of the universe; the poet invokes the end of the
storm's upheaval:

Ritorna domani piú freddo, vento del nord,
. . . .
e tutto sia lente tranquilla, dominio, prigione
del senso che non dispera! Ritorna piú forte
vento di settentrione che rendi care
le catene e suggelli le spore del possibile!
Son troppo strette le strade, gli asini neri
che zoccolano in fila dànno scintille,
dal picco nascosto rispondono vampate di magnesio.
Oh il gocciolío che scende a rilento
dalle casipole buie, il tempo fatto acqua,
il lungo colloquio coi poveri morti, la cenere, il vento,
il vento che tarda, la morte, la morte che vive!

Return tomorrow and colder, north wind . . . and let everything be a peaceful lens, control, the prison of the sense no longer despairing! Come back stronger, north wind, and make dear our chains and seal up every germ of the possible! The streets are too narrow; the black donkeys clattering by in a line strike sparks; from the hidden peak flares of magnesium answer. Oh, the dripping that comes haltingly down from the dark hovels, time turned into water, the long dialogue with the poor dead, ashes, the wind, the wind delaying in coming, death, living death.

The chain can be a comfort; it assures that everything will be in its place, the living and the dead, with no disturbing communication. The conflict of revolt against the chain and longing for the dulling prison in which there is no despair is called a Christian struggle, and it will die away as the storm waters are carried off in culverts, symbols of the chain:

Questa rissa cristiana che non ha
se non parole d'ombra e di lamento
che ti porta di me? Meno di quanto
t'ha rapito la gora che s'interra
dolce nella sua chiusa di cemento.
Una ruota di mola, un vecchio tronco,
confini ultimi al mondo. Si disfà
un cumulo di strame: e tardi usciti
a unire la mia veglia al tuo profondo
sonno che li riceve, i porcospini
s'abbeverano a un filo di pietà.

This Christian conflict, all shadowy words and lament, what of me does it bring to you? Less than what is taken way by the culvert gently interred in its cement cas-ing. A mill wheel, an old tree trunk, the frontiers of the world. A pile of straw is overturned, and emerging late to join my vigil to your deep sleep, porcupines drink at a trickle of piety.

The symbolic porcupines, quiet, timid creatures, find only a trickle left of the storm, thus representing resignation to the universe. Limits are again established, the culvert's form is pleasantly constraining, and the somnolent Clizia will perceive the poet's calmed frame of mind.

The communications between Clizia and the poet in "Notizie dall'Amiata" are magic, and magic events, omens, and talismans are frequent even in the realistic settings in *Le Occasioni*; magic lies perhaps not so much in the nature of the events themselves, as in their mysterious causality. Symbolic poetry with a coherent literal level of sense, that is, allegorical symbolism, makes much use of such effects: magic is important as a poetic technique and does not imply anything more. In "Nuove Stanze" a chessboard and cigarette smoke seem to be part of a ritual by which something will be revealed:

> Poi che gli ultimi fili di tabacco
> al tuo gesto si spengono nel piatto
> di cristallo, al soffitto lenta sale
> la spirale del fumo
> che gli alfieri e i cavalli degli scacchi
> guardano stupefatti; e nuovi anelli
> la seguono, piú mobili di quelli
> delle tue dita.
>
> La morgana che in cielo liberava
> torri e ponti è sparita
> al primo soffio; s'apre la finestra
> non vista e il fumo s'agita. Là in fondo,
> altro stormo si muove: una tregenda
> d'uomini che non sa questo tuo incenso,
> nella scacchiera di cui puoi tu sola
> comporre il senso.
>
> Il mio dubbio d'un tempo era se forse
> tu stessa ignori il giuoco che si svolge
> sul quadrato e ora è nembo alle tue porte.

When the last shreds of tobacco are put out by your gesture in the crystal ashtray, the spiral of smoke slowly rises to the ceiling and is watched by the astonished bishops and knights. And new rings follow it, moving more than those on your fingers. The mirage which cast forth towers and bridges in the air has disappeared at the first breath of breeze; the unseen window opens and the smoke is stirred. Down there another horde is moving: a coven of men who do not know of your incense, in the chessboard of which you alone can make out the sense. At one time I doubted whether you yourself knew the game unfolding on the board and now become a storm cloud at the gates.

The witches' sabbath of history—the time is the late 1930s in Florence—rages outside, but Clizia alone understands it. Some unspoken conclusion has been reached, and, as the bell of the Palazzo Vecchio rings menacingly, history becomes concentrated in what is not just a concave mirror but a weapon:

> Oggi so ciò che vuoi; batte il suo fioco
> tocco la Martinella ed impaura
> le sagome d'avorio in una luce
> spettrale di nevaio. Ma resiste
> e vince il premio della solitaria
> veglia chi può con te allo specchio ustorio
> che accieca le pedine opporre i tuoi
> occhi d'acciaio.

Today I know what you wish; the Martinella is tolling weakly and terrifying the ivory figures in their spectral snow light. But he resists and wins the reward of the lonely vigil who can, with you, oppose your steel eyes to the burning-glass which blinds the pawns.

In this battle of forces the very material Clizia's eyes are said to be made of suggests sinister power: in a later poem, "Gli Orecchini," she appears in a mirror, amid medusa-jellyfish and bombers in the evening air, and infernal hands adjust her talismanic coral earrings.

The ambiguity of the figure of Clizia, who, it is clear, does not represent salvation in a simple antithesis with damnation, is not uncharacteristic of the analogues of redemption in modern literature, where wisdom, although placed in opposition to ignorance, as in "Nuove Stanze," remains nonetheless dark. Knowledge, we recall, is the ultimate phase of the poet's regeneration in Apollinaire, but does not obviate his certain end; indeed, it leads to it.

The storm, a major symbol of Montale's as early as "Arsenio,"

the most famous poem in *Ossi di seppia*, fuses with the imagery of
warfare in *La Bufera ed altro*, just as the rain and lightning were part
of the inner battle of "Notizie dall'Amiata," The apocalyptic conflict is
in itself of the nature of salvation in the modern world, as it emerges
from one poem of *La Bufera ed altro*, which goes as far as any poem
of Montale's in suggesting historical dimensions:

> L'ombra della magnolia giapponese
> si sfoltisce or che i bocci paonazzi
> sono caduti. Vibra intermittente
> in vetta una cicala. Non è piú
> il tempo dell'unísono vocale,
> Clizia, il tempo del nume illimitato
> che divora e rinsangua i suoi fedeli.
> Spendersi era piú facile, morire
> al primo batter d'ale, al primo incontro
> col nemico, un trastullo. Comincia ora
> la via piú dura: ma non te consunta
> dal sole e radicata, e pure morbida
> cesena che sorvoli alta le fredde
> banchine del tuo fiume,—non te fragile—
> fuggitiva cui zenit nadir cancro
> capricorno rimasero indistinti
> perché la guerra fosse in te e in chi adora
> su te le stimme del tuo Sposo, flette
> il brivido del gelo . . . Gli altri arretrano
> e piegano. La lima che sottile
> incide tacerà, la vuota scorza
> di chi cantava sarà presto polvere
> di vetro sotto i piedi, l'ombra è livida,—
> è l'autunno, è l'inverno, è l'oltrecielo
> che ti conduce e in cui me getto, cèfalo
> saltato in secco al novilunio.

> Addio.

The shadow of the Japanese magnolia thins out, now that its purple buds have fall-
en. At the top a cicada hums from time to time. It is no longer the time of the choir
in unison, Clizia, the time of limitless godhead devouring and strengthening its
faithful. Expending oneself was easier, dying at the first wing beat, at the first encounter with the enemy, a diversion. Now begins a harder path, but the shudder of
frost will not bend you, consumed by the sun and deep-rooted, and at the same time
a soft thrush flying over the cold banks of your river; it will not bend you, fragile

and fugitive, to whom zenith, nadir, cancer, and capricorn remained indistinct, so that the war was in you and in him who worships on you the stigmas of your Spouse. The others retreat and shrivel. The file that delicately cuts will fall still, the empty husk of the singer will soon be powdered glass underfoot; the shadow is leaden—it is autumn, winter; it is the beyond that leads you and into which I cast myself, a mullet leaping onto the dry bank under the new moon. Farewell.

Clizia is here at once the sunflower of a solar Christ and the sphere of inner struggle, the "rissa cristiana." The seasonal pattern of the poem comes from spring and summer being associated with real war in *La Bufera*; the fish at the end is not the only example in the volume of this old Christian emblem being used as a symbol of life. With "L'Ombra della magnolia" Montale takes leave of the wartime poems and rounds off the cycle of Clizia in his poetry. Like Apollinaire's symbolism, Montale's grew and changed in personal circumstances, without loss, however, of continuity.

It has been suggested that the role of Beatrice in the *Commedia* is a completely heterodox conception, and certainly the figure of Clizia is even less in conformity with the normal associations of Christianity. That there are analogies between Clizia and Christ bringing not peace but a sword does not make identity: *comparaison n'est pas raison.* Revelation but not regeneration, reverence but not rebirth characterize Montale's symbolic system: as with other modern poetry using fragments of Christian mythology it is doubtful that a clear, consistent theological definition could be made of the content of the Clizia poems. The well-established abstract entities of true allegory are replaced by conceptions that are more image and emotion than idea: the metaphysical is but a facet of the psychological, and it is very wrong to reduce Montale's poetry to the former, whose existence is so tenuous.

Montale's handling of statement and symbolism differs from Apollinaire's not only in that there are more developed scenes, but also in that, as the settings are fuller and more readily grasped, the statements, on the other hand, are often more cryptic, more seemingly unrelated to or in conflict with the imagery. For example, in "Notizie dall'Amiata" the invocation to the wind to strengthen the poet's chains and narrow the range of the possible is followed by the declaration that the streets are *too* narrow. More often, the difficulties of Montale's verse come not so much from expressions that are in themselves difficult, as from the contextual problem. Montale has an especially noticeable taste for enigma occurring in passages that are relatively clear: like his tendency to construct scenes, this reflects unquestionably, as do other elements in his poetry, his study of Dante and his awareness of the effects of traditional allegory.

The magical coloring we have seen in Apollinaire and Montale's symbolism has its counterpart in Lorca's poetic world, where the mysterious event plays a large role. It is unfortunate that translations of the title like "Gypsy Ballads" seem to prejudge the character of Lorca's greatest work, *Romancero Gitano* (1928); the gypsies of his poems are not the nomads and fortune-tellers of tradition (they are not always distinguishable from Spaniards), and the form of the poem bears no resemblance to any British ballad. Folklore is not their point or principal content.

In *Romancero Gitano* Lorca uses imagery that is complexly related from poem to poem, but these images—moon, sea, fish, river, flowers, horses, mountains, hard light, cold, stars, dawn, and things green, black, or silver—do not have stable, recurrent symbolic values: they serve to make of the *Romancero* a coherent whole, a book with a coloring peculiarly its own. It would be a mistake, however, to assign one value to the moon, for example, which is menacing in "Romance de la luna, luna," serene in "Romance sonámbulo," absent in some night poems, used figuratively in "Muerte de Antoñito el Camborio" and "Romance del emplazado," suggests chaos at night in "Muerto de amor," and casts ecstatic light in "Romance de la Guardia Civil española."

It is rather in the narrative structure of the poems of *Romancero Gitano* that we must look for symbolic implications. Gratuitous events, which imply unfathomable, supernatural causality beyond control are an important element; the opening "Romance de la luna, luna" establishes these as threatening. The imagistic detail of the poem supports the quality of gratuitousness (the moon has a "bustle of spikenard") and suggests the uncertain consistency of a reality ("Por el olivar venían,/Bronce y sueño, los gitanos") beyond which mysterious powers are at work. When Saint Christopher, as the wind, pursues the gypsy girl Preciosa in the second poem, we see a further implication in unfathomable causality: it is counter to freedom and the seeking of satisfaction. The wind threatens her precisely as she is making music, while the "water gypsies" are building "pergolas of snails" for their distraction. The imagery of freedom has its most famous expression in the volume at the beginning of "Romance sonámbulo," where it is underscored by the bold use of a first person corresponding to the dream of a wounded young man brought in only later:

> Verde que te quiero verde.
> Verde viento. Verdes ramas.
> El barco sobre la mar
> y el caballo en la montaña.
> Con la sombra en la cintura
> ella sueña en su baranda,
> verde carne, pelo verde,
> con ojos de fría plata.
> Verde que te quiero verde.
> Bajo la luna gitana,
> las cosas la están mirando
> y ella no puede mirarlas.

Green I want you green. Green wind, green branches. The boat on the sea and the horse on the mountain. With shadow around her waist she is dreaming on her veranda, green skin, green hair, with eyes of cold silver. Green I want you green. Beneath the gypsy moon things are looking at her and she can't look at them.

The poem is one of several examples in the book of fragmented narrative with a concealed plot. The interpretation of the poem must lie not in the invention of a plot to fit the episodes but in reading their thematic suggestions. The opening images and the "niña amarga" in her trance, and later hovering over the pool with her "moon icicle," represent a dream-like harmony and freedom, in contrast with the triple opposing elements of the dawn, the wounded young man and his *compadre* seeking the green moon verandas, and the *guardias civiles* in pursuit. An important accessory theme emerges from the conversation of the young man and the older one:

> —Compadre, quiero cambiar
> mi caballo por su casa,
> mi montura por su espejo,
> mi cuchillo, por su manta.
> Compadre, vengo sangrando,
> desde los puertos de Cabra.
> —Si yo pudiera, mocito,
> este trato se cerraba.
> Pero yo ya no soy yo,
> ni mi casa es ya mi casa.

"Friend, I want to exchange my horse for her house, my saddle for her mirror, my knife for her cloak. Friend, I have come bleeding from the passes of Cabra." "If I could, boy, this deal would be already closed. But I am not myself, nor is my house mine."

The older man has lost his identity and therefore his goals of freedom and satisfaction. A whole poem, "Romance de la pena negra," is devoted to this theme, and we see that loss of identity is the opposite and complementary curse to being chosen by malevolent forces—the latter, for example, the case of the summoned man in "Romance del emplazado." The first situation, disappearance of the feeling of identity, as in "Romance de la pena negra," means loss of all direction, inner or outer; the other case involves the intensification of the feeling of mysterious causality through the gratuitousness of events. The latter is made especially perceptible to the reader in "Romance sonámbulo," in reference to the young man, whose death agony is vivid and detailed, while the cause of his wounds is unknown:

> —Compadre, quiero morir
> decentemente en mi cama.
> De acero, si puede ser,
> con las sábanas de holanda.
> ¿No ves la herida que tengo
> desde el pecho a la garganta?
> —Trescientas rosas morenas
> lleva tu pechera blanca.
> Tu sangre rezuma y huele
> alrededor de tu faja.
> Pero yo ya no soy yo,

ni mi casa es ya mi casa.
—Dejadme subir al menos
hasta las altas barandas;
¡dejadme subir!, dejadme,
hasta las verdes barandas.
Barandales de la luna
por donde retumba el agua.

"Friend, I want to die decently in my bed. A steel one, if possible, with sheets of fine linen. Can't you see my wound from chest to throat?" "Your white shirt bears three hundred dark roses. Your blood is oozing and smelling around your sash. But I am no longer myself, nor is my house mine." "Let me at least go up to the high verandas; let me go up! Let me, as far as the green verandas. Verandas of the moon from which water roars down."

They do not find the "niña amarga" and we do not know why; again the narrative technique is omission of causality to produce an effect of supernatural malevolence.

Poems devoted to the archangels associated with the principal Andalusian cities occupy the center of *Romancero Gitano*: as usual, the folklore and locality are incidental to the larger design. "San Miguel (Granada)" is made of three tiers: their juxtaposition at first seems unmotivated, but actually it has a subtle thematic design. The saints represent holiness and beauty, the professed transcendental values of the world:

San Miguel, lleno de encajes
en la alcoba de su torre,
enseña sus bellos muslos
ceñidos por los faroles.

Arcángel domesticado
en el gesto de las doce,
finge una cólera dulce
de plumas y ruiseñores.
San Miguel canta en los vidrios;
efebo de tres mil noches,
fragante de agua colonia
y lejano de las flores.

Saint Michael full of lace, in the bed alcove of his tower, shows his beautiful thighs surrounded by lanterns. A domesticated archangel, in the grimace of twelve o'clock, he feigns a gentle anger of feathers and nightingales. Saint Michael sings in the panes, the ephebe of three thousand nights, smelling of cologne and distant from flowers.

The saint is narcissistic and refined. His worshippers, who form the middle tier, long for a "yesterday of nightingales" or are merely coarse peasants; in neither case do they look up about them outside church:

> Se ven desde las barandas,
> por el monte, monte, monte,
> mulos y sombras de mulos
> cargados de girasoles.
> . . . .
>   Un cielo de mulos blancos
> cierra sus ojos de azogue
> . . . .
> Y el agua se pone fría
> para que nadie la toque.
> Agua loca y descubierta,
> por el monte, monte, monte.

You can see from the verandas mules on the mountain and shadows of mules loaded with sunflowers. . . . A sky of white mules closes its quicksilver eyes . . . and the water turns cold so no one will touch it, open, wild water on the mountain.

The magnificent sky and torrent symbolize the one true value: freedom. In comparison the saint is fussy and constrained, salvation merely pretty. In "San Rafael (Córdoba)" we have a picture of the church's heaven: closed funeral carriages arrive at the Guadalquivir, and there rises from the river a vision of a celestial Cordova, a paradise of classical architecture, guarded by a fish—the saint—and boys, in distant allusion to the story of Raphael and Tobias. The triptych of archangels is completed by Gabriel of Seville, whose skin is night apple, his muscle silver, his chest jaspar. Flower images abound as he announces her pregnancy to a gypsy woman. He has the appearance of a finely formed, slightly epicene gypsy boy, the type of Antoñito el Camborio in the two following poems, and it is important to stress the connection between the holy and beauty or artifice, the divine as precious, destructible, and even associated with the perishable such as youth, flowers, and fruit. Archangels are of course exempt from earthly damage, but Antoñito el Camborio, "worthy of an empress," who is a mortal image of the divine in the two poems devoted to him, is arrested by *guardias civiles* and murdered by his cousins, who are jealous of his skin, polished with oil and jasmine. Antoñito, "moreno de verde luna," is received by angels at his death; they treasure his fragile beauty but have not protected him. The impression that beauty and holiness are subject to destruction is made explicit in the final poem of the cycle: when the *Guardia Civil* destroys the gypsy city in "Romance de la Guardia Civil española," Saint Joseph is wounded, and the Virgin is powerless before the onslaught at the "gate of Bethlehem."

The sense of an end is heightened in the *romances* dealing with Antoñito, where he represents the line of gypsies dwindled into effeteness and into a perfection of grace never to be duplicated. The death brought by the *Guardia Civil* to the gypsies in general in the last *romance* sums up the triumph of death over beauty and freedom. The center of the *Romancero* had dealt with archangels, but we see in the end that holy figures of beauty cannot resist the ultimate reality of nothingness: the celestial Cordova is a mirage, Saint Michael an impotent narcissist. The articulations of the cycle of the *Romancero Gitano* are more complicated, however, than a simple antithesis between beauty and death. The theme of freedom is used as a contrast to the saint's peculiar beauty in "San Miguel," and Antoñito no longer represents the gypsies who wandered alone on the mountains; elsewhere, as in "Romance sonámbulo," freedom is the antithesis of death, as we might expect. Death is the greatest sign that we are subject to an unknown pattern of causality, a force that could be called fate—the idea is more present than the word in *Romancero Gitano*. The assumption that death is not random but part of a concatenation of events means that it is the true transcendental power and therefore establishes its antithetical relationship with religious conceptions as well as with freedom. The double antithesis, the use of three thematic centers, gives Lorca's poem cycle an unusual, subtle pattern, in keeping with the tendency of some modern poets to avoid merely single antitheses as a structural principle.

The dark thematics of *Romancero Gitano* recur in pronounced form in the later *Poeta en Nueva York*, especially in the Christmas section, and confirm that Lorca's vision is more truly demonic than that of Eliot in *The Wasteland* or other poets to whom the word is sometimes applied. It certainly sets him apart as well from the surrealists, with whom he is often compared. The gratuitous event in the latter, as in Apollinaire, tends to be surprising and interesting rather than threatening. The fact of Lorca's having chosen a narrative form in *Romancero Gitano* makes it to my mind a more powerful means of symbolizing demonic causality than the more purely imagistic *Poeta en Nueva York*, the technique of which bears closer textural analogies to surrealist style. Narrative is less frequent in experimental modern poetry than the pattern of image and statement: Lorca's achievement stands out all the more for it.

Yeats' poetic thought is often spoken of slightingly, with little sense of how powerful and ingenious a synthesis he made. To be sure, many of its details, as they appear in his chief exposition, *A Vision* (1925), are vague, but he accomplished the extraordinary task of devising a philosophy that includes a metempsychotic cycle and release, a cyclic view of history, a transcendental view of art, a lower transcendental existence of the soul as yet unreleased, dualisms reconciled with unitarian patterns, and the simultaneous presence of the incompatible ideas of tragedy and absolute redemption. Merely one or two aspects of this vast design would have sufficed as material for most poets; Yeats, however, did not want to sacrifice any of the patterns he had admired in religious thought and poetry.

The basic shape of this philosophy of the soul he borrowed from occultism, though divested of its customary concern with emanation and original fall: the soul passes through a graded series of human incarnations before achieving its release, the latter associated with the sun and symbolized by dance. Yeats' great ingeniousness lay in substituting for the progressive brightening and lightening of the soul, such as we find in occultist systems like Hugo's, a twenty-eight phase cycle dominated by the moon and so constructed that evolution through it could be taken, like the moon's cycle, as a waxing and waning of precious spiritual powers. In other words, the soul's cycle functions as a growth from and return to the original inchoate state.

Usually such cycles are iterative and are not combined with any idea of release from cyclic movement such as we find in Yeats' dance in the sun. One might say that the soul passes through a tragic cycle before regeneration. Yeats' poems focus ordinarily on the cycle and not on the ultimate release; in other words, their point of view is human more often than divine, absolute, and all-embracing. Thus Yeats' system recognizes both a dualistic conception based on the full and dark of the moon, and an ultimately unitarian vision of the ending of lunar dominance.

Within the moon cycle there are two phases through which the soul passes without incarnation, for they do not support life: these are the first or dark of the moon and the fifteenth or full. The first phase, which is also the last before release, is called Hades in "Byzantium" but it is also called heaven by the soul:

> *My Soul.* I summon to the winding ancient stair;
>   Set all your mind upon the steep ascent,
>   Upon the broken, crumbling battlement,
>   Upon the breathless starlit air,
>   Upon the star that marks the hidden pole;
>   Fix every wandering thought upon
>   That quarter where all thought is done:
>   Who can distinguish darkness from the soul?
> . . . .
>   Think of ancestral night that can,
>   If but imagination scorn the earth
>   And intellect its wandering
>   To this and that and t'other thing,
>   Deliver from the crime of death and birth.
> . . . .
>   Such fullness in that quarter overflows
>   And falls into the basin of the mind
>   That man is stricken deaf and dumb and blind,
>   For intellect no longer knows
>   *Is* from the *Ought*, or *Knower* from the *Known*—
>   That is to say, ascends to Heaven . . .

The Soul is drawn toward the insentient state symbolized by the dark of the moon, not realizing that its ultimate solar regeneration will follow; the pessimism is ironic in the larger scheme albeit meaningful to the Soul caught in what it sees as the tragic uselessness of the cycle of fecundity. The Self replies:

> I am content to live it all again
> And yet again, if it be life to pitch
> Into the frog-spawn of a blind man's ditch,
> A blind man battering blind men
> . . . .
> I am content to follow to its source
> Every event in action or in thought;
> Measure the lot; forgive myself the lot!
> When such as I cast out remorse
> So great a sweetness flows into the breast
> We must laugh and we must sing,
> We are blest by everything,
> Everything we look upon is blest. ("A Dialogue of Self and Soul")

Yeats' system encourages divergent points of view as between God and man, self and soul. The crime of birth and death is a judgment dependent on one way of looking at the wheel of incarnation; there is no absolute fall or original sin in Yeats' thought, merely the illusion of one fostered by the individual's travail. The incarnate soul is not only excercised by the thought of the dark of the moon and insentience but also by the peculiar fifteenth phase:

> To such a pitch of folly I am brought,
> Being caught between the pull
> Of the dark moon and the full,
> The commonness of thought and images
> That have the frenzy of our western seas. ("The Double Vision of Michael Robartes")

The vision Michael Robartes has of the fifteenth is that of a dancer flanked by figures emblematic of wisdom:

> On the grey rock of Cashel I suddenly saw
> A Sphinx with woman breast and lion paw,
> A Buddha, hand at rest,
> Hand lifted up that blest;

> And right between these two a girl at play
> That, it may be, had danced her life away,
> For now being dead it seemed
> That she of dancing dreamed.
>
> Although I saw it all in the mind's eye
> There can be nothing solider till I die;
> I saw by the moon's light
> Now at its fifteenth night.

The dancer also symbolizes the state of ultimate release, and here we see the peculiar quality of the fifteenth phase: it also is a release, but a relative and temporary one; there is lunar respite for the soul as well as the ultimate solar one. In Yeats' short play "Purgatory" a murder under the full moon is intended to stop the cycle of birth and death; it is a violent, mistaken action, undertaken because of the seemingly dualistic character of the world: the inhuman full moon seems to represent the absolute good and therefore demands, as the main character sees it, immediate expiation of the crime of incarnation. The wiser Self of "Dialogue of Self and Soul" realizes that the crime is relative, like the fifteenth phase, and he alone can forgive himself, there being no judging power, only the absolute of the ultimate solar release. (This impersonal conception of the divine is characteristic of occultism.) However, awareness of evil is most intense to the soul in phase fifteen, and since tragic art springs from this, we must not deprecate its importance in the dialectic chain of states of the soul.

Since the soul in phase fifteen is out of incarnation and in purgatory, so to speak, or in the state where the consciousness of evil is the most clear, this phase represents an absolute vision within the bounds of the life cycle; the fifteenth phase, being transcendent, is therefore analogous to the work of art: in both, soul becomes the simulacrum of a body, thought becomes image. Art can thus be identified with the aspiration toward the temporary release and antilife of phase fifteen:

> O sages standing in God's holy fire
> As in the gold mosaic of a wall,
> Come from the holy fire, perne in a gyre,
> And be the singing-masters of my soul.
> Consume my heart away; sick with desire

And fastened to a dying animal
It knows not what it is; and gather me
Into the artifice of eternity. ("Sailing to Byzantium")

Eternity is, of course, relative, as is art and everything else in the lunar cycle, to the ultimate solar transformation of the soul, but within this limited dualism of life and art we recognize the temporal-transcendental antithesis of life and the pure contemplation of beauty, as we find it in early Yeats and late nineteenth-century French poets. "I hail the superhuman," says the soul, the generalized soul who speaks "Byzantium."

The unpurged images of day recede;
The Emperor's drunken soldiery are abed;
Night resonance recedes, night-walkers' song
After great cathedral gong;
A starlit or a moonlit dome disdains
All that man is,
All mere complexities,
The fury and the mire of human veins.

Before me floats an image, man or shade,
Shade more than man, more image than a shade;
For Hades' bobbin bound, in mummy-cloth
May unwind the winding path;
A mouth that has no moisture and no breath
Breathless mouths may summon;
I hail the superhuman;
I call it death-in-life and life-in-death.

The allegory of the first stanza is of the soul passing into phase one (starlit) or fifteen (moonlit) and seeing life's dualistic urges and complexities as nugatory. The "image" is the way souls appear in the fifteenth phase, and we recognize the ambiguous way the transcendental is inimical to life in late nineteenth-century representations of beauty. Like all fine allegory the literal level is carefully worked out, here the sea being life surrounding the night city of the soul:

At midnight on the Emperor's pavement flit
Flames that no faggot feeds, nor steel has lit,
Nor storm disturbs, flames begotten of flame,

Where blood-begotten spirits come
And all complexities of fury leave,
Dying into a dance,
An agony of trance,
An agony of flame that cannot singe a sleeve.

Astraddle on the dolphin's mire and blood,
Spirit after spirit! The smithies break the flood,
The golden smithies of the Emperor!
Marbles of the dancing floor
Break bitter furies of complexity,
Those images that yet
Fresh images beget,
That dolphin-torn, that gong-tormented sea.

The purgatorial flames in Yeats do not have an absolute moral value because there is no ultimate evil; rather they cleanse as much in an aesthetic sense, allowing the pure pattern of the phases to appear. Knowledge and art, which bears knowledge, come closer to representing an absolute value than do ordinary moral qualities alone. With knowledge we see that the cycle is not evil:

The purity of the unclouded moon
Has flung its arrowy shaft upon the floor.
Seven centuries have passed and it is pure,
The blood of innocence has left no stain.
There, on blood-saturated ground, have stood
Soldier, assassin, executioner,
Whether for daily pittance or in blind fear
Or out of abstract hatred, and shed blood,
But could not cast a single jet thereon.
Odour of blood on the ancestral stair!
And we that have shed none must gather there
And clamour in drunken frenzy for the moon.
. . . .
For wisdom is the property of the dead,
A something incompatible with life; and power,
Like everything that has the stain of blood,
A property of the living; but no stain
Can come upon the visage of the moon
When it has looked in glory from a cloud. ("Blood and the Moon")

The moon stands for a realization, especially in art, of the nature of the phases through which the soul passes and of the fact that evil, while it must be realized and recognized, is relative to the larger pattern. The irony is of course that in its normal incarnate phases the individual has not wisdom but only the contradictory urges of the soul toward the lunar absolutes of dark and full and of the self toward perpetuating the crime of birth and death.

The historical references in "Byzantium" and "Blood and the Moon" bring us to another extraordinary dimension of Yeats' thought: making a division unknown to the main occultist tradition, he ascribes to history an iterative, cyclic pattern in contrast to the one-time evolution of the soul through its phases. The vision of the *tragique* of life, which late nineteenth-century poets symbolized by the solar cycle, is projected onto the unfolding of history by Yeats. The details of his system need not concern us here, save to note that medieval Byzantium represents a high point, symbolized by phase fifteen of the soul. What is important is that like all iterative cyclic systems Yeats' represents an escape from the terror of history through knowledge of its processes. Here visions of beauty and of raging crowds in ragged lace give way to the zero point of the historical cycle symbolized by the dark of the moon:

> The cloud-pale unicorns, the eyes of aquamarine,
> The quivering half-closed eyelids, the rags of cloud or of lace,
> Or eyes that rage has brightened, arms it has made lean,
> Give place to an indifferent multitude, give place
>
> To brazen hawks. Nor self-delighting reverie,
> Nor hate of what's to come, nor pity for what's gone,
> Nothing but grip of claw, and the eye's complacency,
> The innumerable clanging wings that have put out the moon.
>
> I turn away and shut the door, and on the stair
> Wonder how many times I could have proved my worth
> In something that all others understand or share;
> But O! ambitious heart, had such a proof drawn forth
> A company of friends, a conscience set at ease,
> It had but made us pine the more. The abstract joy,
> The half-read wisdom of daemonic images,
> Suffice the ageing man as once the growing boy. ("Meditations in Time of Civil War")

The abstract joy is in knowledge, which is redemption from history, even from such visions of the return of evil as this one rising out of images of the Irish Civil War:

> Violence upon the roads: violence of horses;
> Some few have handsome riders, are garlanded
> On delicate sensitive ear or tossing mane,
> But wearied running round and round in their courses
> All break and vanish, and evil gathers head:
> Herodias' daughters have returned again,
> A sudden blast of dusty wind and after
> Thunder of feet, tumult of images,
> Their purpose in the labyrinth of the wind;
> And should some crazy hand dare touch a daughter
> All turn with amorous cries, or angry cries,
> According to the wind, for all are blind.
> But now wind drops, dust settles; thereupon
> There lurches past, his great eyes without thought
> Under the shadow of stupid straw-pale locks,
> That insolent fiend Robert Artisson
> To whom the love-lorn Lady Kyteler brought
> Bronzed peacock feathers, red combs of her cocks. ("Nineteen Hundred and
>   Nineteen")

(Herodias' daughters are the wind in Irish folklore; Robert Artisson was an evil alchemist.) Aside from Byzantium, Yeats' images of history are usually of the turning points: Dionysus' death, the conception of Helen ultimately giving rise to the Trojan War, the Second Coming, "Phantoms of Hatred and of the Heart's Fullness and of the Coming Emptiness" as in "Meditations in Time of Civil War"; what this focusing upon the articulations of history means is that its historicity is dispelled, and only its iterative, design-giving elements are left. From the standpoint of the specific moment, history may be an absolute evil, just as life is for the soul aspiring to phase fifteen or the end of the lunar cycle, but most mythic visions of cycles are consolations against the circumstances of the moment and free man from them. From this comes the tragic joy Yeats once expressed:

> The gyres! the gyres! Old Rocky Face, look forth;
> Things thought too long can be no longer thought;

For beauty dies of beauty, worth of worth,
And ancient lineaments are blotted out.
Irrational streams of blood are staining earth;
Empedocles has thrown all things about;
Hector is dead and there's a light in Troy;
We that look on but laugh in tragic joy.
. . . .
Conduct and work grow coarse, and coarse the soul,
What matter? Those that Rocky Face holds dear,
Lovers of horses and of women, shall,
From marble of a broken sepulchre,
Or dark betwixt the polecat and the owl,
Or any rich, dark nothing disinter
The workman, noble and saint, and all things run
On that unfashionable gyre again. ("The Gyres")

The varied points of view on life and the soul in Yeats' poetry come from an elaborate dialectic pattern. Phases one and fifteen of the soul's journey appear to be opposites, the fifteenth representing transcendental awareness, but they are both part of the lunar cycle which itself will end in the sun. Phase fifteen is particularly crucial, since its transcendental state will be transcended. Phase one, which consists of inchoate formlessness is not simply the beginning but also the end of the lunar cycle: paradoxically nothing can exist—civilization or the regenerate soul—without being reabsorbed at least briefly into the primordial unity of chaos. The negative qualities of phase one, like the absolute-seeming character of phase fifteen, are dialectical stages. All the other phases, those of incarnation, which Yeats describes in *A Vision*, are subordinate to this design but important because they represent the point of view of life and embody its dualism: the pull toward the apparent absolute and that toward generation. The cycle of fecundity is necessary to reach the absolute of phase one, even if it is a cancelling of phase fifteen in the metempsychotic order. We see in the opposition of phase fifteen and the phases of incarnation, the antithesis of life as fecundity or death and of inorganic art as life, which marked late nineteenth-century symbolism. Drawing on occultism of a kind widespread in romantic France, Yeats used the myth of solar unity to move beyond this dualism, but he did not minimize its importance in the dialectic chain: indeed the significance of dialectic in poetry is to give full value to all intermediary stages. His use of the moon as his major symbol is indeed significant for the relation of his art to that of the *symbolistes:* the moon is beautiful, lifeless, and, while concrete, is not part of organic nature on earth. The peculiar qualities of the moon make it the perfect symbol for expressing at once a distaste for the merely natural and a love of the image, firm, bright, and clearly delineated.

The disinclination to see any significance in nature, which is such a distinctive feature of Yeats' poetry, is matched by Rilke's abandonment of the dense visual imagery of *Neue Gedichte* in his later work. What Rilke has to say in the *Duineser Elegien* (1922) is not perhaps so difficult to understand as it is unexpected. The explicit statement of it in the seventh and ninth elegies is thus preceded by a lengthy preparation in which the reader is made to assume a particular point of view about life through imagery.

In the first and second elegies the speaker thinks of crying out; the voice of God is mentioned hypothetically; the rustling words of those who died young reach the speaker; the cosmic wind ("Wind voller Weltraum") blows; newly invented dirge music echoes in space; the air is full of "ewige Strömung" or flux; in general, sound waves are more important than sight and suggest vastness. Notions of existence are fluid: beside the stronger *Dasein* of the angels, the distinction between the living and the dead is not sharp; man evaporates in his feeling; he is a gasp of air; lovers only temporarily feel corporeal solidity and then exist less; the Greeks in their statues represented the necessary limits and tentativeness of human touch. "Is" and "exist" are used emphatically and somewhat cryptically; the feeling that much is implied which is not yet explained is increased by odd expressions about man's needing something or things' needing him, and a general alienation in the "interpreted" world. There is little clarifying or outlining imagery of dark and light: night is invoked as even further effacing distinctions which are not at all clear-cut; the objects that are named are not described in a detailed, circumstantial way. These elegies are a grand prelude to the whole, conceived like it on a large scale, and explainable in the slightest detail by later elegies.[2] Their structural characteristics are those of the meditation: some traditional rhetoric of apostrophes and exclamations persists, but the movement is often associative or elliptical.

Lovers are an important class of beings in the elegies; they are represented as privileged but hindered in their spiritual aspirations by the very physical existence of the partner. In the third elegy the sexual instincts underlying love's spirituality are explored in a lengthy description of the unconscious of a boy infant with its jungles, archaic memories, and blood-sea. This picture of primeval lust is the most concrete one in the elegies; we begin to sense already that there is a hierarchy of images in the elegies, and that these are the lowest. The representation of the unconscious in the third elegy is typical of the tendency to spatialize abstract things including time and emotion. At the beginning of the fourth, man's life is symbolized by a confusion in the seasons, simultaneous flowering and withering. The mind of the lover is put into images fairly typical of Rilke's odd mixture of the concrete and abstract:

> Treten Liebende
> nicht immerfort an Ränder, eins im andern,
> die sich versprachen Weite, Jagd und Heimat.
> Da wird für eines Augenblickes Zeichnung
> ein Grund von Gegenteil bereitet, mühsam,
> dass wir sie sähen; denn man ist sehr deutlich
> mit uns. Wir kennen den Kontur
> des Fühlens nicht, nur was ihn formt von aussen.

Aren't lovers forever reaching verges in each other, lovers who looked for spaces, hunting, home? Then, for the sudden sketchwork of a moment, a ground of contrast is painfully prepared, to make us see it. For they are very clear with us. We don't know our feeling's shape but only what forms it from outside.

A little later a child left alone is pictured as standing in the "Zwischenraum" between world and toy. Throughout the elegies the relative lack of solidity of the ordinary world of objects is opposed to all kinds of figurative visual representations. Rilke carries very far in the elegies the tendency we saw earlier in Mallarmé and some other poets toward perturbing ordinary categories of vocabulary.

The most elaborate images in the elegies are all metaphors, an especially striking one being in the fourth elegy the play in the theater of the heart, in which the angel shakes the puppet. This of course embodies the gesture of the angel snatching up the speaker envisaged at the very beginning of the first elegy. The play is the course of life represented by the seasonal cycle, the imagery of which, with birds, trees, and flowers, had already been introduced at the commencement of the fourth elegy. The speaker thinks, as he watches the play, about his childhood and then about dead children, ones who did not complete the cycle. I mention the thematic and imagistic relationships among the parts of the fourth elegy to stress the elaborate connections underlying what appear to be sudden elliptic leaps in the continuity of the elegies.

The puppet theater is complemented by an acrobatic performance in the fifth elegy, which turns out to be a metaphor for life and especially that of lovers. The mixture of abstract and concrete in curious space and motion images is especially pronounced here; the performance takes place on a carpet lost in the cosmos, which is simultaneously in Paris in the midst of a "Rose des Zuschauens." The sixth elegy is that of the hero; with it the themes of the early dead, the lovers, the angels, and the cycle of life, which are introduced in the first elegy, are lengthily elaborated. At the beginning of the seventh, we see rising chains of existence: spring, summer, summer nights, and stars in the natural order; creatures, lovers, heroes, children, the young dead, and angels in the spiritual one. Existence is *Dasein*, a word used almost as if it were a sensation, and we realize that as materiality diminishes in the chain of being, *Dasein* increases.

The drawing together of themes at the beginning of the seventh elegy is announced by a temporal expression, *nicht mehr;* no longer will the speaker lament or long plangently for something exterior and unattainable. Suddenly two complementary truths are uttered:

> Nirgends, Geliebte, wird Welt sein, als innen. Unser
> Leben geht hin mit Verwandlung. Und immer geringer
> schwindet das Aussen.

Nowhere, beloved, can world exist but within. We spend our lives transforming things within. And ever diminishing, the outer is vanishing.

Historically we are at the end of an epoch not only of great visual art but of human things, houses or objects "once prayed to or tended or knelt to." We recognize here the category of the sacred; the age of the sacred is over, supplanted by the profane, and a new sacred age will not follow soon in the cyclic movement of history, the "dumpfe Umkehr der Welt." But what is precious and will not last objectively can be transformed and made to exist, to have *Dasein,* in the inner world. In the ninth elegy the earth yearns to become invisible, which is why it needs us, and transformation is elaborated upon: "Hier ist des S ä g-l i c h e n Zeit," "Now is the time of the tellable." The word replaces sight: this is a Word Discarnate unlike the logos of Christian and para-Christian poetic tradition. Its salvation—for we, the transitory, are the saviours of the perishable—is not accompanied by any imagery, and here we see the radical novelty of Rilke's style in the *Duineser Elegien:* all the imagery of flux and uncertain outline in the earlier elegies and the elusive mingling of concrete and abstract in the figurative tends to dissolve the sense of ordinary reality and prepare us for the ultimate transformation into the word. However, most modern poets who reject the superficial solidity of the world are exponents of the image, the picture of the transcendental or the symbol mediating between the spiritual and dead matter. Rilke's radical conception of the word as pure transcendency seems to do away with poetry, at least the imagistic kind of poetry of the early twentieth century, altogether. Perhaps a similar reticence about the capacities of imagery prevented Yeats from writing poems on the solar regeneration of the spirit, but most poets have found in symbolism an adequate means of expressing the invisible. It is curious that in the tenth elegy, after the rejection of all but the imageless act of speaking, "Tun ohne Bild," Rilke falls back on a personification allegory about the City of Pain and the journey of the dead. The technique continues the mingling of concrete and abstract in the elegies but seems somehow unauthentic after the conclusion of the ninth elegy: "Erde, ist es nicht dies, was du willst: u n s i c h t b a r/in uns erstehen?"

A single spring suffices before we die into the imageless, according to Rilke's ninth elegy—however, that spring is necessary, and without it pure transcendency would have no meaning. Rilke uses an unusually large amount of discursive language in his late work, while other poets dealing with the cycle of spirit tend, on the contrary, to rely more on imagery. It does not matter in the case of an orthodox Christian poet like Ungaretti, whose late poem *La Terra Promessa* superimposes the story of Dido and Aeneas, the Christian quest for rebirth, Ungaretti's personal journey to Italy (he was born and raised in Alexandria), and the aspirations of an autumnal civilization. More complicated are the works of poets such as Dylan Thomas or Georg Trakl, where Christian imagery does not have an automatic point of reference in doctrine. Stefan George's apocalyptic book *Der Stern des Bundes* inextricably mingles the social, aesthetic, and prophetic, so that one hardly knows whether theology, art, or politics is the dominant matter.

It emerges from what we have seen that, far from being concerned primarily with the theme of poetry and its creation, many modern poets have been engaged in revelation and prophecy of a broader sort. Within the narrow context of one tradition—Yeats and English-language poetry, say—such preoccupations may appear peculiar, especially when they draw on the motifs of magic or esoteric knowledge. However, we can now see that they form part of a large pattern of symbols and hypotheses. Furthermore, the suggestion of metaphysics usually emerges only with a poet's full maturity: his symbolism has at first a psychological value around which more ambitious theories and configurations gradually crystallize. But the language—even in the case of a Christian poet like Ungaretti—retains much that is individual not to say idiosyncratic, however closely an abstract formulation of one poet's thought may resemble another's: salvation, rebirth, and regeneration are very approximate terms compared with the shades of meaning in particular poems. This is the reason why we find in many of these poets abstract terms or even entire statements combined with highly symbolic passages: something approaching a general idea is modified by the meaning—sometimes obscure—implicit in imagery. Symbolism alone is not always comprehensible, nor does statement suffice. The relationship of the two is one of the most characteristic and individual of stylistic traits: a poet like Yeats or Rilke in the *Duineser Elegien* may rely heavily on statement, whereas symbols proliferate in Dylan Thomas. Each poet finds his way between generalization and the multiplication of particulars.

The very notion of particulars, however, demands qualification: the idea of the literary symbol has an important element of ambiguity. On the one hand, we may think of a kind of archaic, prelogical vividness and discreteness of individual details, one prior to abstraction and classifications; on the other hand, symbols can be considered highly rationalized, fitting, as many of them do, into typologies and inviting translation into general terms. It would be tempting to assert that traditional allegory is a rationalized construction, whereas modern symbolic poems work through the accumulation of particulars alone. For purposes of this study we have assumed that older symbolism is somewhat more rational than the polemics over Dante and Spenser strictly allow us to and that modern poetry does not include its share of facile or obvious symbols, good and bad.

When we tentatively fit together our various observations on recurrent patterns in modern poetry, it becomes clear that the phenomena of mood symbolism and schematic symbolic configurations are not without some relationship to each other: rhetorical intentions—generality of meaning or discriminations of argument—may be feeble or absent. The representation of psychological content, sometimes in great irrational detail, replaces persuasive discourse or even, as in the case of poems with concealed plots, the ordinary expectation of the full rendering of externals. Furthermore, the link with fiction is one of the clearest signs that, as the latter's rhetoric became obscured,[3] many writers ceased to conceive of the poet in his traditional roles of natural philosopher, lover, purveyor of wisdom, or prophet even, and felt him rather to be simply another man tense with a stream of fantasies, fears, and desires. When the poem uses not altogether cryptic symbols or even intermittent discursiveness to convey some universal process such as death or release from bondage, the general spiritual tonality or mood of the poem communicates itself far more than does any exact notion of what mode or process is involved. The patterns are there, often analogous to the great generalities of Christianity, but, as in Montale's verse, which is so characteristic in this respect, we are at a loss to make out what the poem could mean in a real metaphysical sense. This elusiveness of image and statement separates much modern symbolism from allegory, whose obscurities derive not from the inexistence of a doctrine behind it but are merely passing failures of rhetorical effectiveness and persuasive manipulation.

When patterns of feeling replace argument partially or altogether, insistently unusual features of style, real schemata or patterns of language will almost inevitably play a large role in a successful poetic texture. While these may be analyzable according to the old rhetorical theory of ornament and persuasive figures, it is merely mechanical detail that makes an expression of Mallarmé's comparable to one of Racine's: the heightening of communication or *auxesis*, which classical rhetoric had as its goal, may actually be replaced by a progressive darkening of the subject in the recurrent stylistic patterns of modern poetry. Such patterns are not always matters of imagery: tenses, sentence structure, pronoun and prepositional usage, and interplays of sound, all may violate standards not only of previous poetry, but of subsequent poets' work as well, since the period of high modernism and radical experimentation reached its peak some decades ago. Ultimately these explorations of language, beyond their varying aesthetic merits, have as a whole the enormous cultural significance of being the manifestation in art, well before our critical faculties could fully comprehend such phenomena, of the concern for language and its analysis which has taken such new impetus and directions in the course of this century.

Appendix

UN COUP DE DÉS

A THROW OF THE DICE

JAMAIS

QUAND BIEN MÊME LANCÉ DANS DES CIRCONSTANCES

ÉTERNELLES

DU FOND D'UN NAUFRAGE

WILL NEVER, EVEN IF IT IS CAST FOR ETERNITY BY A MAN
WHOSE SHIP IS WRECKED,

SOIT
que

l'Abîme

blanchi
étale
furieux

sous une inclinaison
plane désespérément

d'aile

la sienne

par

---

supposing that the abyss of ocean, whitened, slack, angry, beneath a despairingly flat slope of sail like a wing (the ship's wing already fallen because of its incapacity to rise in flight and already covering the wavelets, shearing the ocean's surface flat) sucks in the shadowy shape

avance retombée d'un mal à dresser le vol
et couvrant les jaillissements
coupant au ras les bonds

très à l'intérieur résume

l'ombre enfouie dans la profondeur par cette voile alternative

jusqu'adapter
à l'envergure

sa béante profondeur en tant que la coque

d'un bâtiment

penché de l'un ou l'autre bord

---

buried deep under the double sails to the point of bringing the sails'
wingspread down to its gaping depth—sucks in the shape which is the
hull of a ship leaning to one side or the other of the double sails, supposing all this,

LE MAÎTRE

surgi
    inférant

             de cette conflagration

                          que se

                    comme on menace
         l'unique Nombre qui ne peut pas

                                    hésite
                       cadavre par le bras
       plutôt
           que de jouer
             en maniaque chenu
                   la partie
                 au nom des flots

                                un

                        naufrage cela

THE MASTER, no longer in the habit of his former navigational calcu-
lations or the seamanship forgotten with age (in times past he took
the helm), the Master, rising, inferring from the sea and sky, like a
vast conflagration at his feet, that the Unique Number that can be no
other is being readied, shaken, combined in the palm of his hand
clutching it, as if to threaten his destiny and the winds, he the Master,

        de l'horizon unanime

prépare
    s'agite et mêle
        au poing qui l'étreindrait
un destin et les vents

être un autre

            Esprit
                pour le jeter
                    dans la tempête
                en reployer la division et passer **fier**

écarté du secret qu'il détient

envahit le chef
coule en barbe soumise

direct de l'homme

        sans nef
            n'importe
                où vaine

---

a Mind up to the task of casting the dice and passing on proudly, hesi-
tates, like a dead man separated by his arm from the secret in his
hand, rather than playing the waves' game, like a crazy white-haired
old man (one wave splashes over his head, drips off like a beard—this
is now Man's catastrophe, without any useless ship, anywhere),

ancestralement à n'ouvrir pas la main
crispée
par delà l'inutile tête

legs en la disparition

à quelqu'un
ambigu

l'ultérieur démon immémorial

ayant
de contrées nulles
induit
le vieillard vers cette conjonction suprême avec la probabilité

celui
son ombre puérile
caressée et polie et rendue et lavée
assouplie par la vague et soustraite
aux durs os perdus entre les ais

né
d'un ébat
la mer par l'aïeul tentant ou l'aïeul contre la mer
une chance oiseuse

Fiançailles
dont
le voile d'illusion rejailli leur hantise
ainsi que le fantôme d'un geste

chancellera
s'affalera

folie

---

he the Master, with the instinct of his race, fears not to open his fist, which he is clenching and waving over his useless head, and cast the dice as a legacy after he is gone to his double-natured son (the final eternal demon has led the old man from nowhere to this ultimate confrontation with the probabilities of chance and the dice) his son, his boyish double, whom the waves have caressed, smoothed, cast back and washed and preserved from the fate of hard old bones scattered

N'ABOLIRA

---

with the ship's timbers, for his son was born from a frolic of the sea and the master, when the sea tried its idle luck by means of the old man or the old man was trying his luck against the sea—this was a betrothal whose veil of illusion, their mutual obsession, spurting forth like the ghost of a gesture, will tremble and fall away, for it was madness—A THROW OF THE DICE WILL NEVER ABOLISH

COMME SI

Une insinuation

au silence

dans quelque proche

voltige

—AS IF a simple curve, curling up ironically in the silence, or the mystery itself, plummeting down with a roar into some near whirlpool of hilarity and horror, should be fluttering around the abyss

simple

enroulée avec ironie
        ou
              le mystère
                    précipite
                          hurlé

tourbillon d'hilarité et d'horreur

autour du gouffre
              sans le joncher
                    ni fuir

            et en berce le vierge indice

                      COMME SI

---

of sea, neither sinking into it nor darting away, and should rock
gently on its pure edge AS IF

282

plume solitaire éperdue

sauf

a simple curve like a feather frightened and alone except for the fact
that a midnight-blue cap meets it, grazes it, and immobilizes it against
its velvet, which a dark laugh crumples, for this derisory stiff white
feather points too boldly at the heavens not to distinguish by its nar-

que la rencontre ou l'effleure une toque de minuit
et immobilise
au velours chiffonné par un esclaffement sombre

cette blancheur rigide

dérisoire
en opposition au ciel
trop
pour ne pas marquer
exigüment
quiconque

prince amer de l'écueil

s'en coiffe comme de l'héroïque
irrésistible mais contenu
par sa petite raison virile
en foudre

---

row shape him—the bitter prince of the reef—who wears it like a heroic helmet, he, irresistible but contained by his virile little thunderclap of an intelligence

soucieux

expiatoire et pubère

muet

La lucide et seigneuriale aigrette
au front invisible
scintille
puis ombrage
une stature mignonne ténébreuse
en sa torsion de sirène

par d'impatientes squames ultimes

(the bright, lordly, dizzying feather on the invisible forehead shines, then leans over a tiny dark creature standing with her twisting siren's body just long enough to slap her impatient, bifurcated tail scales against a rock, which first seemed an edifice then vanished into mist,

rire

      que

        SI

de vertige

debout

  le temps
     de souffleter
bifurquées

    un roc

  faux manoir
     tout de suite
       évaporé en brumes

      qui imposa
        une borne à l'infini

---

having momentarily placed a limit on infinity) he the prince, full of cares, expiatory, and pubsecent, with his silent laughing at the fact that IF IT

C'ÉTAIT

issu stellaire

CE SERAIT

pire

non

davantage ni moins

indifféremment mais autant

WERE THE NUMBER on the dice, born of the stars, IF IT EXISTED, other than as a fragmented illusion appearing to a dying man, IF IT BEGAN AND CEASED, appearing when denied, and closed when it appeared, finally, through some spreading profusion of rarity IF THE NUMBER APPEARED, the evidence of the total insofar as there was one, IF IT SHONE, IT WOULD BE (worse neither more or less,

EXISTÂT-IL
autrement qu'hallucination éparse d'agonie

COMMENÇÂT-IL ET CESSÂT-IL
sourdant que nié et clos quand apparu
enfin
par quelque profusion répandue en rareté
SE CHIFFRÂT-IL

évidence de la somme pour peu qu'une
ILLUMINÂT-IL

LE HASARD

Choit
la plume
rythmique suspens du sinistre
s'ensevelir
aux écumes originelles
naguères d'où sursauta son délire jusqu'à une cime
flétrie
par la neutralité identique du gouffre

---

hardly mattering but just as much) CHANCE (for A THROW OF THE DICE NEVER WILL ABOLISH CHANCE). The feather falls, rhythmically suspended in the catastrophe and is buried in the primeval foam, from which, not long ago, its delirious movement rose up to a height made indistinguishable by the identical and neutral oneness of the sky and sea.

RIEN

de la mémorable crise
ou se fût
l'événement

NOTHING (of the memorable crisis or else the event had probably been accomplished in view of some null result—on the human plane) HAS PROBABLY TAKEN PLACE (an ordinary high place voids forth the absence of any event) BUT THE PLACE (some sort of low surface

accompli en vue de tout résultat nul
humain

N'AURA EU LIEU
une élévation ordinaire verse l'absence

QUE LE LIEU

inférieur clapotis quelconque comme pour disperser l'acte vide
abruptement qui sinon
par son mensonge
eût fondé
la perdition

dans ces parages
du vague
en quoi toute réalité se dissout

---

splashing in order, as it were, to disperse abruptly any sign of the
empty act of casting the dice, which, otherwise, by its illusion, would
have given some factual basis to the loss of the ship in these realms of
indeterminacy in which all reality is dissolved)

EXCEPTÉ
à l'altitude
PEUT-ÊTRE
aussi loin qu'un endroit

EXCEPT, at the altitude, PERHAPS, as far as a place can fuse with the beyond (aside from the interest it generally has because of its obliquity and declivity of light in the vicinity of—it must be the Wain, hence the North) A CONSTELLATION, chilly in oblivion and abandonment but not so much so that it cannot record, on some empty and

fusionne avec au delà

hors l'intérêt
quant à lui signalé
en général
selon telle obliquité par telle déclivité
de feux

vers
ce doit être
le Septentrion aussi Nord

UNE CONSTELLATION

froide d'oubli et de désuétude
pas tant
qu'elle n'énumère
sur quelque surface vacante et supérieure
le heurt successif
sidéralement
d'un compte total en formation

veillant
doutant
roulant
brillant et méditant

avant de s'arrêter
à quelque point dernier qui le sacre

Toute Pensée émet un Coup de Dés

---

higher surface, the successive star-strokes of a total sum being formed
and keep vigil, in doubt, turning, luminous, and meditative, before
stopping at some final point which marks its consecration. All Thought
Emits a Throw of the Dice.

Notes

CHAPTER I

1 Baudelaire's use of the word *imagination* strikes me as insignificant, as does his quoting an English source on the subject late in his career.

2 The theory of this poetry was formulated by Samuel Johnson in his essay on Denham. Samuel Johnson, *Lives of the English Poets* (3 vols.; London: Oxford University Press, 1961), I, 54–62.

3 Mallarmé's use of *idée* is not usefully elucidated by relating it strictly to any specific philosophical system; as used by him and others, the Idea is sometimes transcendental beauty, sometimes the structural principle of the artwork, and sometimes the image evoked by a word.

4 Aside from the sections of *Hérodiade* Mallarmé published, we now have further fragments and his notes. See Stéphane Mallarmé, *Noces d'Hérodiade: Mystère*, ed. Gardner Davies (Paris: Gallimard, 1959).

5 The quotation is from a letter to Edmund Gosse not in Stéphane Mallarmé, *Correspondance*, ed. Henri Mondor (3 vols.; Paris: Gallimard, 1959–1969). See Suzanne Bernard, *Mallarmé et la Musique* (Paris: Nizet, 1959), 75. I find Mallarmé's idea more subtle as a structural principle than the one of reconciliation of opposites, which supplemented the romantic organic theory.

6 See the preface to the 1903 edition of Edouard Schuré, *Histoire du Lied* (Paris: Perrin).

7 See the interview in Jules Huret, *Enquête sur l'évolution littéraire* (Paris: Charpentier, 1901), 280–85.

8 Letter of 16 May 1873 to Edmond Lepelletier. See Paul Verlaine, *Oeuvres complètes*, ed. Jacques Borel (2 vols.; Paris: Club du Meilleur Livre, 1959), I, 1035.

9 Letter of 17 May 1867 to Eugène Lefébure. See Stéphane Mallarmé, *Correspondance 1862–1871* (Paris: Gallimard, 1959), 246.

10 Letter of 3 May 1868 to Eugène Lefébure. See *Ibid.*, 273.

11 In Jules Huret's *Enquête*. See Stéphane Mallarmé, *Oeuvres complètes*, eds. Henri Mondor and G. Jean-Aubry (Paris: Gallimard, 1945), 869. By his phrase the "objective correlative," T. S. Eliot seems to designate mood symbolism.

12 See Richard Ellmann, *The Identity of Yeats* (New York: Oxford University Press, 1954), 128. Perhaps this is the best place to mention that Yeats, who knew little French, is only the best of a number of late nineteenth-century poets in English who were working out all kinds of rather *symboliste* ideas. See Lothar Hönnighausen, *Präraphaeliten und Fin de Siècle: Symbolistische Tendenzen in der Englischen Spätromantik* (Munich: Wilhelm Fink Verlag, 1971).

13 Ernst Morwitz, *Kommentar zu dem Werk Stefan Georges* (Düsseldorf: Helmut Küpper, 1969).

14 See John J. Espey, *Ezra Pound's Mauberley: A Study in Composition* (London: Faber and Faber, 1955), 49.

15 The earlier versions are given in the notes to Mallarmé, *Oeuvres complètes*, 1450–59.

16 The word *drap* is Corbière's correction in his own hand for *jour*.

17 Jules Laforgue, *Oeuvres complètes* (5 vols.; Paris: Mercure de France, 1925), I, 131–32, 182; IV, 66; *Mélanges posthumes* (Paris: Mercure de France, 1903), 116; *Lettres à un ami* (Paris: Mercure de France, 1941), 68.

CHAPTER II

1 Jules Laforgue, *Lettres à un ami* (Paris: Mercure de France, 1941), 68.

2 The best statement of this is to be found at the end of the essay on Baudelaire in Paul Bourget, *Essais de psychologie contemporaine* (Paris: Lemerre, 1883).

3 See Peter Bien, *Kazantzakis and the Linguistic Revolution in Greek Literature* (Princeton: Princeton University Press, 1972). For Cavafy see 221–22.

4 Some patterns have been studied in Rolf Kloepfer and Ursula Oomen, *Sprachliche Constituenten moderner Dichtung: Entwurf einer descriptiven Poetik: Rimbaud* (Bad Homburg: Athenäum, 1970).

5 See David Perkins, *A History of Modern Poetry: From the 1890s to the High Modernist Mode* (Cambridge, Mass.: Harvard University Press, 1976), 458.

CHAPTER III

1 Letter to Henri Cazalis, April, 1866. Stéphane Mallarmé, *Correspondance 1862–1871* (Paris: Gallimard, 1959), 207–08.

2 Stéphane Mallarmé, *Oeuvres complètes* (Paris: Gallimard, 1945), 368, 378, 647, 648, 871.

3 The tradition of mystic verse in French was not well-known. Rimbaud probably came to know Madame Guyon's work; he would have read about her in Jules Michelet's *Histoire de France* (19 vols.; Paris: A. Le Vasseur, 1830–1867), 15, and in Jules Michelet, *Le Prêtre, la Femme et la Famille* (Paris: Flammarion, n.d.). He evidently studied at least the first of the four volumes of Jeanne-Marie Bouvier de la Motte Guyon's *Poésies et Cantiques spirituels* (4 vols.; Cologne: J. de la Pierre, 1722), forbidden in France but published in Germany. See especially I, 13, 71, 110, 111, 145, 165, 174; II, 132, 144; III, 155. Mme. Guyon was one of the few French mystics.

4 For a detailed analysis of *Une Saison en enfer* see John Porter Houston, *The Design of Rimbaud's Poetry* (New Haven: Yale University Press, 1963), 137–200.

5 It is extremely interesting to see the beginnings of the religious inspiration in Verlaine's work: "Par instants je suis le pauvre navire," "La tristesse, la langueur du corps humain," "Ce soir je m'étais penché," "Luxures." These appear to date from his association with Rimbaud. "Crimen amoris" and "Du fond du grabat" are an interpretation of the same material we find in *Une Saison en enfer*.

CHAPTER IV

1 There is a valuable introduction, with translations, to these poems: Glauco Cambon, "Eugenio Montale's 'Motets': The Occasions of Epiphany," *PMLA*, LXXXII (December, 1967), 471–84.

2 There is one comprehensive, excellent study of the elegies: Jacob Steiner, *Rilkes Duineser Elegien* (zweite, durchgesehene Auflage; Bern: Francke, 1969).

3 I allude, of course, to Wayne Booth, *The Rhetoric of Fiction* (Chicago: University of Chicago Press, 1961).

Index